THE WORLD CRISIS AND INTERNATIONAL LAW

The knowledge economy, a seeming wonder for the world, has caused unintended harms that threaten peace and prosperity and undo international cooperation and the international rule of law. The world faces threats of war, pandemics, growing domestic political discord, climate change, disruption of international trade and investment, immigration, and the pollution of cyberspace, just as international law increasingly falls short as a tool for managing these challenges. Prosperity dependent on meritocracy, open borders, international economic freedom, and a wide-open Internet has met its limits, with international law one of the first casualties. Any effective response to these threats must reflect the pathway by which these perils arrive. Part of the answer to these challenges, Paul B. Stephan argues, must include a re-conception of international law as arising out of pragmatic and limited experiments by states, rather than as grand projects to remake and redeem the world.

Paul B. Stephan, the John C. Jeffries, Jr., Distinguished Professor of Law, David H. Ibbeken '71 Research Professor of Law, and Senior Fellow of the Miller Center of Public Affairs at the University of Virginia, has taught and written about international law and the world economy for over forty years. Besides his academic life in the United States, he has lectured and published in China, Russia, the United Kingdom, France, Germany, Switzerland, Austria, Georgia, Montenegro, Australia, Mexico, Brazil, and Israel. He also served in the US Departments of the Treasury, State, and Defense, and advised the IMF, the World Bank, and the OECD.

The World Crisis and International Law

THE KNOWLEDGE ECONOMY AND THE BATTLE FOR THE FUTURE

PAUL B. STEPHAN
University of Virginia

CAMBRIDGE
UNIVERSITY PRESS

Shaftesbury Road, Cambridge CB2 8EA, United Kingdom

One Liberty Plaza, 20th Floor, New York, NY 10006, USA

477 Williamstown Road, Port Melbourne, VIC 3207, Australia

314–321, 3rd Floor, Plot 3, Splendor Forum, Jasola District Centre, New Delhi – 110025, India

103 Penang Road, #05–06/07, Visioncrest Commercial, Singapore 238467

Cambridge University Press is part of Cambridge University Press & Assessment, a department of the University of Cambridge.

We share the University's mission to contribute to society through the pursuit of education, learning and research at the highest international levels of excellence.

www.cambridge.org
Information on this title: www.cambridge.org/9781009320979

DOI: 10.1017/9781009321020

First published 2023

A catalogue record for this publication is available from the British Library

Library of Congress Cataloging-in-Publication Data
NAMES: Stephan, Paul B., author.
TITLE: The world crisis and international law : the knowledge economy and the battle for the future / Paul B. Stephan, University of Virginia.
DESCRIPTION: Cambridge, United Kingdom ; New York, NY : Cambridge University Press, 2023. | Includes bibliographical references and index.
IDENTIFIERS: LCCN 2022044743 (print) | LCCN 2022044744 (ebook) | ISBN 9781009320979 (hardback) | ISBN 9781009320993 (paperback) | ISBN 9781009321020 (epub)
SUBJECTS: LCSH: International law. | World politics–1989-
CLASSIFICATION: LCC KZ3410 .S746 2023 (print) | LCC KZ3410 (ebook) | DDC 341–dc23/eng/20221201
LC record available at https://lccn.loc.gov/2022044743
LC ebook record available at https://lccn.loc.gov/2022044744

ISBN 978-1-009-32097-9 Hardback
ISBN 978-1-009-32099-3 Paperback

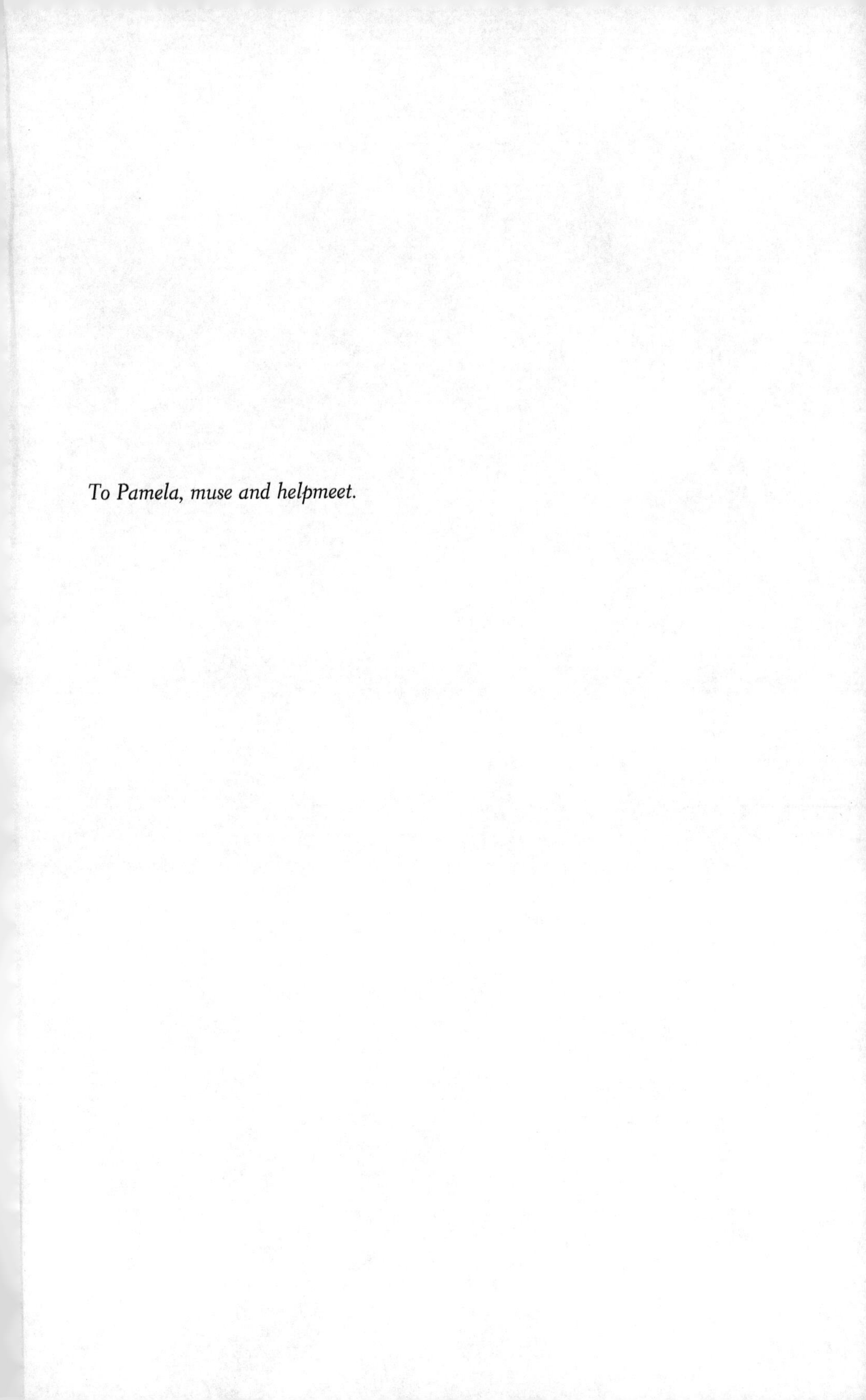

To Pamela, muse and helpmeet.

Contents

PART III BATTLEGROUNDS

PART IV INTERNATIONAL LAW FUTURES

Figures

Preface

This is my COVID-19 book. But for the shutting down of the international meetings, conferences, and research that keep me busy in normal times, I would not have turned to this project. It reflects many years of study, reflection, and teaching, but more pressing demands always got in the way. The pandemic silenced those demands.

This book is not a memoir, even though I put myself in it in a few places as an observer of current events. Nor is it a work of social science, although I draw on the research of many economists, political scientists, sociologists, and social theorists to illuminate the narrative. I have no doctorate in any discipline; the *juris doctor* is a bit of flim-flam, sufficient to denote the legally trained professional but not necessarily an advanced academic degree. Rather, as I say in the book, I am a hack, a jobbing international lawyer telling a story about the changes in the world economy over the last thirty years and the place of international law in these events. I find the story compelling and the implications for the future blood-curdling, and hope at least a few readers will agree.

As I mention in the book, during my academic career I have had the privilege of occupying, by way of secondment, positions in several departments of the US government, including as Counselor on International Law to the State Department's Legal Adviser (in the George W. Bush administration) and as Special Counsel to the Department of Defense's General Counsel (in the Trump and Biden administrations). Nothing in this book reflects any views other than my own, and certainly not those of the US government or any of its organs. Similarly, I have taken part in several legal proceedings, domestic and international, on which this book touches. In these pages, however, I draw on no classified, private, or privileged information to which any public or private position has given me access. Any inference that insider knowledge lurks here would be mistaken.

I am grateful to Bill Burke-White for arranging my inclusion in a Perry House symposium at the University of Pennsylvania on international law and cities, and to Charles Reid, who invited me to take part in a University of St. Thomas Law School symposium on sovereignty. The two events, the first occurring just before COVID-19 struck and the second displaced by the pandemic, gave me a chance to sketch out the ideas that form the backbone of my story.*

Many friends and colleagues have read various drafts and provided great comments and criticism. I fear that memory holes may render this list incomplete, but I acknowledge the helpful comments, insights, and criticism of Anne van Aaken, Ken Abraham, Jack Beatson, Bill Bratton, Kathleen Claussen, Rebecca Crootof, Bill Dodge, Kristen Eichensehr, Michael Froomkin, Jean Galbraith, Richard Gard, Baird Garrett, Jack Goldsmith, Mitu Gulati, Andrew Kent, Suzanne LaPierre, David Law, Tom Lee, Julia Mahoney, Paul Mahoney, Lauri Mälksoo, Sean Murphy, Delphine Nougayrède, Bernard Oxman, George Rutherglen, Rich Schragger, Mike Seidman, David Sloss, Jill Snyder, Cindy Spaulding, Adriana Stephan, Andy Thomson, Bakhtiyar Tuzmukhamedov, Pierre Verdier, Mila Versteeg, Matt Waxman, David Westin, and Ted White. Participants in workshops at Miami Law School and under the auspices of the ASIL's International Law in Domestic Courts Interest Group helped set me straight, or at least tried as best they could. Two anonymous reviewers of my proposal for Cambridge University Press clarified my thinking and saved me from blunders. My extraordinary Dean, Risa Goluboff, has provided great support throughout; I am proud to be part of the institution she leads. The University of Virginia Law School's wonderful research librarians got me into places I never thought I could go and made their diligence and creativity something almost to be taken for granted, did I not know better. Pamela Clark, always my most trenchant critic and an insightful and supportive reader and editor, sustained me throughout with love and bemusement. During the final months of preparation of this book, she allowed me to surmount a disabling sports injury by waiting on me, quite literally, hand and foot. My gratitude to her has no bounds.

* Paul B. Stephan, Foreign Relations and the City, in CITIES, GEOPOLITICS, AND THE INTERNATIONAL LEGAL ORDER – REPORT AND THOUGHT PIECES (2019), available at https://global.upenn.edu/perryworldhouse/cities-geopolitics-and-international-legal-order-report-and-thought-pieces; Paul B. Stephan, *Sovereignty and the World Economy*, 17 *U. ST. THOMAS L.J.* 649 (2021).

Abbreviations

AfD *Alternative für Deutschland* (Alternative for Germany), a German populist political party.

AI Artificial intelligence.

BIT Bilateral investment treaty.

BRICS Brazil, Russia, India, China, and South Africa, a group identified in 2001 by a Goldman Sachs partner as the most significant of the so-called emerging-market countries.

CDC Center for Disease Control and Protection, an agency of the US Department of Health and Human Services.

CJEU Court of Justice of the European Union, the legal organ of the European Union, known as the Luxembourg Court and formerly the European Court of Justice.

COMECON Council for Mutual Economic Assistance, the international organization that managed economic coordination between the Soviet Union and its allies.

DARPA Defense Advanced Research Projects Agency, an agency of the US Department of Defense.

DFC International Development Finance Corporation, a publicly owned US corporation that superseded OPIC in 2018.

ECB European Central Bank, an organ of the European Union.

ECHR European Convention on Human Rights, a multilateral treaty in force in Europe since 1953 that establishes the European Court of Human Rights and imposes duties on states.

ECtHR European Court of Human Rights, also known as the Strasbourg Court, the judicial organ of the Council of Europe and thus responsible for applying and interpreting the European Convention on Human Rights.

EEC European Economic Community, the most important component of the European Communities from 1957 to 1993.

EU European Union, the successor to the European Communities.

FDA The Food and Drug Administration, an agency of the US Department of Health and Human Services.

FIRRMA Foreign Investment Risk Review Modernization Act of 2018, legislation that authorizes regulation of foreign investment in the United States.

FPÖ *Freiheitliche Partei Österreichs* (Freedom Party of Austria), an Austrian populist political party.

GATS General Agreement on Trade in Services, one of the Uruguay Round agreements signed in 1994.

GATT General Agreement on Tariffs and Trade, adopted in 1947 and incorporated into the Uruguay Round agreements.

GDP Gross Domestic Product, an economic statistic that measures the size of a country's economy.

GDPR The General Data Protection Regulation, a 2016 legislative act of the European Union.

ICANN Internet Corporation for Assigned Names and Numbers, a US nonprofit entity that administers the internet's domain-name system.

ICC International Criminal Court, established by the 1998 Statute of Rome.

ICJ International Court of Justice, the judicial organ of the United Nations.

ICSID International Centre for the Settlement of Investment Disputes, a member of the World Bank family of international organizations.

IEEPA International Economic Emergency Powers Act, a 1977 US statute that authorizes sanctions against foreign states and nationals as well as their assets.

IMF International Monetary Fund, the Fund.

ISDS Investor–state dispute settlement, a system of arbitration based on BITs and often ICSID.

ITO International Trade Organization, a proposed international organization under the 1948 Havana Charter that never came into being.

JCPOA Joint Comprehensive Plan of Action, a 2015 agreement between Iran and China, France, Germany, Russia, the United Kingdom and the United States to limit Iran's nuclear program.

KSRF	Constitutional Court of the Russian Federation (*Konstitutsionnyy Sud Rossiyskoy Federatsii*).
MAI	Multilateral Agreement on Investment, a failed 1998 proposal of the OECD.
MFN	Most-favored nation obligation, commonly found in trade and investment treaties.
NAFTA	North American Free Trade Agreement, signed in 1992 and superseded in 2018.
NATO	North Atlantic Treaty Organization, a military alliance founded in 1949.
NIEO	New International Economic Order, a concept propounded by newly independent states in the 1960s and 1970s as an aspiration for international economic law.
OECD	Organisation for Economic Co-operation and Development, the successor to the OEEC.
OEEC	Organisation for European Economic Co-operation, the entity that administered the Marshall Plan between 1948 and 1961.
OPIC	Overseas Private Investment Corporation, a publicly owned corporation that promoted US overseas investment from 1971 to 2018.
ÖVP	*Österreichische Volkspartei* (Austrian People's Party), an Austrian political party.
PIGS	Portugal, Italy, Greece, and Spain, the members of the Eurozone with the worst sovereign-debt problems after the Great Recession.
PLA	People's Liberation Army, the military arm of the People's Republic of China.
PSPP	Public Sector Purchase Programme, a facility of the European Central Bank meant to address the sovereign-debt problems of EU member states.
TRIPS	Agreement on Trade-Related Aspects of Intellectual Property, one of the Uruguay Round agreements.
UNCTAD	The United Nations Conference on Trade and Development, an organ of the United Nations.
WHO	World Health Organization, an organ of the United Nations.
WIPO	World Intellectual Property Organization, an organ of the United Nations.
WMD	Weapons of mass destruction.
WTO	World Trade Organization, established by the Uruguay Round Agreements.

1

The Crisis Arrives

We live in a dark time. Not so long ago we thought a new dawn had broken when the Cold War ended, bringing universal peace, general prosperity, worldwide connectivity, human rights, and the international rule of law. Instead, disillusion has overtaken us in the wake of shocks and abounding threats. We face uncivil politics, economic anxiety, and tribal conflict throughout the rich world. Authoritarian nationalists seem the coming thing around the world, rich and poor alike. Peace and prosperity do not. Many believers in the liberal international order now feel, like Marxists in the 1980s, that history has turned against them.

Consider the threats: under Trump the United States broke international as well as domestic norms and abandoned many commitments, few of which the Biden administration seems ready to restore; after Brexit the European Union shows further signs of unraveling; corrupt and brutal strongmen rule in important-if-not-rich countries such as until recently Brazil, China, Russia, and Turkey; and China's international ambitions sow discord in both the rich world and the global South.[1] Populism in India means Hindu nationalism and

[1] Throughout this book I use the term "West" to denote the part of the world that prospered while aligned with the United States and Western Europe during the Cold War, as well as the states, especially in Europe, that have changed sides since, and "South" to denote today's revisionist states that were either nonaligned or identified as socialist during the Cold War. The current members of the European Union fit into the "West" category, as well as most of the members of the Organisation for Economic Co-operation and Development (OECD), while the five BRICS (Brazil, Russia, India, China, and South Africa) epitomize the revisionist South. Argentina, Mexico, and Turkey seem closer to the South, although they also illustrate the fluidity and contingency of the categories. The terms are obviously metaphorical rather than geographically literal. The West includes Japan and South Korea, and the South, China and Russia, notwithstanding where they lie on the globe. A rough but useful proxy would put the forty-two states that have sanctioned Russia for the Ukrainian invasion in the camp of the West, while assigning to the South the fifty-two states that did not join the first US General

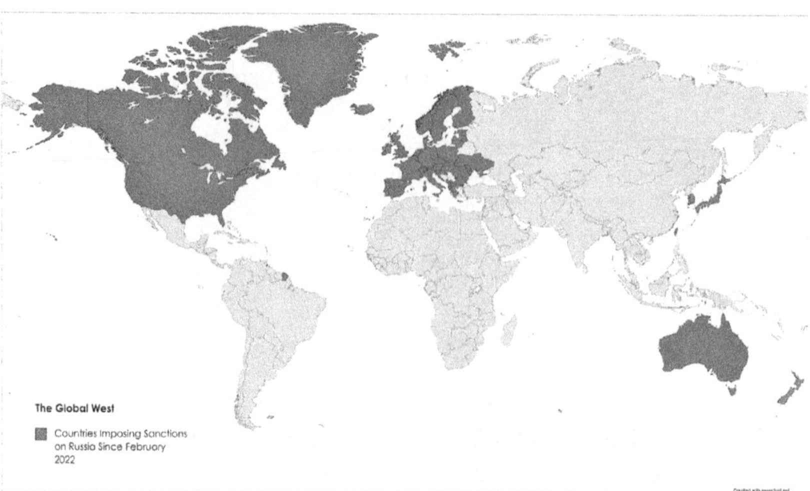

FIGURE 1.1 The West: states sanctioning Russia for its invasion of Ukraine.

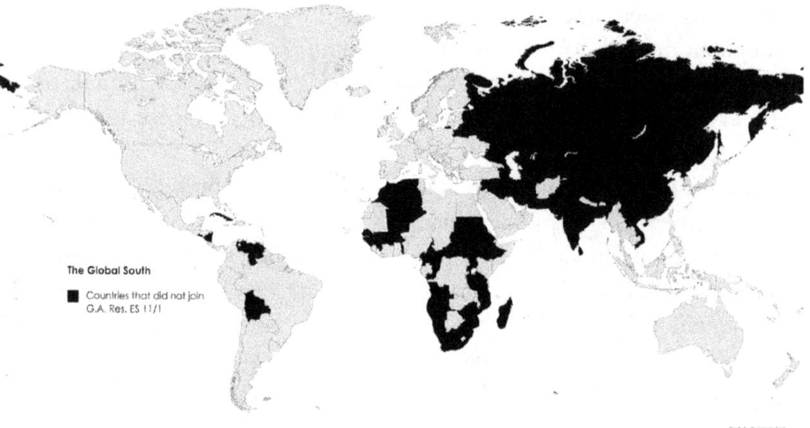

FIGURE 1.2 The South: states that did not join the UN General Assembly Resolution condemning the Russian invasion

new forms of suppression of opponents of the regime. A worldwide retreat from political and economic liberty has transformed the international landscape. Meanwhile we witness Russia's second invasion of Ukraine and await China's conquest of Taiwan, terrified of these prospects yet struggling to respond.

Assembly Resolution condemning the invasion (as against 141 who did). Notably, the first group contains less than 15 percent of the world's population but produced more than 59 percent of its economic output in 2020. The second has more than 57 percent of global population but only a bit more than a quarter of economic output. Figures 1.1 and 1.2 show these groups.

But wait, there's more: technological innovation had promised to remake the world and liberate us all. Now it offers such dystopian prospects as the amplification of political dysfunction, unsustainable inequality, deep fakes, pervasive surveillance, and the erasure of privacy. The internet, rather than challenging dictators from the bottom up as people had hoped, became a means of wielding state power from the top down. The surveillance state took over just as more life moved online. Private internet firms do their own part to destroy privacy and safety in cyberspace. Liberty, representative democracy, and the rule of law seem in retreat everywhere in the cyber world.

Then COVID-19 came. The social isolation necessary for staunching contagion brought crazy theories and actions that shredded the social compact. The already intolerable wedge between haves and have-nots now looms even larger. Low-wage frontline workers bore more than their share of the disease's toll, while poor children fell further behind their well-off peers when schools shut down. The scramble for vaccines made winners out of the tech-savvy and the well-connected while exposing the offline to greater risk of death and disease. Distrust of national public health authorities, whose blunders and mistakes at the start of the pandemic reflected the enormity of the challenge and the extent of the gaps in the knowledge needed, fed vaccine resistance and bizarre alternative medicines. Disruptive protests against lockdowns and mask and vaccine mandates erupted in Australia, Austria, Canada, France, and Germany, among other supposedly advanced and contented societies. Rejection of authority thwarts herd immunity in much of the world. China compounded the problem by combining unstainable lockdowns with exclusive reliance on its own subpar vaccine, ensuring that its vast population remains a reservoir to sustain the virus. North Korea, which simply closed its borders and did not avail itself of any vaccine, reinforces that reservoir.

This turmoil has deeply compromised the international rule of law. The decade after the Cold War ended saw international organizations (both global and regional) proliferate. National governments embraced new limits on their sovereignty to advance international projects for economic governance, the waging of war, and respect for human rights. Without new formal commitments, except in Europe, they accepted open migration as a norm. Civil society grew and prospered, clamoring for a role in making and applying international law at the expense of national governments. The World Wide Web and the explosion of connective devices spawned cyberspace. Visionaries saw this sphere as a place that could overtake nation states and host a new global community based on individual empowerment through connection and data.[2] It seemed that the new technology could mobilize the masses to oust authoritarians and hold the corrupt to account. As with migration, states responded to the internet revolution with an implicit global compact of laissez-faire.

The twenty-first century became the place where the hopes of the 1990s went to die. The 1990–91 Gulf War had seemed to give the UN Security Council an effective veto over major uses of armed force in international relations. The North Atlantic Treaty Organization (NATO) bombing of Serbia exposed that settlement's shallow roots even before the new century began. The 9/11 attacks and the US response – the unhappily named global war on terror as well as the coalition war on Iraq – blew it up. The Orange, Rose, Cedar, and Tulip Revolutions in Ukraine, Georgia, Lebanon, and Kyrgyzstan seemed a new form of people's power, undergirded by smartphones, but all they promised turned to ashes, as did the later Arab Spring. The return of the Taliban to Afghanistan brought an abrupt end to an especially costly and quixotic nation-building project and raised deep doubts about the prospects of others, Iraq in particular. The 2022 Russian invasion of Ukraine brought a nasty coda to these pacific hopes.

The 2008 world financial crisis shattered the rich world's confidence in both global finance and advanced capitalism. In its wake, the center-left and center-right in Europe and the United States fell back in the face of onslaughts from both political extremes. International governance suffered directly. Targets of a surging anti-globalization movement included the World Trade Organization (WTO), set up in 1994 to promote and regulate trade; the International Monetary Fund (IMF, also known as the Fund) and regional financial institutions such as the European Central Bank (ECB), which imposed painful austerity on spendthrift governments; and international courts, whose judgments face scorn from prominent states in both the rich West and the revisionist South. Then came Trump, Brexit, the rise of national populist parties in much of Central and Eastern Europe, and a different kind of national-populist politics dominating Brazil, China, India, Mexico, the Philippines, Russia, and Turkey, as well as smaller states such as Venezuela. What these movements share is a hostility to the international status quo. Meanwhile, places where war and misery fester – the Middle East and the Horn of Africa in particular – got even worse as the new century rolled along.

[2] Lawrence Lessig, Code and Other Laws of Cyberspace (1999).

WHY INTERNATIONAL LAW

Many people will wonder what these obviously bad developments have to do with the degradation of the international rule of law. Outside a hermetic world of specialists, most question the importance of international law generally. Among US legal academics, many, I suspect a majority, find it boring, the province of high-minded idealists too good for the world in which we live. I agree that many international lawyers too often get the causal arrow backwards, seeing international law as contributing to desired practices and institutions where it instead rests on them. Still, we can learn a lot about the world and its maladies by looking at international law.

First, international law serves as the canary in the coal mine, providing an early warning of threats to peace and prosperity. When a powerful state upends widely held views of international law and backs up its claims with consequential actions, as Germany did when it annexed Sudetenland in 1938 and Russia when it annexed Crimea in 2014, it puts the world on notice of new dangers independent of injury to the rule of law.

Second, the techniques and values of international law can work either as instruments to advance human cooperation for the good or as a means of eroding trust and social capital to the harm of humanity. International law provides a framework for setting expectations about the future. Fulfillment of those expectations inspires people to come together to tackle new challenges. Frustration pushes people toward disengagement or despair. Either way, international law matters.

THE KNOWLEDGE ECONOMY AND THE ROAD TO DARKNESS

How did we get to this dark place, and how do we get out? At the heart of the story is the knowledge economy. It is that portion of economic activity that uses constantly evolving knowledge as a factor of production as well as economic activity that produces knowledge. Think of a cutting-edge civilian or military aircraft, a physical good the value of which depends mostly on the technological expertise and innovation used in its production and the knowledge (pilot training and data collection) it creates when put to work. Technological breakthroughs drove economic development throughout history, from the new grains that made cultivation and cities possible thousands of years ago to the use of steam power to drive the industrial revolution. What makes the knowledge economy different is the pace of technological change, requiring a steady stream of breakthroughs to spur production, as well as the growing share of knowledge in the economy's products.

Over the last sixty years or so engineering feats from computers to semiconductors to lasers to massive data storage to coding breakthroughs transformed the way we work and live. The technological giants – Alphabet, Amazon, Apple, Facebook (now Meta), Tencent, Cisco, Huawei, Big Pharma, Boeing, Siemens, and their ilk – represent only the tip of the knowledge sector. This new way of making things and providing services – an economy where research, learning, and technological innovation add the most value – generates enormous wealth, betters the lives of billions, and raised hundreds of millions out of extreme poverty. Most recently, it gave us both remote communication – Zoom and other conferencing apps – to let the more fortunate of us keep doing our jobs and sustain a kind of connection with those we love during the pandemic, and ingenious mRNA vaccines that protect us from COVID 19.

I use the term "knowledge economy," and not "globalization," advisedly. I hated the g-word since it first appeared. It describes a cluster of effects, readily apparent over the last thirty or forty years, but doesn't offer a coherent conception of its subject or an account as to why it matters. Globalization in some form has shaped the world since the mid-nineteenth century, when steam ships and telegraphs drove connectivity, free movement of goods and capital, and imperialism.[3] But while technological breakthroughs and knowledge gains brought economic change since the dawn of history, the knowledge economy is a new thing. In it, mind work does not simply contribute to meeting the world's needs and wants, but dominates.

A focus on globalization, rather than the knowledge economy, also invokes different implicit assumptions about how change happens. Globalization refers to, among many things, the lowering of barriers to the movement of people and things around the world. This perspective suggests that globalization constitutes the outcome of particular public policy choices, often associated with laissez-faire ideology. The faces of globalization become, if only in caricature, Margaret Thatcher, Ronald Reagan, and Milton Friedman.[4] Centering the knowledge economy, by contrast, means looking at impersonal forces over which governments exercise only sporadic and often feckless influence. It takes heroes, villains, and ideology out of the story and instead looks at many people competing to adapt to a challenging world through new ways of doing things.

3 J. Bradford DeLong, Slouching towards Utopia: An Economic History of the Twentieth Century (2022).

4 John Gray, False Dawn: The Delusions of Global Capitalism (1999); Fiona Hill, There Is Nothing For You Here: Finding Opportunity in the Twenty-First Century (2021).

Foregrounding globalization is like talking about climate change (something we can observe) without taking into account emissions of carbon dioxide (something that brings about what we observe). Serious scholars use the term, and I appreciate their work.[5] This book, however, gets at the underlying economic, social, and political forces that remade our world. What observers see as an output (the present state of globalization) reflects an input (the knowledge economy), which we can analyze and understand, even if not completely.

The distinction is critical. Taking the knowledge economy as our subject allows us to focus on knowledge workers, its essential element. These people are good at producing, managing, and distributing knowledge, broadly conceived. At its core, the knowledge economy depends on talent, skills, and the many forms of intelligence. What it does not do is reward and elevate people who are, by the standards of the gifted, not similarly blessed. The contemporary politics that make our world dark reflect largely battles between the knowledge economy's winners and losers.

Many observers, economists, philosophers, social scientists, legal academics, education theorists, and journalists alike, have explored the knowledge economy. I draw on their work throughout this book. Since the mid-2010s, political theorists and public intellectuals have grappled with the degradation of liberal-democratic politics and the growing threats to peace and prosperity as authoritarianism rises around the world. This book fits within that trend. It is, however, the first to connect the knowledge economy directly to our present discontents.

This new mode of production we call the knowledge economy brings us great things based on extraordinary scientific accomplishments and imaginative brilliance. It also fuels struggles around the world through its relentless production of inequality, dislocation, insecurity, and distrust. These are the unintended but profound consequences of an economy that aims to reward skill and talent above all else.

The knowledge economy's paradoxical effects rest on the same factors that explain its success. Economists identify scalability and locality as the twin pillars of this mode of production. Both share an essential feature: developing knowledge through research, experiments, trial and error, and the odd breakthrough costs a lot, while passing on learned knowledge does not. Once people figure out how to profit from a new insight, whether physical,

5 Anthea Roberts & Nicolas Lamp, Six Faces of Globalization: Who Wins, Who Loses, and Why It Matters (2021); Richard Baldwin, The Great Convergence: Information Technology and the New Globalization (2016).

technical, social, or abstract, repeating the performance isn't so hard. Think of a pharmacological breakthrough, like the COVID-19 vaccines we now rely on (to live normal lives). Discovery, development, and testing of the drugs cost billions of dollars. Making and shipping doses cost next to nothing. Thus scaling up the application of a particular bit of knowledge to an ever larger market almost always increases profits, overturning the physical world's historic economic law of diminishing returns. Extraordinary profits result. This is scalability.

At the same time, useful knowledge grows fastest when knowledge workers have dense connections with their peers. Brainstorming, swapping insights and observations, and watching each other try and fail does a better job of producing more valuable knowledge (valuable in the economic sense, knowledge that directly affects the value of goods and services society offers to people) than isolation. Hence the knowledge economy leads to knowledge clusters. Silicon Valley is everyone's favorite example, but many other densely populated communities do this as well. This is locality. Notwithstanding the experiments with telecommuting that the pandemic forced on us, in-person connectivity will continue to dominate this economy.

Knowledge is key to flourishing in today's world. Yet not everyone can be a knowledge worker. Moving into the knowledge sector involves years of education, training, and experimenting, as well as hard-to-acquire skills such as focus, discipline, and tolerance for risk-taking. As one sector rises, others fall back. Workers who do not have the skills that the knowledge economy demands cannot swiftly remake themselves, and many have no hope of ever doing so. Losing ground and hope for themselves and their families, those the knowledge economy leaves behind embrace the politics of resentment and resistance.

The resulting anxiety and distrust have many targets – political, cultural, and educational élites, migrants, local minorities (ethnic and sexual) – but one is those international legal regimes that support the knowledge economy. Populists see international law as foreign and therefore suspect, dedicated to advancing the interests of the hated élites, and full of false promises. The WTO, the international financial institutions, and supranational structures such as the European Union, human rights treaties and courts, trade agreements and foreign investment protection regimes, and international and regional treaties protecting refugees and immigrants have taken hits over the last decade and seem on the verge of collapse.

Locality has a lot to do with these politics. Knowledge workers cluster because productivity relies on connection. The demands of knowledge productivity also mean buying a lot of day-to-day support so that knowledge workers can devote their time and energy to their well-rewarded jobs. Simple economics dictates that as the demand for less skilled work – housekeeping, childcare, food services, transportation, building maintenance and construction, and the like – goes up, either incumbent workers will get paid more (a price effect) or more workers will come to that market (a supply effect). Throughout the world, the supply effect seems to dominate the market for urban low-skill service providers, with immigration the delivery system.

Many migrants come to knowledge clusters, both knowledge workers who can capture the value of their skills through high compensation (whether material or moral) and service workers who do jobs that do not require much training or certification. The latter typically come from places with poor prospects, often profound rural poverty. We can see these two kinds of migration at work in places in the rich West such as New York, London, Silicon Valley (San Jose), Singapore, and Tokyo, as well as Bangalore, Mumbai, the Pearl River Delta (Guangzhou, Hong Kong, and Shenzhen), and Shanghai in the rising global South.

Locality has competitive and distributional consequences. The rise of an industry in a particular place tends to drive out less successful businesses. We thus find the losers from the knowledge economy living where the knowledge workers and the low-wage service workers who support them do not. This physical separation sharpens political disputes.

At the heart of this book is a conflict – the battle for the future – that will decide whether we endure lives of misery amid global disasters, or instead find ways of surviving the looming threats. The battle is a struggle between knowledge workers (who can market their skills globally), poor migrants (those who sustain knowledge workers, increasingly people from poor countries who flock across borders to great urban centers), and the despairing (people whose worked in the economic sectors that the knowledge economy superseded and find adapting, especially migrating domestically or internationally, hard). That struggle underlies most international controversies today and manifests itself, among other arenas, in fights over international law, including control of the internet, immigration, cross-border trade and investment, and ultimately the authority of most international institutions.

COVID-19 made all this worse. It drives inequality and social division. Knowledge workers benefit from technological workarounds that let them remain productive and, more importantly, well-paid. Meanwhile not just the elderly, but the poor and socially marginalized suffer. Already stressed parts of society, especially people of color and low-skill migrants living in crowded, multigenerational homes while working in urban service sectors, pay a terrible price in death and long-term morbidity. During the pandemic, the market value of tech companies skyrocketed, as did the fortunes of their owners. Lower-paid service providers too often lost their jobs, got sick, or died. School closures meant that their children lost what chances they might have had to vault into the knowledge class; privileged kids had online access, tutors, private schools, and dutiful parents to cushion the effects of the shutdown. Vaccine resistance, anti-masking, and quarantine violations sundered families and communities.

States met a borderless, global challenge – a real war against a merciless, impersonal pathogen – not by coming together, but rather with parochialism and lost trust. Revisionist states seeking to disrupt the international status quo, principally China and Russia, exploit the social media that quarantined people around the world look to as a substitute for normal human contact. They sow distrust in liberal democracy, established institutions, and fellow citizens with different backgrounds and beliefs.

Many people got to distrust and disillusionment without any outside help. International organizations, first and foremost the World Health Organization (WHO) and the WTO, failed to check the beggar-thy-neighbor policies of the rich world states, which hoarded personal protective equipment, tests, and vaccines that could contain the global threat. The failure of the West to meet the vaccine needs of the South, coupled with the distrust of many people in the South of the solutions offered, ensures the resilience of the virus and the ongoing vulnerability of humanity.

I do not argue that the knowledge economy dictates outcomes. Economic events create incentives that influence behavior, sometimes powerfully. These incentives compete with other forces that mold culture, societies, and institutions. A world driven crazy by COVID-19 is not one where the economic concept of rationality reigns supreme. This book shows that the knowledge economy has done much to shape the present world, not only to the good. My contribution is to connect that insight, not original with me, to the forces that overturned the ambitions of the immediate post-Cold War period and threaten our world today. I do not claim that this is the whole story, only that it is one that needs telling.

So there's a lot not to like about the knowledge economy. Yet the world cannot simply walk away from it. As COVID-19 shows, knowledge and global cooperation are indispensable to overcoming great crises. The looming threat of climate change, somewhat forgotten during the immediate unrest, persists. Any response that sustains prosperity across the planet while lowering the carbon footprint, if such a way can be found, will depend on the knowledge economy. The world will need all the talents of its ablest people, effectively organized and motivated, to meet the challenges in the pipeline. However we bridge our widening social inequality, if we do so at all, sidelining of the very people whom we need to come up with solutions to our other deep problems cannot be the answer.

Yet it also seems clear that we cannot go back to the status quo ante. The liberal commitment to free movement of people, capital, goods, and services, as well as the aspiration to judge all states by the standards and values of the western liberal democracies, have, as maximalist projects, proved unsustainable. Deference to international bureaucracies and judiciaries has dissipated. The 1990s have left the building and won't come back. International cooperation formalized as law must be redone if the international law project is to survive in any fashion.

THE PLAN OF THIS BOOK

Two lenses, historical and economic, show us how we got here and, perhaps, how we can move on to something better. Part I of this book provides a broad narrative of events. The expansion and creation of international organizations took place in the aftermath of the fall of the Iron Curtain and the opening of historically autarkic economies around the world. This part explains how the ideas of liberal internationalism guided these steps. Challenges to the new regimes emerged early in the twenty-first century, first from terrorism and then through the world financial crisis. Confidence in the purposes and management of the international organizations eroded. A rising China became a strategic risk where it had been an essential economic partner. Cyberspace became a source of both misinformation and insecurity. Things first changed gradually, then all at once. This account concludes with a look at the many faces of national populism around the world and the ravages of the COVID-19 pandemic.

Part II of the book does political economy. Not myself trained as an economist or any other kind of social scientist, I take the path of legions of law professors who borrow from those fields based on a sense of what seems credible and consistent with observed evidence. Drawing on the research of these scholars, I unpack the knowledge economy and its international dimensions.

This part shows how economic dynamism driven by the search for more and better ways to do things underlies not only international economic liberalism but also commitments, at the international as well as national level, to free expression and nondiscrimination, including open cyberspace. It details the ways that the knowledge economy has a geographical, but not national, dimension, favoring urban knowledge clusters while spawning deindustrialization in national heartlands. It explores the chasm between residents of great global cities, both rich and poor, and people outside these cities that see marginalization and immiseration as their fate. This chasm fuels the dysfunctional politics in so many places in the West and the growing geopolitical tensions between West and South.

We also must consider the possibility that a knowledge economy enclosed within one large authoritarian country might enjoy better prospects than a system of globally distributed production and worldwide consumption held together by the institutions of liberal internationalism. We may be heading toward a second-best world of increasingly national markets supported by technological accomplishments that make managing an illiberal state easier. If international cooperation fails because of the deep conflicts that the knowledge economy spawns, advanced capitalism in one country might prevail. This is to say that the twenty-first century might be China's.

The arguments found in this part do not rely on strict economic determinism. I share the taste of most contemporary historians, at least in the United States, for contingency and multicausal, complex stories. My point is simply that the students of the knowledge economy, mostly but not only economists, make a good case about its importance, growth, and structure. As such, the knowledge economy contributes to forces that shape, even though they do not compel, both individual behavior and political arrangements that end up expressed as law. I emphasize the knowledge economy in this book mostly because I think it is important, but also because most practitioners of international law and international relations do not know as much about it as they should. The knowledge economy is not everything, but, to paraphrase Vice President Biden's exclamation when Congress adopted the Affordable Care Act, it's a big deal.[6]

Part III of this book brings the historical and political-economic perspectives to bear on the work of international law. The twenty-first century presents serious challenges to international legal regimes supporting peace and security, immigration, trade and investment, and law-based resolution of international disputes. Not only do important actors flout rules that we thought had rested on a broad state consensus, but they defy specific orders by international tribunals vested with the authority to issue them. The book takes a deep dive into these stories to show that they are not isolated incidents, but rather form a pattern. The backlash against liberal internationalism is about more than trade, investment, and migration. Rather, fights in these fields are part of a general struggle representing a broad rejection of the ambitions of the liberal international regime.

6 As people might remember, an open mic caught Biden's remark, which included an emphatic adjective between big and deal.

Part IV considers where the world is headed and the prospects for restructuring international law. It argues that risks of cataclysms even greater than COVID-19 loom before us, and that the world could find itself turned into a republic of misery and privation.[7] Global warming looks perilous, but let's not overlook new wars and the spread of weapons of mass destruction, new pandemics, worldwide financial collapse, greater toxicity of cyberspace, and even more adept national-populist regimes that thrive on conflict and violence. Bleak futures seem all too evident. Perhaps we are doomed.

Giving up all hope, however, seems too cheap and easy. To hold back the potential catastrophes, political leaders and entrepreneurs as well as international lawyers must discover where international cooperation still makes sense. Part of the search for effective responses to the lurking global threats includes finding ways to restore confidence in organized responses to global problems. International law remains a useful tool for making these solutions work. Restoring a consensus in its favor will take time, however, and must proceed in modest steps. Smallball must replace visions. The extinction events might get here first, but we can't go any faster.

I offer conjectures about how the smallball story might play out. Many of the existing international legal structures, I speculate, likely will retrench or disappear. In particular, the WTO, the European Union, the International Criminal Court (ICC), and the present investor-state dispute settlement (ISDS) regime may not survive in their present forms, if at all. There remain, however, projects where the benefits may be sufficiently great to overcome current obstacles. These include protecting cybersecurity and big data, safeguarding the integrity of the international financial system, resetting international economic law, restructuring investment protection without private litigation against states, and inducing multinational businesses to stay away from the greatest human rights atrocities. Rather than relying on international organizations, leadership of these projects will belong to one or a few states, acting as norm entrepreneurs herding other states toward acquiescence. It will be a long time before we return to the bureaucratic and structural experiments that sprang up in the aftermath of the Cold War.

Progress in these areas will not solve the big problems coming down the road – global warming and the environmental cataclysms that result, new pandemics, growing inequality, the spread of weapons of mass destruction, and enduring regional conflicts. But enough experience with successful cooperation may

7 Walter Scheidel, The Great Leveler: Violence and the History of Inequality from the Stone Age to the Twenty-First Century (2018).

restore the potential of international law to help out when states turn to these perils. These first steps only begin the process, but they are essential.

Turning Mark Antony on his head, I come here to praise international law, not to bury it. The knowledge economy's obvious gains distracted us from its costs. We adapted international law to serve that economy without thinking about those whom these changes harmed. We have reaped the consequences in the populist backlash. Yet, I argue, the international law toolkit still contains valuable instruments for coping with the great challenges the world is throwing our way. The trick is in recognizing what hasn't worked and finding new ways of using the tools that we have.

MY PRIORS

In a world increasingly drawn to crude categories as a substitute for patient and creative analysis, I feel a duty to declare my priors up-front. If nothing else, sketching an intellectual genealogy for this book will help readers decide whether it is worth their time to pay attention to it. I wish that people would not fall back on ideological labels as a substitute for work, but I also don't want anyone to feel cheated.

Here I will describe my convictions, although I appreciate that others will want to show how I must be wrong about them. I do not pretend to be a philosopher or a political theorist and don't intend to become one now. What follows is where I think I am coming from, speaking as a humble jobbing international lawyer who tries to tell good stories.

I believe that partisan politics as well as superficial use of the terms liberal and conservative represent a profoundly clunky way of thinking about law and policy, especially international law. In my youth I identified with the New Left and hung out with people aligned with the Black Panther Party. Later, I became a student of Soviet politics, economics, and ideology and worked briefly as a political analyst in the Central Intelligence Agency. I then moved into law. An interest in matters considered vital to national security provided a common thread throughout my career. At the same time, I became ever more mindful of how swiftly events can upend the assumptions on which these considerations rest. Through good fortune more than ability, I had the privilege of serving as an international lawyer in the Clinton, George W. Bush, Trump, and Biden administrations, as well as a consultant to the International Monetary Fund, the World Bank, and the Organisation for Economic Co-operation and Development. In every instance I never held positions of real authority but had a chance to watch government, both national and international, at work up-close.

I still harbor the values and ideals that inspired me in youth, except that I now believe millenarian expectations are dangerous rather than liberating. The confounding of my sense of a revolution in American society and culture at the end of the 1960s, followed by the even more violent crushing of my hopes for Russia at the end of the 1980s, taught me to suspect promises and prospects of radical change generally. I lack a commitment to either US political party or to the particular bundle of policy prescriptions defined as progressive or conservative. Accordingly, my narrative reflects a skeptical eye cast upon all political packages. I greatly admire my colleagues in government, gifted lawyers and experts whose judgment and public-mindedness amaze me. I stand in less awe of the politicians to whom they report.

My critique of the knowledge economy as a base and international law as a superstructure (with apologies to Marx, from whom I draw but do not follow) comes from inside liberal internationalism as I understand it. Deep humility coupled with an irresistible desire to improve on what we know and can do seem to me the heart of the liberal enterprise. Humility does not exclude unconventional, even audacious conjectures, but rather demand recognizing the difference between a hypothesis and an established fact. I have strong convictions, but all remain subject to overturning. Without confronting the data, carefully considering a full range of arguments, and pressing on in the face of great obstacles, we don't get vaccines, the internet, or Paxlovid. Of course, without a deeply interconnected world we don't get pandemics either, or at least not ones that take over our lives so quickly and completely.

The concept of liberal internationalism itself is problematic. Other terms, such as neoliberalism, cosmopolitanism, and globalism, confuse the picture and carry political valences that I want to avoid. Liberal internationalism, as I understand it, involves the application of the methods of liberalism – free inquiry, radical skepticism, disentanglement from tribal loyalties, and an aspiration to advance human flourishing – to projects that take into account as well as build interdependence among states and peoples of the world. My understanding of the concept, I hasten to say, does not conform to any school of international relations theory, whether rational interest, liberal institutionalism, or any other ism.

While acknowledging and trying to surmount liberal internationalism's shortcomings, I reject any ideological orthodoxy that would shut down the process of open inquiry when it threatens some revealed truth. Maintaining that a person can't ask certain questions or follow the evidence wherever it leads us prevents us from making the world less bad and fails to help the victims of injustice. I accordingly reject arguments that would limit attempts to learn from experiences of people around the globe just because their worlds seem different, weird, or even an affront to our most cherished values. Raised as I was as a Calvinist, my remaining tie to that faith is dutiful adherence to the path of Reverend Bayes, a Presbyterian minister and mathematician.[8]

QUESTIONING MY PRIORS AND THE POSSIBILITIES OF LIBERALISM

I accept attacks on liberal internationalism that highlight its hubris and emptiness. The first tends to come from the left, which shows how liberalism hides the misery and humiliation it inflicts.[9] The second comes more from the right, which argues that it cuts off people from a real sense of connection and common purpose.[10] What motivates this book is a wish to take these charges on board without abandoning the fundamental principles of discovery based on skeptical, compassionate, and courageous inquiry.

Internationalism for me is not a rejection of the nation state or an embrace of a cosmopolitan attitude for moral or aesthetic reasons. Rather, it is a recognition, I think unavoidable, of the nature of the contemporary world as deeply and variously interconnected. We cannot grapple with this world, either to ward off danger or to make it better, without accepting this essential reality. It does not follow, however, that this recognition makes more international law and international organizations the default preference. To the contrary, I will argue that in many cases, the best international norm is one of getting out of the way of states that apply innovative solutions to particular problems.

What this book seeks to do is to save liberal internationalism from itself. International law seems as good a place as any to face that challenge. International law, like any legal system, rests on beliefs about how the world works. It succeeds or fails based on how it uses its special techniques, reflecting those beliefs, to make people's lives better or worse. The heart of this book's argument is that a big part of the international law project of the late twentieth century came undone, but that liberal commitments demand that we try to learn from these failures and to do better. Accordingly, we should neither deny the blunders nor give up on using international law's resources to help people around the world have better lives, if they are fit to the task.

8 Thomas Bayes, *An Essay towards Solving a Problem in the Doctrine of Chances*, 53 PHILOSOPHICAL TRANSACTIONS 370 (1763).

9 SAMUEL MOYN, NOT ENOUGH: HUMAN RIGHTS IN AN UNEQUAL WORLD (2019).

10 PATRICK DENEEN, WHY LIBERALISM FAILED (2018).

Liberalism, a posture that tries to learn from as many ways of living together as possible, does not go well with triumphalism. It demands circumspection, a quality at odds with the contemporary world that rewards attention more than accomplishment. It comes with a sense of tragedy, an understanding that things often do not turn out as hoped. As this book considers, there may be no way out of the present mess or the ones still to come, and all we have left may be despair. The case for the liberal enterprise does not rest on historical inevitability, but rather on an intuition that, whatever its shortcomings, it remains the best way to make sense of and meet the challenges of a disordered world. This book proceeds in that spirit.

PART I

The Rise and Fall of Liberal Internationalism and the New World Order

This part traces a historical arc that begins with the collapse of communism and ends with a world in crisis. At the start, a consensus took form among most governments, if not necessarily in academia or civil society, that something called liberalism had prevailed, that liberalism dictated certain attitudes and ideas about the world lumped together under the label "liberal internationalism," and that this framed an agenda for building up international institutions and obligations through commitments freely undertaken by national governments. Technological optimism lubricated the path. People in the knowledge industries as well as many academics and governments believed that the democratic connectivity embodied in the new World Wide Web and related tools would empower ordinary people and lead to more and better international projects that would marginalize obstructive states.

This cheerful consensus about the inevitability of liberalism and liberal internationalism did not stick. First it frayed, then it tore apart. The last eight years have left us shaken, anxious, and lost. This part reminds us of the path we took to get to the dark place where we now live. Although the knowledge economy lies behind many of these developments, these chapters only occasionally note its role in the events recounted. This part describes what happened; the next part looks to the knowledge economy to explain what went on beneath the surface.

2

The End of Communism and the Embrace of the Washington Consensus (1989–2000, Part I)

This chapter tells how the rich world, starting with the United States, sought to remake the former socialist space into a buttress of an integrated world economy. The 1990s was for many people a long-promised fulfillment, the capstone to what Henry Luce in 1941 had called the American Century.[1] The socialist world, authoritarian and autarkic, suddenly embraced the principles of liberal democracy and economic openness. Dismantling the oppressive political systems, first of Eurasia and then of right-wing regimes in places like South Africa, Indonesia, and Chile, happened quickly. Establishing stable representative democracies based on liberal economies was the ultimate goal. The leaders of the West saw themselves as up to the task. Cheerleaders such as journalist Thomas Friedman prophesized a new international order based on interconnectivity and global markets.[2] For liberals, it seemed as if the world was going their way.

History has moments that provoke a sense of shocking transformation. Even though we know that a point straddles decades of accumulating events and that we can't understand its significance for many years (if ever), we still insist that something profound happened.[3] The death of communism was one of those moments. It meant rejecting the means by which the Soviet Union both controlled its own territory and dominated its dependencies in Central and Eastern Europe. It discredited the theoretical structure of communist ideology that guided, or at least legitimized, a form of political, social, and economic

1 Alan Brinkley, The Publisher: Henry Luce and His American Century (2010).

2 Thomas L. Friedman, The Lexus and the Olive Tree: Understanding Globalization (1999).

3 Pierre Nora, *Between Memory and History*: Les Lieux de Mémoire, 26 Representations 7 (Spring 1989).

organization ruling in much of the world. The mechanism and ideology had shown wear and tear for decades, but the end came quickly.

Elections in June 1989 brought the Solidarity movement to power in Poland, the first of the Soviet Union's European satellites to slip its grasp. President Mikhail Gorbachev announced the end of the Soviet Union on (western) Christmas Day 1991. A lot happened in those thirty-one months. Yugoslavia came undone. Every Central and East European state north of the Balkans installed new governments pledged to break with the Soviet model and embrace liberal democracy. The Romanians shot the Ceauşescus. The Rolling Stones came to Prague to perform for Vaclav Havel. The Soviet-supported Sandinista regime in Nicaragua consented to democratic elections that brought its ouster. The Rao government in India, with Finance Minister Manmohan Singh taking the point, began dismantling state controls of the economy and barriers to international trade and investment. Deng Xiaoping's new path for China became manifest. The apartheid regime in South Africa released Nelson Mandela from prison and began negotiating the terms of its liquidation, thereby opening up the country to greater foreign trade and investment. The UN Security Council blessed an armed intervention to oust Iraq from Kuwait, its first such action since 1950. References to 1989 as an *annus mirabilis* abounded, and some went so far as to declare the end of history.[4]

Only Cuba and North Korea seemed not to have gotten the message, although China's path remained obscure. China did not formally renounce Marxism–Leninism and remains today under the control of a party that brands itself as communist. It crushed a student-led protest movement in Beijing's Tiananmen Square only days before the Polish election, killing hundreds if not thousands of demonstrators. But its economic opening up and the profound expansion of its economy during the 1990s convinced many that it had become a valuable component of the new world order. People believed that, the name of its ruling party aside, China had become a nationalist state shaped by Confucian principles, not a surviving outpost of the transformative evangelical ideology that had swept over the world in the years after World War II.

All this unfolded against another revolution, one that changed the way people could see, hear, and shape the world. Online connectivity became an option, especially in the rich West. Technological breakthroughs in satellite communications made in the 1960s had, by the 1980s, transformed the way news media could collect and broadcast images and sounds globally and

[4] Francis Fukuyama, The End of History and the Last Man (1992).

instantaneously. Video cameras were still too expensive to support a great mass of content originators – that would change in the next century – but more networks could put their people on the ground in newsworthy spots and, using the satellites, process and broadcast the content in real time. The Gulf War was the first where billions around the planet could watch what an air war looked like from the perspective of the target. The CNN effect was born.

This effect did two things. First, it gave leaders in charge of newsworthy places, especially those with a risk of violence or visible suffering, a sense that the whole world actually could watch. Second, it gave the global news providers confidence that they could curate the narrative. Doubtless their principal interest was in securing viewers, preferably with trust, but "normal" editing also entailed shaping the narrative to make it easy on the viewers. Curating had a reductive function, screening out complexities that would confuse or annoy the audience.

The producers of these news outlets, to be sure, did not call themselves curators, in the sense of assembling words and sounds to make a point. They edited the news, but not (they sincerely believed) based on their political convictions. Most thought that they edited, and that editing reflected commonsense assumptions, shared by everyone they knew, about what their audience wanted and should be led to want. They aspired to elevate their audience, but within the context of values and assumptions about the ways of the world that they thought were broadly held and good.

Managing the news in this fashion made great sense in a world of limited news outlets. Presenters admired for their acumen and erudition could speak with the voice of God, as people in the industry said of Walter Cronkite. They helped build and bolster a consensus about what counted and what made sense and made it easy to dismiss dissidents as disgruntled cranks and oddballs. Other kinds of knowledge élites, in politics, education, and cultural institutions, similarly held sway, confident in their qualities and good intentions. As technological change later disrupted these industries and blurred the distinction between legacy information providers and revisionists, imposing mainstream sensibilities and assumptions became more of a political choice, and less of an unassailable best practice.

At the cusp of the collapse of the Soviet Union, one particular instance of cable news curating had a dramatic and enduring impact. In August 1991, a segment of the Soviet leadership put President Gorbachev under house arrest and declared an emergency government to respond to growing instability, especially the risk that the various union republics would secede. Although it was the month when the great mass of Muscovites leave for vacation, many people took to the streets in Moscow to protest this attack on the reform

FIGURE 2.1 Russian President Boris Yel'tsin addresses the crowd standing atop of a tank in front of the Russian government building, August 19, 1991. Source: Associated Press.

process. Large demonstrations, previously unthinkable, had become commonplace there since the start of 1991. The locus of resistance became the square outside the "White House," the home of the Russian Federation's parliament. A tank appeared in that square, recalling immediately the global image of a protestor–tank encounter that fixed the meaning of the tragic Tiananmen Square protests two summers before. Compare Figures 2.1 and 2.2. Instead, the tank stopped and Russian President Yel'tsin mounted it. The crisis was over. This was people power embodied, viewers thought, personal courage and good ideas prevailing over the dark forces of the dying past. A new era was dawning and Yel'tsin would lead it.

The lens both captured and made history, much as Hegel understood Napoleon, "the world spirit," when he saw the emperor enter Jena in 1806. What the television viewers did not see, because the newsgatherers and their editors believed they would not want to see, was the background to the great confrontation between man and tank. If the cameras had panned out, they would have shown a block of the capital's shops lined, as was typical at that time, with consumers stoically waiting to get in. The hopeful customers did

FIGURE 2.2 A Chinese man stands alone to block a line of tanks heading east on Beijing's Changan Blvd. in Tiananmen Square, June 5, 1989. Source: Associated Press.

not know what would be on the shelves but took the presence of a line as a signal that something desirable was inside. They waited not for a new dawn of history to break or for the drama of violence between the army and the protestors to resolve. Rather, they needed to get through their day as best they could as hard-pressed members of a dysfunctional society. They had no reason to believe that the events captured by the cable news cameras would make any difference in their already challenging lives.

As this pairing of global news reality and ordinary life suggests, two narratives about these events emerged. In the West, the popular account linked freedom to democracy and proclaimed that the people in the Soviet-dominated world had come to see markets and competition, both economic and political, as the only way to the good life. A counternarrative to the West's story bubbled up within Russia, maintaining that frustrated bosses trying to grab a larger share of social plunder had more to do with the winding down of the Soviet system and its imitators. During the 1990s, policymakers in the West acted as if they believed the first story. By the twenty-first century, the arc of events in the former Soviet space pointed in the other direction.

From within the post-Soviet space, the plunder story had a lot going for it. To understand why it made sense to people who lived there, recall how the economy was supposed to work. State planning meant that an independent government agency (in the Soviet Union this was the State Planning Committee called Gosplan), divorced from the enterprises that made and bought things, issued orders telling the enterprises which one would make how much of something for which customers. To comply with the plan, enterprises relied on the agency to order its suppliers to provide the needed inputs. These enterprises in turn had to render its products to customers designated by the agency. Practice varied among states that used this system, but in general buyers and sellers could negotiate only secondary terms such as delivery schedules and a certain range of quality features. Price and quantity terms in these contracts came from the agency.[5]

Market fundamentalists argue that this approach to economic management has a great deficiency: it blocks the creation of valuable information on capacity, desire, and informed expectations about the future that open transactions can reveal. State planning, by contrast, depended on judgments by bureaucrats in the planning agency about which resources would do the most good where. These bureaucrats made their decisions based more on power than information. Because the system mandated that they keep their distance from the enterprise, they lacked working knowledge of how production and consumption actually work. More importantly, they owed their jobs to people who cared more about maintaining the existing power structure than about economic results.

Of course, in the rich West large enterprises frequently contain multiple stages of production – think of General Motors and its acquisition of Fisher Body after World War I – and operate the same way, by fiat rather than outsourcing decision-making to the market. Many economists believe that the "make or buy" decision – the choice between buying a component of a product on the market versus making it oneself – is complex and interesting, not self-evident.[6] Countries that hewed to the Soviet model, however, did not allow enterprises to experiment with this choice, but instead mandated "make" all the way down. Some allowed limited exceptions for small-scale consumer goods and services, such as the produce from household gardens. As a general rule, however, the entire production process from raw materials, labor, and know-how to finished goods and services made its way under state planning.

The market fundamentalists weren't wrong about lost information but missed a far graver problem with the Soviet model of economic management. Planning rested on power rather than data, and those who exercised power faced few external political constraints. In most of the countries saddled with

5 Olympiad S. Ioffe, *Law and Economy in the USSR*, 95 HARV. L. REV. 1591 (1982).

6 Benjamin Klein, *Vertical Integration as Organizational Ownership: The Fisher Body–General Motors Relationship Revisited*, 4 J. L. ECON. & ORG. 199 (1988); R. H. Coase, *The Acquisition of Fisher Body by General Motors*, 43 J. L. & ECON. 15 (2000).

this system, a single party dominated, making it impossible for outsiders to hold underperformers to account. Rather, removal of decision-makers depended on the party, and the party looked after its own. In most of the states that adopted state planning, the system evolved into one where patronage, transactional alliances, and corruption held sway, not technocratic expertise.

Two aspects of this system, neither inevitable but both pervasive, drove this process. First, "socialist" political leaders saw themselves in competition with western "capitalists" and wanted economic results to display the superiority of their system. Thus they demanded high levels of production that denied enterprises any slack. They called this taut planning. Second, the system employed the principle of one-man leadership to give a single person (mostly men) full authority as well as accountability for the performance of each enterprise. Enterprise directors thus faced both a deep challenge and an opportunity: meeting production quotas was hard because the suppliers of their inputs typically could not meet their own ambitious production targets, but any goods that they managed to make and hold had great value because of the general overall scarcity of anything worth having.

Over time, a dynamic of hoarding, bribery, cooked books, and plunder took hold. A vivid example was Uzbekistan in the 1970s. This large Soviet republic was a cotton mono-economy where half the supposed annual output did not exist, although state records claimed otherwise. Fraud backed by the raw power of party functionaries allowed the state cotton enterprise to deceive Gosplan and the Moscow leadership. As in Uzbekistan, throughout the Soviet-style countries successful management increasingly meant achieving an edge in hiding assets from the state and identifying the best superiors to bribe. For superiors, success turned increasingly on the ability to harvest bribes.

In these countries, the formal hierarchical structure of political authority, running down from the top party organs through sectoral and regional bodies to the production units, increasingly diverged from the real-world ability to get rich through graft. As this gap grew and became more evident, those supposed to be on top attempted increasingly ambitious reforms to restore the ordained order, which the real-world winners managed to turn to their own benefit. Eventually the formal system imploded and the nominal foundation of power – the Communist Party of the Soviet Union and its clones elsewhere in the empire – disappeared.[7]

Getting rid of the party structures led many in the rich world to believe that the ideology and values of the party were also abandoned. What these

7 Paul B. Stephan, *The Fall: Understanding the Collapse of Soviet Communism*, 29 SUFFOLK U. L. REV. 17 (1995).

outsiders failed to see was that actual practice in these societies rested on hoarding, bribery, cooked books, and plunder, and that discarding the formal political structures didn't change these fundamentals. The transactional approach and the centrality of patronage networks remained after the party structures disappeared. These were the system's ideology and values and, as it turned out, its legacy.

Consider a slightly stylized example, drawn from actual events during the final years of the Soviet Union. Someone in the relevant ministry would relabel stocks of high-quality petroleum as waste oil, meaning it supposedly had no commercial value. Once relabeled, the oil could be sold to a foreign customer, typically a Cypriote entity due to the favorable tax treaties, with the low price for waste oil remitted to the state entity that held the stocks. From the Cypriote entity title in the oil would pass among several closely held companies, trusts, or other entities located in tax havens with strong bank secrecy laws. At the end of the daisy chain of transactions, a commodities trader (in those years often Marc Rich, a US fugitive from justice working out of Switzerland) would buy the petroleum at the world market price, many times more than the price paid to the state entity. The difference, an extraordinary profit buried in the daisy-chain entities that but for these transactions would have gone to the state, would be doled out among the persons who reclassified the petroleum, other government officials who supported the transaction (often officials in the security services), and entrepreneurs on their way to becoming oligarchs.

People estimate that roughly $20 billion a year left Russia this way from 1989 onwards. Other resource-rich countries saw similarly laundered flight capital. Some of the money nested in London, New York, Lausanne, Los Angeles, and other cosmopolitan fleshpots, often as real estate. Perhaps the larger portion of these assets returned home as "foreign" direct investment. A few businesspeople became publicly and fabulously rich; their partners in government did as well or better but more quietly.

This story illustrates only a part of the world transformation that seemed to crystalize in 1989–91. An extreme form of government failure – a term that the economist Anne Krueger coined to compare bad state economic management to the market failures that justify government intervention in the economy – explains why the Soviet Union collapsed.[8] Reforms in Latin America, Africa, and South and East Asia had their own histories and complicated explanations. China lacked the vast internationally marketable

8 Anne O. Krueger, *Government Failures in Development*, 4 J. ECON. PERSP. 9 (1990).

natural resources that cursed the Soviet Union, and India had a democratic multiparty politics that did not sit easily with Nehru's founding commitment to Soviet-style economic management. Government failure and persistent corruption features in many of the accounts of the reforms at the end of the 1980s, but not all and not necessarily to the same degree. To the extent that the collapse of the Soviet Union framed the transformation, however, looking behind that collapse and exploring its footprint on the present remain useful.

Believing that the transformation represented an "aha!" moment and a triumph for liberal institutions and ideology, entrepreneurs, economists, bankers, accountants, and lawyers poured into the suddenly liberalizing countries, hoping to create emerging markets out of what had been state satrapies. The policy formula was fairly straightforward: privatize as much and as fast as possible; open up the country to foreign investment and trade; get rid of state subsidies that distort the market for mass commodities such as food and fuel; and build a tax system as a substitute for government ownership of enterprises as well as a more transparent instrument for economic governance.

Those offering these policies – technocrats from international and regional public financial institutions, rich-world national ministries of finance, civil society organizations such as the Open Society Foundation, universities, and the private sector, backed up by western political leaders – typically had greater confidence in the quality of the advice than those who received it. Many countries nevertheless tried to implement these reforms, whether from inspiration, a lack of any better idea, or a concern that walking away from an ascendant West might have unhappy consequences. Most of the countries in Central and Eastern Europe and Eurasia had spent their last years as Soviet-style states accumulating significant international indebtedness. This debt gave the international financial institutions (principally the IMF and the World Bank plus the OECD, a provider of technocratic expertise rather than finance) leverage over financial and economic policy. For a few heady years, the in-country representative of these institutions would sit next to the office of the president, prime minister, or minister of finance of the debtor states, offering advice that sometimes seemed suspiciously like commands.

My part in the reform project provides an example of the larger transformational agenda. From 1993 to 1998 I worked as an international technical expert, mostly in the former Soviet space. I focused on the tax piece of the program. Tax reform was only one element of the structural reform program that western experts and their sponsoring organizations presented to the emerging market states. Each of these projects had its own set of tasks and backstory.

I had an ongoing consulting contract with the US Department of Treasury but also took on assignments from the Fund, the Bank, and the OECD. Since 1979 I had taught Soviet law and US tax law at the University of Virginia and belonged to civil-society groups that made connections between Soviets and Americans. I had visited the Soviet Union dozens of times, done workshops and taught classes at the leading academic institutions, and in December 1991 shared the last day of official business with the leaders of the Soviet parliament and its constitutional review tribunal. As no one else in the US legal academy had such a bizarre combination of interests, opportunities abounded for me to advise the new post-Soviet states on creating tax systems as an instrument of economic reform.

The economists and tax lawyers I encountered along the way were highly skilled professionals, many brilliant and inspiring. Some had worked on tax reform in the global South, especially places such as the Dominican Republic and Malawi that had embraced new approaches to economic development early on. None had spent much time, if any, in the pre-reform Soviet-model countries, which had had no need of their services. These western experts largely assumed that politicians and policymakers wanted to integrate their economies with the world economy and that no competing model for managing the challenges of this integration existed.

What stays with me still is the range of people with whom we partnered in the Russian government. Incumbent leaders of the tax bureaucracies, principally the Ministry of Finance and the State Tax Service, seemed in 1993 deeply skeptical of outsiders and their advice. They hosted us because their political masters expected them to, but they regarded our meetings as something to be endured. In contrast, the civil society people, who seemed the most enthusiastic reformers, clever, incisive, and talking a great Chicago school, were a joy to work with. Disturbingly, a few of these folks ended up with unaccounted wealth and amazing bling.

The person on the Russian side with whom we had the most extensive and closest relationship was Sergey D. Shatalov, a physicist who had represented the Academy of Science in the first (more or less) democratically elected Russian parliament. The son of a Soviet Army general, he had credibility within traditional political circles, but also was an independent and admirable thinker. As one of the more numerate people in the parliament, he gravitated to tax policy and authored early Russian tax legislation. He was in the White House, the parliament's home, when Yel'tsin's troops fired on it in October 1993, after which Yel'tsin dissolved the legislature. Briefly in civil society, and then back in government as a deputy minister, he became the point person for the Tax Code, a project consummated at the end of the decade. He later took the lead in President Putin's use of the tax system to reassert national control over energy resources and to suppress oligarchs who had gotten above themselves. He retired a few years ago without any detectable signs of exceptional personal wealth. I respect him greatly, even though we became adversaries of a sort when the victims of some of his tax practices sought my help to obtain international justice.

Other experts in accounting, banking, bankruptcy, finance, and the like had their own stories. There was no master plan. Efforts to theorize what the reform project stood for developed mostly after the reforms were under way. Most of the advisers were not ideologues or political philosophers, but rather people with technical skills trying to solve problems. Even so, several background assumptions ran through these endeavors, a skein of commitments that, if not fully theorized, still formed a fairly coherent view of the world. The term "Washington Consensus," developed originally to explain the George H. W. Bush administration's approach to a Mexican financial crisis, morphed into catchall for these ideas.[9] I offer here a sketch of what reformers then took for granted as well as a synopsis of the fault lines that later undid the consensus.

MARKETS ARE USEFUL

In a complex and dynamic environment, people making their way in life need constantly updated information about the present state of the world as well as useful predictions about the future. When functioning properly, markets do this. Economists speak of "revealed preferences" or "having skin in the game" to distinguish the information conveyed by consequential choices – spending from a budget, when any one choice means forgoing others – from cheap talk. Market-based information can become what economists call a public good. It is nonrivalrous, which is to say that consumption of the information by any one person won't affect the ability of any other user to take advantage of it, and can be made to be nonexclusive, which is to say that it can be openly distributed at little cost to consumers. Accordingly, appropriately behaving markets, once up and running, can greatly enrich a society just from the information they create.

The technical advisers who came to the emerging markets of the 1990s urged their advisees to create markets to accompany privatization. Goods and

9 John G. Williamson, *Lowest Common Denominator or Neoliberal Manifesto? The Polemics of the Washington Consensus* in CHALLENGING THE ORTHODOXIES 13 (Richard M. Auty & John Toye eds., 1996).

services that previously were doled out by state organs through the planning process had to be made tradeable. This entailed two steps, putting those commodities into the hands of actors who had the right incentives to trade or use and creating mechanisms through which actors could transact with like-minded persons in trades that would stand up to later regret.

The first step, advisers believed, typically meant "privatization," transferring goods and services to people who would capture the gains, and suffer the losses, of the trade-or-use decision. The second meant putting the resources of the state, expressed through its legal system, behind property and contract rights, so that traders could count on their transactions surviving envy and remorse. These steps would set in motion a process by which, in theory, goods and services would find their "highest and best use" by winding up in the hands of people who valued them the most.

Privatization required mechanisms to move the state-owned assets destined for private ownership into the hands of people capable of making trade-or-use decisions. The choices were fraught, because under the Soviet model administrators, while not owners, still derived considerable benefits from their authority. In many places these administrators held on to enough power to effectively veto the decisions of the newly installed political leaders. In a few places, the international financial institutions had enough clout to overcome the incumbent administrators' veto, but these tended to be smaller countries with many reasons to resent and distrust the Soviet Union (such as the Baltic states, the Czech Republic, Hungary, and Poland).

The Czechs pioneered the voucher privatization method, perhaps the simplest and seemingly the most transparent means to put publicly owned assets into private hands. The state would convert state-owned enterprises slated for privatization into stock companies, put the companies' shares in a trust, and then put the shares up for auction. It would concurrently distribute to citizens vouchers that they could use to bid in these auctions. Those who got the distributed vouchers could sell them or wait for the auctions. Some auctions were restricted to vouchers, while others allowed cash, which in practice meant foreign bidders.

This system had at least two problems. First, the decision to accept foreign money as an alternative to vouchers need not rest on objective, technocratic factors. Insiders could steer the decision in ways that allowed them to extract a return from the choice. Second, a fair per capita distribution of vouchers meant that most wound up in the hands of people largely unfamiliar with market transactions, creating what economists call information asymmetries (significant discrepancies in knowledge among participants in a transaction). More sophisticated actors could buy up the untested vouchers, gambling that naïve distributees would undervalue them. These gambles sometimes led to great fortunes, as voucher entrepreneurs flipped their hoards for valuable privatized enterprises, which they could either sell to foreign investors or manage themselves.

In other states where cooked books and looting were already well-established, privatization enlarged the field for rigged transactions. As the "waste oil" example illustrates, what Russians called "spontaneous" privatization meant fraud and embezzlement. Not only did assets end up in the hands of shady characters without the public getting anything in return, but the shady characters ended up not with free and clear title to their assets, but rather living under a sword of Damocles. Just as the avenues of power allowed the spontaneous transactions to go forward, new arrangements among those in power could reverse them. Finding ways of holding powerful actors at bay, rather than identifying market opportunities, became the key skill for survival. Under these conditions, markets no longer do the work they could do, because sellers and buyers cannot confirm what they are getting.[10]

FINANCIAL MARKETS PROVIDE USEFUL INFORMATION

The international economic institutions had an especially strong faith in the ability of financial markets to generate information and therefore value. Transactions tied to currency exchange and interest rates made by sophisticated actors and staking trillions of dollars served as a kind of continuing audit on the performance and prospects of national economies. This market is huge. In 2019, according to the Bank for International Settlements, the nominal value of daily trades in currencies and interest rates averaged $6.6 trillion and $6.5 trillion respectively. As formerly state-dominated economies opened themselves up to the outside world, this information would measure the wisdom of their policy choices and the risk of backsliding. World financial markets would do a better job than any team of experts in letting national policymakers know whether they were heading in the right direction.

States under the autarkic model for managing international economic relations, of which the Soviet Union represented an extreme example, had used currency restrictions as a form of economic governance, limiting access to foreign currency to discourage imports of foreign goods and services as well as licensing access for approved transactions. These licenses, valuable only because of the restriction, often became a means of rewarding insiders.

[10] Paul B. Stephan, *Toward a Positive Theory of Privatization: Lessons from Soviet-Type Economies*, 16 INT'L REV. L. & ECON. 173 (1996).

Freeing up financial markets thus resulted not just in generating better information on the quality of macroeconomic policies, but also in shutting down a particular pathway for corruption. The foreign advisers also pushed countries to relax or eliminate restrictions on "capital account" currency transfers, that is funds for financing investments rather than short-term consumption. They believed that western investors, rather than domestic politicians, would make better decisions about where to put capital to promote new enterprises and jobs.

Pre-reform, states had accepted inflation, overt or disguised by the absence of market prices, as the cost of giving their subjects tangible benefits such as subsidized food and fuel without offsetting taxes. The international economic institutions regarded inflation as a tax on investment, and thus as an obstacle to private economic activity. They promoted anti-inflationary policies as a means to foster both foreign and domestic investment, which would help private markets do a better job of measuring success and failure. Typically, this means discouraging governments from running deficits, even at the cost of cutting back social safety nets.

To be sure, not all the prominent people tied to the international economic institutions embraced these prescriptions. Joseph Stiglitz, who as an academic economist had done groundbreaking work on information asymmetries, saw the consensus policies as simplistic and more likely to harm than to help. Serving as the Bank's chief economist from 1997 to 2000, he argued that financial markets had significant downsides, especially insufficient means to link transactions to their mid- and long-term consequences.[11] His criticisms, however, had little impact during the 1990s, however much they have since become accepted wisdom. His reward was the 2001 Nobel, but not any immediate policy impact.[12]

Financial crises in 1997 and 1998, first in Asia and then in Russia, bolstered Stiglitz's critique of the international financial institutions' approach to financial markets. Much of the foreign investment in these emerging markets had taken the form of marketable financial instruments, rather than as strategic direct investment that tied the investors' fortunes directly to the fate of particular enterprises. The form maximized flexibility, meaning the investors could pull out at the first sign of distress. The problem was that the time preferences of the investors did not align with those of the consumers of the

[11] Joseph E. Stiglitz & Bruce Greenwald, Toward a New Paradigm in Monetary Economics (2003).

[12] Many people, especially humanists and social scientists who do not do economics, object to confusion of the legacy Nobel prizes with the Sveriges Riksbank Prize in Economic Sciences in Memory of Alfred Nobel, first awarded in 1969 and to Stiglitz in 2021. I do not understand the aversion: fifty years of practice have established the prestige and relative rigor of the newer prize.

finance, whose projects needed patience to pay off. In theory, smart people could have designed contracts to bridge this gap, but asymmetries in information and the rush to reform let these possibilities slip by.

The elimination of controls on the export of foreign currency from capital account, as prescribed by foreign advisers, exacerbated the problem. Investors could pull out at the first sign of trouble, which often came not from the country in question but from another with similar characteristics. Thus in 1997 financial troubles in Thailand spread quickly to other countries in the region and panic became self-fulfilling, as foreign capital fled and local markets collapsed. "Hot money" and "contagion" became the terms that impeached the institutions' policies.

COMPETITION MAKES MARKETS WORK AND INTERNATIONAL COMPETITION MAKES THEM WORK BETTER

Markets reveal information better if sellers and buyers can bid against each other and can base their bids on accurate facts and reasonable conjectures. Barriers to competition exclude fact-based bids and discourage potential bidders from uncovering and exposing fraud. Restraints on competition thus contribute to information gaps that frustrate markets from providing the social benefits that they otherwise might produce.

Embracing these core beliefs, foreign advisers sought to lower barriers to competition, especially at the border. The principle of comparative advantage, a pillar of market theories since at least the dawn of the nineteenth century, maintains that states should find their niche in the world economy so as to maximize the value that they can realize from their endowments. Taken to its logical conclusion, the principle indicates that states should remove border barriers to products (goods and services) and capital (financial and human). What results are the "four freedoms" embraced, for example, in EU and US domestic law, free flow of goods, services, capital, and people.

However useful competitive markets are to help us assess public and private economic choices, the information they provide is not as valuable when we already know that the status quo is dysfunctional. States embarking on a restructuring of their economy, as were so many at the beginning of the 1990s, already understand that past policy choices brought them to a bad place. Competitive markets can help observers assess the wisdom of choices about how to get out of the mess, but in the early stages most of the information they deliver simply reports that the mess still exists. The value of market assessments of these decisions increases only over time as we learn more about their implementation and credibility.

Throughout modern history, many states successfully delayed their exposure to international competition until they implemented development plans. During the latter part of the nineteenth century, the United States lurked behind high tariff barriers to incubate its manufacturing industries; the power to do this was one of the objects of the Civil War. South Korea's transformation during the 1960s and 1970s provides a powerful lesson. It hid behind high trade barriers while transforming itself from a country that was substantially poorer than North Korea in 1955 to an international economic force in the 1980s.

To be sure, history also contains many examples where political leaders made bad choices and ended up making their countries poorer and more vulnerable to global markets. After World War II, for example, countries such as Argentina and Uruguay lost ground because of import-substitution policies that did not reflect local needs and capacities. In an ideal world, the reforming governments would collaborate with the institutions to determine which reforms best fit a country's endowments. The institutions instead pushed for tearing down the barriers without waiting for a plan.[13]

German reunification provides a powerful example of the instant-liberalism response to Soviet-style political and economic control. Leonard Bernstein conducting Beethoven's Ninth at the shattered Berlin Wall embodied the thrill of those days. What too few paid attention to was the rather crude response to the millions of East Germans who had gained their skills and knowledge – what economists call human capital – in the old system. Germany made a huge one-off wealth transfer by converting East German Marks into West German Deutschmarks at a wildly inflated price. It otherwise left the incumbent residents to the mercies of an open economy. Talents and habits that fit within one structure collapsed in value when transported to another one. Thirty years on, deep and sharp contrasts between the five *Ossi* Länder and the historic West Germany remain, not the least in a disposition for extreme national populism in their politics.

COMPETITION NEEDS POLICING TO WORK

Competitive markets do not spring up on their own. Private actors have every reason to rig markets so as to increase their profits at the expense of the general

[13] Dani Rodrik, The Globalization Paradox: Democracy and the Future of the World Economy (2011).

welfare. Left to their own devices, incumbents will fix either prices or output and bar others from entering their markets. When a single producer does this, we call it abuse of monopoly power; when multiple producers combine for the same purpose, we call it a cartel.

Since the late nineteenth century, the rich world has sought to suppress this form of market subversion. Even though considerable disagreement continues about the definition of particular market abuses and the right mix of tools to suppress them, every rich country in the world today has some kind of competition policy embedded within its legal system. The logic is straightforward. Privatization and an increased role for markets make sense only if the markets work. Markets work only if they operate free of arrangements and subterfuges that harm general welfare. Identifying and rooting out market structures that make people worse off is at the heart of competition policy.

State-planned economies dispensed with competition in favor of specialization under state supervision. The transition to markets meant requiring both newly private firms and government regulators to imagine how competition should work. Having worked in a world where hoarding and patronage dominated business activity, covert collaboration seemed much more natural than open competition. Government officials had trouble grasping what competition policy looks like in practice, as they knew about it (if they knew anything at all) only from studying foreign practice.

TAXATION IS THE PREFERRED REGULATORY INSTRUMENT

Because the old planned-economy systems encouraged fraud and embezzlement, foreign advisers and the reformers who listened to them sought to optimize transparency in economic regulation. Compared to other forms of regulation, tax offers advantages. It demands only a payment, rather than a change in behavior, even though the payment has a behavioral response as its purpose. To the extent that the law defines the conditions for taxation with clarity, the regulated person knows where they stand and can proceed accordingly. The precision of tax rules is usually preferable to discretionary regulatory standards such as "public interest" or "public convenience," which encourage the regulated to invest in coopting the regulatory authority, often to the advantage of incumbents over potential new entrants.

Complementary to the substitution of taxation for direction regulation was the design of tax systems with as little complexity as possible. Complicated rules may capture the nuances of the many circumstances in which taxpayers find themselves, but at the cost of uncertainty, taxpayer opportunism, and administrative arbitrariness. Especially if a society is new to tax, as most of the reforming countries were, making the administrators as much like automatons as possible seemed best. Thus reformers advocated broad tax bases with few if any exceptions. The broader the tax base, the lower the rate needed to produce a given amount of revenue. Achieving this means the behavioral impact of the tax will be minimized, except for those behaviors that the government deliberately wishes to encourage or suppress. In the United States, the 1986 Tax Reform Act achieved something close to this tax nirvana, and the international financial institutions advised policymakers to follow the same policy, if not necessarily adopting the US model.

These general preferences seem especially relevant to states where regulatory capacity – skills and experience-based judgment – are in short supply. The countries moving away from state planning lacked expertise in all kinds of economic regulation, not just tax administration, but the foreign advisers believed that learning how to run a tax system was generally easier than other forms of regulation of private activity. The transparency of tax systems, it was hoped, would also make corruption easier to detect, an important feature in a world where it prevailed.

LAW OFFERS A PREFERRED CHANNEL FOR TELLING PEOPLE WHAT SOCIETY WANTS FROM THEM

Given that the Washington Consensus reflected the views of economists, an observer might wonder how law and lawyers came to play such a large role in the new post-Soviet world. For some economists, more than lawyers themselves, law serves as a near-magical means of forming preferences and shaping behavior. Markets work, these economists believe, because the legal system creates and enforces property and contract rights. Taxes work because law proclaims them and people take the proclamation seriously.

The relationship between law and culture presents fascinating questions. What is relevant here is that many economists did not systematically take them up until the end of the 1990s. Andrei Shleifer, the Harvard economist who did much of the important research on this topic, previously had shaped the US program to reform the Russian economy. His Russian experience had not been a happy one, resulting in a US criminal indictment in 1997 that evolved into a civil suit with a significant settlement. The 1998 Russian financial crisis exposed the reforms' shortcomings. To Shleifer's credit, he drew on his time in Russia to critically examine what he and his teammates too often took for granted at the beginning of the decade.

The experts who came to reform the former state-planned systems embraced a division of labor under which they would draft new laws and shepherd their adoption, while their counterparts in the host government would see to implementing and enforcing the law. On its face this seemed sensible. The experts thought they understood how laws worked in the West and what they looked like on paper, while the host governments knew their people and how to lead them.

Two problems with the division of labor arose. The experts stopped paying attention after their laws were enacted, rather than trying to understand their effect. Host governments learned that they did not need to follow through on a reform, as long as they let the desired laws go on the books.

Illustrative was a 1995 Russian law setting out the fundamentals of corporate law. The Soviet system had no such thing, as marshalling private capital to support private endeavors was exactly what the old system had outlawed. Prominent US corporate law professors saw an opportunity both to test their ideas for better law for all societies and to adapt their theories to the particular shortcomings of Russia. They thought that they had taken into account Russia's weak judiciary and its businesspeople's habit of self-dealing. The bright-line rules they proposed defined forbidden insider transactions and imposed on them the draconian sanction of instant invalidity. So transparent a scheme, they argued, could not be subverted easily and would allow investors to trust their projects. The Russian parliament adopted their proposal with remarkably little tinkering.[14]

This triumph of a technocratic vision soon became, if not a disaster, deeply disappointing. The advisers, as they admitted a few years later, had not appreciated either the resourcefulness of Russian legal formalism or the corruptibility of Russian law enforcers.[15] The bright lines could be used not as a shield to protect investors but as a sword to destroy incumbents in favor of rising oligarchs with local power bases that coopted the regional judiciary. US-endorsed corporate law became a means of carrying out raids of existing firms, spawning legal instability and eroding investor confidence. These developments ground down the business sector until the next decade, when a reconsolidating state power reestablished its control over private enterprise. State planning had ended, but the old system of patronage and tribute based on embezzlement and bribery remained and could overwhelm the best intentions of the most brilliant foreign advisers.

[14] Bernard Black & Reinier Kraakman, A *Self-Enforcing Model of Corporate Law*, 109 HARV. L. REV. 1911 (1996).

[15] Bernard Black, Reinier Kraakman, & Anna Tarassova, *Russian Privatization and Corporate Governance: What Went Wrong?* 52 STAN. L. REV. 731 (2000).

INVIDIOUS DISCRIMINATION WASTES HUMAN POTENTIAL AND HARMS SOCIETY AS WELL AS INDIVIDUALS

In theory, communist ideology was internationalist to its core and thus looked to people of all races and ethnic backgrounds to advance the socialist cause. As to women, the picture was more complex. The upper echelons of the various communist parties as well as the most prominent professions remained almost completely out of reach to women, notwithstanding rhetoric to the contrary. Women were expected to enter the labor force, whether partnered or not, with crèches providing support for children during the working day but husbands by cultural tradition doing nothing within the home. Meanwhile ethno-national loyalties and identities ran through the actual politics in these systems. Whoever was seen as the "other" – in Russia this meant largely Central Asians, people from the Caucasus, and Jews – faced high, often unsurmountable barriers to the commanding heights of politics and academia.

One of the goals of post-socialist reform was to unleash the talents of the people whom the old regimes had cast aside. The western advisers urged reformers to include women and minorities in leadership positions as well as to create opportunities for them in the emerging private sector. They saw discrimination as a holdover from the old regime, in need of eradication every bit as much as state planning itself.

These were natural positions for the West to take. The triumph of liberalism and the defeat of communism confirmed the individual as the principal agent as well as the object of history and society. Fulfillment, not solidarity, became the foremost value of the age, notwithstanding the name of Poland's resistance movement. Freed from the shackles of the past, the new human would seize the freedoms embraced by the new order to realize their worth. Society would not let unfounded prejudice get in the way of this central goal.

This antidiscrimination principle is deeply appealing. Practicality, however, can be a problem. The principle rests ultimately on a hope of historical amnesia. Liberating society from its past, and people from the social construction of status, is harder than it looks. Moreover, moments of radical transformation turn out to be less than ideal for erasing long-term historic resentments and prejudices. Transformations tend to sort people out into winners and losers, and losers are eager to find reasons why their setbacks are not their fault. Old ways of thinking come back, even if the second time is farce rather than tragedy.

* * *

The inflection point of 1989–91 seemed to validate a bundle of liberal ideas about the world economy, good domestic governance, and the core value of respect for individuals based on talent rather than background. Acting on their confirmed beliefs, governments in the rich world launched a program of reform, restructuring, and assistance for the states that had lived under the discredited regimes. The pathway to a bright future seemed clear. Obstacles existed but were largely unforeseen.

3

New International Organizations and Their Ambitions (1989–2000, Part II)

Liberal internationalism meant not only remaking the South in the image of the West, but working at the international level to help liberal democracy and free markets flourish. The alphabet soup of organizations formed in the West in the wake of World War II were repurposed, and new ones created. Those who saw themselves as the victors of the Cold War built a new, thicker, and more elaborate body of international law made and administered by international bodies. International governance, both global and regional, took off as an alternative to national sovereignty.

As these reforms accumulated, people came up with increasingly ambitious arguments about the manifest destiny of liberal internationalism. Prominent academics promoted a theory of democratic peace to demonstrate the desirability, and hence the inevitability, of liberal democracy. History taught, they maintained, that coupling liberal reforms of domestic states to greater protection of liberalism at the international level would bring about not only prosperity, but less war.

These liberal internationalists argued that prosperity promotes peace by dissolving at least some discontents and protecting from risk of violent ruptures in the social fabric. But adding liberal democracy to prosperity does even more. The theorists argued, based on substantial evidence, that liberal democracies do not go to war against each other. Entrenching liberal democracy both domestically and internationally thus translates into peace. Representative democracy based on the rule of law and checks on government by a robust press and civil society complement market freedoms. The institutionalization of liberal democracy becomes the path to a bright global future.[1]

[1] Bruce Russett, Grasping the Democratic Peace: Principles for a Post-Cold War World (1993); Anne-Marie Slaughter, *The Liberal Agenda for Peace: International Relations Theory and the Future of the United Nations*, 4 Trans. L. & Contemp. Prob. 377 (1994).

Chapter 4 recounts how the twenty-first century provided ample falsification of the democratic peace concept. The 1990s, however, was a time when its predictions seemed compelling. Accordingly, shortly after its (assumed) triumph over communism, the West undertook to create a new international legal environment. Paralleling the surge in rich-world exports of specialized expertise in finance, economics, and law was a boom in international institution-building based on the liberal internationalist premises of the technical assistance. The end of the political, economic, and ideological commitments that had riven the world opened the door to greater international cooperation based on what were supposed to be shared values, interests, and understandings of how things worked. Institutions developed in the West to deal with its share of the world economy now extended to the rest of the world, while startup or transformed international organizations took up projects to shape the new world order.

Institutions and organizations are not exactly the same thing. The Catholic Church is an institution more than an organization, while the World Health Organization is at most the latter. The difference is cultural rather than formal. Lawyers concentrate on the organizational form, as that is where the issues that matter to us lurk. Policymakers create organizations in the hope that they become institutions, entrenched and resonant with layers of meaning and significance.

The end of World War II saw the birth of many international organizations – the United Nations, the Fund, the Bank – meant to manage international cooperation in a way that would make it harder for the things that led to World War II – a worldwide economic crisis and piecemeal wars of conquest evolving into global warfare – happen again. The 1990s recapitulated this process by expanding the old organizations and creating new ones.[2]

The enlargement of international organizations began within the Fund, the Bank, and the OECD, encountered in Chapter 2 as the architects of the restructuring of the formerly socialist countries. It soon spread to other areas of international governance and human rights. The financial bodies came first because most of the states taking leave of state planning found themselves mired in debt. They had foreign-lender loans they could not repay and also lacked the wherewithal to pay for the goods and services that they needed (or wanted) to import. The answer to these problems was more credit, but the international entities controlled how much of this these states could receive and on what terms.

2 Paul B. Stephan, *The New International Law: Legitimacy, Accountability, Authority, and Freedom in the New Global Order*, 70 U. Colo. L. Rev. 1555 (1999).

To say that these organizations "control" access to credit may surprise some, as the international financial institutions themselves do not lend that much money to states. The Fund provides limited lines of credit to national central banks, the Bank concentrates on development projects, and the OECD hands out no money at all. What they do instead is certify whether a state has agreed to comply to their satisfaction with an economic reform program that, in their view, will put that state in a better position to honor its debts. This "conditionality" function, historically the province of the Fund, became during the 1990s a joint project of the three legacy international financial entities.

These legacy organizations, as they increased their role within the formerly state-planned economies, also restructured their membership to fit their new mission. The victors of World War II, China and the Soviet Union included, had imagined the Fund and the Bank as instruments for rebuilding the war-shattered states. Within months of their inception, however, the Soviet Union made clear that it would not take part in the endeavor, for which the United States supplied almost all the money and intended to shape according to its lights. The Stalin regime induced the few Central and Eastern European states that had originally signed up to back out.[3] China meanwhile collapsed into civil war and then revolution (1945–49), then suffered the cataclysms of Mao's Great Leap Forward (1958–62) and Cultural Revolution (1966–76).[4] During this time the Republic of China in Taiwan occupied China's seat at the Bank and the Fund.

For the next forty years, these bodies supported the western side in the Cold War. The Fund functioned as a bank that helped states out of fiscal difficulties; the Bank functioned as a fund that supported infrastructure and other development projects. Mostly they rewarded countries that did not align with the Soviet Union once the Cold War got under way. They also handed out aid in the rich world by organizing the restructuring of national economies during the economic shocks of the 1970s. The United Kingdom's Labour Government under James Callaghan, for example, received a vital bailout through the Fund's 1976 loan, the largest program the Fund had ever undertaken. The conditions tied to the loan set the country on a path to Thatcherism, which came into its own three years later.

3 Benn Steil, The Battle of Bretton Woods: John Maynard Keynes, Harry Dexter White, and the Making of a New World Order (2013).

4 Frank Dikötter, Mao's Great Famine: The History of China's Most Devastating Catastrophe, 1958–1962 (2010); Frank Dikötter, The Cultural Revolution: A People's History, 1962–76 (2016).

The OECD has its origin in the Marshall Plan, formally the Organisation for European Economic Co-operation (OEEC). The United States organized the OEEC in 1948 to take over the task of European reconstruction that the victorious allies in 1944 had assigned to the Fund and the Bank. The United States decided that, as it had to supply all the funding for remaking war-torn Europe, it wanted full control over the instrument in charge of the project.[5] When, in 1961, the OEEC's success became manifest, the United States and the beneficiary countries converted it into the OECD, an entity devoted to smoothing the workings of liberal economies. Rather than handing out aid, it promotes best practices in areas such as competition and tax policy. A growing roster of non-European countries sought membership so as to take part in the conversation about how best to manage advanced capitalism in an increasingly prosperous world. Canada joined at its founding, along with several European countries that had not belonged to the OEEC. Japan came in 1964, Finland in 1969, Australia in 1971, and New Zealand in 1973.

Both the Fund, traditionally headed by a European, and the Bank, always led by an American, came to roost in impressive headquarters across the street from each other and only a few blocks from the White House (as well as the Metropolitan Club). The OECD occupies a beautiful chateau on the verge of the Bois de Boulogne in the 16th Arrondissement, near many great restaurants. As physical manifestations, they convey the message that one can do well by doing good. As the 1980s unfolded and the triumph of the western vision of good order and governance emerged, they perched as hopeful midwives for the new world aborning.

These stalwarts of the Cold War's winning side transformed themselves from bloc organizations to universal ones. The Fund and the Bank expanded their membership by 20 percent between 1989 and 1993, remaking themselves as proponents of fiscal stability and economic growth for virtually all the world's states. The OECD, always a smaller club of wealthier countries, expanded its membership by a quarter during the 1990s, mostly by taking in countries from Central and Eastern Europe.

Other international organizations remade themselves as they brought in the former socialist states. Liberalizing international trade had been a core project for the West since the end of World War II. The General Agreement on Tariffs and Trade (GATT) began life at the time of the Marshall Plan as a road map for reducing state-imposed barriers to international trade in goods. Originally conceived as part of a full-blown international organization like

5 Benn Steil, The Marshall Plan: Dawn of the Cold War (2018).

the Fund and the Bank, the GATT lost its corporate identity as a result of the US pivot toward hegemonic leadership of its bloc at the outset of the Cold War. The International Trade Organization (ITO), established by the 1948 Havana Charter and, as a legal matter, taking the same structural form as the United Nations, the Fund, and the Bank, never happened. Instead, the GATT became a treaty (only provisionally applicable, not ratified) with substantive rather than institutional commitments. The Agreement relied at first on a tiny staff borrowed from the United Nations' Geneva resources. It initially had no stand-alone grandiose headquarters.

Like the Fund and the Bank, the GATT became an instrument of one side of the Cold War. Of the twenty-three founding members, only Czechoslovakia fell within the Soviet orbit, and it left the GATT after the 1948 communist takeover of its government. China similarly left after its regime change. After 1959 Cuba stopped doing much with the GATT, although it never left.

As conceived, the GATT was meant to fight the last war. It sought to ward off the kind of retaliatory tariff hikes that had fed the Great Depression, the global economic crisis of the early 1930s that aided Hitler's rise to power and greased the path to World War II. It hosted multilateral negotiations on lowering tariffs, battled against workarounds that could substitute for protective tariffs, and offered dispute settlement services to the parties to the Agreement through ad hoc arbitration. This exclusive focus on tariff reduction meant lower barriers for physical goods, the only commodities subject to this form of border taxation.

By the 1980s, the GATT had become a flourishing international institution, astride a crucial and burgeoning economic sector that it managed with a soft touch and increasingly legalized pronouncements. Even a few "socialist" countries – Hungary, Poland, Romania, and Yugoslavia – joined during the 1960s and 1970s. It achieved its narrow but critical purpose – keeping down trade barriers on a wide range of goods, mostly those made in the rich world – very well. The South after decolonization got special regimes (called the Generalized System of Preferences) that still allowed rich countries to continue protecting their own producers of low-technology goods such as agricultural products and textiles.

When the world changed with the end of the Cold War, the GATT remade itself as the World Trade Organization, the kind of full-blown international institution that the postwar visionaries had hoped for in the ITO. The 1994 Uruguay Round Agreements created an organization, founded a permanent appellate court to ride herd over its dispute resolution business, and added new economic sectors to its jurisdiction. By first terminating the GATT, the rich countries that dominated these negotiations made an offer that the rest of the world couldn't refuse – join the new regime or live with legal anarchy in international economic relations. The formerly socialist countries queued up for membership. By the end of 2000 the WTO had 140 members, up from 84 GATT parties in 1989.

The new international agreements bundled into the WTO regimes reflected the Washington Consensus described in Chapter 2. Recognizing that tariff reduction had gone about as far as it could, the framers of these agreements pivoted to freeing up cross-border trade in services, unifying health and safety standards through committees of international experts, and strengthening the legal protection of intellectual property, and, to a lesser extent, of capital mobility. As services had assumed a larger role in the world economy, promoting international competition here became more important to those who thought more competition meant greater prosperity. Making intellectual property mandatory, rather than a local option for states, would in theory bolster innovation everywhere. In the short term, it would increase royalty payments from poor countries to rich ones, where most intellectual property then originated. Insisting that health and safety standards conform to international scientific standards, a strategy intended to suppress disguised trade barriers, helped rich-world producers who had the greatest knowledge about and influence over those standards.

Not only did the WTO expand in size and scope, but it upgraded its institutional bite. In its early days, the GATT relied on diplomats to mediate trade disputes, employing pragmatic bargaining more than legal formalism. During the 1950s and 1960s trade lawyers, especially veterans of government ministries, took over dispute resolution. The GATT sponsored arbitration panels, formed from a list of state-nominated trade law specialists. These panels would offer their views, often in the form of elaborate legal opinions. The disputants, however, had no formal obligation to comply. A panel opinion took effect only if adopted by consensus of the GATT parties. This meant a dissatisfied state could veto any and all panel decisions that did not go its way. The panel opinions instead served as a focal point for settlements.

Under the WTO, the arbitral panels remained in place, but dissatisfied states could appeal only to the appellate body, a permanent working court. The seven members of the court, chosen by the members and acting through three-member tribunals, could affirm, reject, or revise panel decisions. States that disagreed with an appellate body decision could seek recourse from the membership as a whole, but unless a consensus of the members (including the state that had prevailed in the appeal) held otherwise, the appellate decision would stand. The Appellate Body soon developed an extensive body of case law, on which a growing industry of civil society and academic specialists fed.

The WTO Appellate Body embodied a distillation of the ideas that flourished after the end of the Cold War. The existing consensus held that promoting competition and markets was the desired end and should rely on legal commitments to achieve its ambitions. Accordingly, disinterested legal experts, not economists or diplomats, should have the last say on what an increasingly ambitious international regulatory regime meant. States still remained free to negotiate their own settlements, taking the form of a customs union or a free trade agreement. As of 1995, the effective date of the Uruguay Round Agreements, these negotiations took place in the shadow of a profoundly different legal regime. The designers of the WTO paired economic liberalization based on greater international control of national policies with legal rulings handed down by an international court. This pairing blended the supposed transparency and disinterest of law with the substantive agenda of reining in national control over economic life.

MAKING THE WORLD SAFE FOR INTELLECTUAL PROPERTY

One thing that distinguished economic activity in the West from the parts of the world that followed the Soviet model was the extension of property law to fruits of knowledge. Patent, copyright, and trademark law had developed first in Europe. The United States built patent and copyright law into its 1789 Constitution but for a long time was reluctant to protect foreign rights. It did not extend federal protection to trademarks until after World War II. As the world economy grew after the war, intellectual property played a growing role in the West's trade and investment. Greater legal protection followed.

The concept of intellectual property rests on the idea that the law will reward inventors and creators by giving them a monopoly of some fixed duration over the economic exploitation of their creation. Typically, creators license their work to producers or publishers who pay a fee, called a royalty, tied to sales. The returns to creators thus depend on both the market success of their ideas, reflected in what people pay for their use, and the resources states devote to enforcement of the monopolies through punishment of pirates.

The Soviet model treated ideas as it did all other factors of production, something to be commandeered and managed by the state as part of its overall control over economic life. Because market sales did not exist, royalties tied to what people paid for products could not reflect the value of an idea's contribution to production. Instead, state bodies handed out rewards to creators as they saw fit. These rewards often lacked much connection to the idea's contribution to economic life, but rather reflected the status of creators and their patrons in the political structure. A notorious case was that of the faux-biologist Trofim Lysenko, who between 1928 and 1953 reaped great rewards from the Soviet state for agricultural "discoveries" that depended on faked research and had catastrophic results for those who implemented them. Even after Stalin's death in 1953, rewards to both scientists and artists depended more on political favor than economic usefulness or audience reception. Lysenko lost influence but never had to answer for all the harm he caused.

Treaties that mandated international protection for domestically created intellectual property had sprouted up long before the collapse of the Soviet system. Once the international economy took off in the wake of the end of socialism and autarky, and digital technology exploded, states doubled down on the international portability of intellectual property. Accordingly, the Agreement on Trade-Related Aspects of Intellectual Property (TRIPS), one of the achievements of the 1994 Uruguay Round, mandated states to adopt intellectual property laws that corresponded to the West's practice.

Not to be outdone, the World Intellectual Property Organization (WIPO), an organ of the United Nations, served as host for negotiations for new multilateral treaties designed to build a top-down intellectual property rights system adapted to the digital revolution. These include the 1996 Copyright Treaty and the Performances and Phonograms Treaty. These WIPO instruments require their parties (much of the world) to implement measures to deter digital copying and to outlaw private attempts to bypass copy-protection technologies deployed by rights owners.

The thinking behind TRIPS and the WIPO treaties was fairly simple. Intellectual property rights inspire creators to do more, and more valuable, work, and the best way to protect these rights is to crack down on piracy. States in the South objected to a regime that resulted in significant payments from users in the South to rights owners in the West. Critics in civil society and academia argued that the treaty negotiators were largely beholden to incumbent rights holders, overlooked the ways that overly aggressive anti-copying measures deterred valuable experimentation and innovation, and forced on states outcomes that their domestic legislatures did not want but tolerated due to the take-it-or-leave-it nature of multilateral treaties. As the WTO and WIPO illustrate, the renewal of international organizations in the wake of the Soviet collapse meant further empowering the masters of the burgeoning knowledge economy.

PROTECTION OF FOREIGN DIRECT INVESTMENT

Complementing the remaking of the international trade regime was the rapid expansion of international investment protection. Businesses distinguish between direct investment, which gives the investor a role in the management of the target project, and portfolio investment, which only supplies financial capital in the form of debt or equity. Portfolio investment sends market signals about the target's performance but otherwise does not interfere with the target's planning and execution of its projects. Direct investment, by contrast, typically brings knowledge and know-how along with the infusion of capital. From the investors' perspective, direct investment allows the transfer of skills and insights to the South in return for a share of management and a fair return. For populists in the South and their allies in academia and civil society in the West, direct investment more often represents a form of colonialism that exploits workers and resources in the South without sufficient compensation or much technology transfer. At least in its conception, the international investment regime sought primarily to encourage direct investment and regarded its critics with incomprehension.

Investment protection treaties began as bilateral commitments between rich western states and developing countries. While formally symmetrical, the treaties had the practical effect of offering exceptional legal protection to rich-world investors moving capital into poorer countries. These treaties appeared not long after end of World War II but gained greater salience in the mid-1960s and proliferated in the 1990s.

In 1965, the World Bank offered a treaty, the Convention on the Settlement of Investment Disputes between States and Nationals of Other States (the ICSID Convention), that created a new member of the Bank's family of international organizations, the International Centre for the Settlement of Investment Disputes. The Convention presumes a separate agreement between the investor's home state and the host state, a bilateral investment treaty (BIT), that provides investors with specific protections and designates ICSID as a provider of arbitral services. ICSID offers a means through which investors can arbitrate claims against host states over failures of protection. Other treaties function outside the ICSID regime. Brazil, India, Russia, and South Africa in particular stayed out even though they joined many BITs. As a result of ICSID and the BITs, ISDS, a system that provides aggrieved investors direct access to international arbitration with offending states, took off.

For the first quarter century of its existence, ISDS did little real work. Then in the 1990s thirty-eight new states joined the ICSID Convention, mostly from the former socialist world. Through 1990, investors had made a total of 26 claims under the regime; in the next decade alone 56 were filed, 253 in the decade after that, 465 in the 2010s, and 66 in 2021 alone. Investor arbitration, initially the turf of a handful of international lawyers, became an important revenue source for many law firms. States that hosted foreign investment sometimes found themselves saddled with multimillion dollar awards for what arbiters believed to be ill-treatment of their guests in violation of the treaties.

The rapid growth of international investor arbitration paralleled a shift in the substantive standards that applied to states. The United States first propounded what it believed to be the duties of host countries toward foreign investors through a statement by Secretary of State Cordell Hull regarding actions by Mexico. Hull focused on outright expropriation – a seizure of property. He advocated not a ban, but, borrowing the standards of the Takings Clause of the Fifth Amendment to the US Constitution, a requirement that the seizure have a public purpose and the duty of the host state to fully compensate the investor for its loss.

The postwar BITs represented an evolution of international law (not unlike developments in US takings law) that extended legal protection to de facto expropriations resulting from onerous regulation. They also imposed on host states complementary duties such as fair and equitable treatment as well as full protection and security. These changes allowed investors to challenge regulatory measures that had a plausible public purpose but concentrated supposedly inordinate costs on the investor. From the perspective of critics of global capitalism, the new approach allowed multinational businesses to obstruct needed environmental, health, and safety regulations by demanding compensation for the cost of compliance.

Opposition to the new investment protection regime popped up as soon as the treaties were proposed. One critique, initially tied to the political left but later taken up by the right, saw the protections as empowering global capital at the cost of the common good. An essential part of sovereignty, the argument went, was a nation state's right to decide what measures its people needed to deal with the harms that accompany industrial (or postindustrial) progress. A different thread, invoking a kind of nationalism that resonated with both the left and the right, objects to foreign experts using international law to override, or at least make more costly, the policy choices of politically accountable domestic actors. The first criticism was substantive and turned on how the observer saw the connection between global capitalism and social welfare. The second was procedural and had atavistic undertones, pitting cosmopolitan eggheads against the twentieth-century equivalent of honest yeomen.

Even before the 1990s had ended, the ambitions to expand international investment law provoked pushback. The OECD, perhaps inspired by the WTO's regulatory creep, in 1997 proposed a draft Multilateral Agreement on Investment (MAI) that would have superseded BITs while still relying on the ICSID system for enforcement. The MAI generally sought to broaden the substantive scope of investor protection. Western civil society and academics loudly objected, mostly on the grounds that the instrument allowed global capitalism to further erode sovereignty in the South. More importantly, Canada and France took strong exception to rules that would restrict the protection of "cultural" industries – arts and entertainment, especially films and music – from foreign influence. Both were willing to die on the hill where the future of Francophonie was at stake. In 1998, the OECD abandoned the project.

THE RISE OF SUPRANATIONAL ORGANIZATIONS

An effort to reorganize the richest regions of the world through "supranational" law – a form of international law that applied to a subset of states, typically neighbors – complemented the upgrading of the international financial organizations as well as international trade and investment law. In Europe, this involved a transformation, as well as an expansion, of the European Communities project. The drive toward "ever closer union" in Europe began in 1952 with the European Coal and Steel Community. Initially, the architects created a customs union that imposed a common schedule of duties on imports into all the members. Over time the membership grew and the commitments to permit free movement of products and production increased.

The Soviet bloc had created its own supranational economic structure in 1949. The Council for Mutual Economic Assistance (COMECON) coordinated links among the state-owned enterprises of its members, which in effect meant almost all significant economic activity. The Soviet Union dominated the organization, and its non-European satellites – Cuba, Mongolia, and Viet Nam – joined during the 1970s. It passed into oblivion in 1991 alongside the Soviet Union.

The death of COMECON inspired the western Europeans to transform their organization into a more ambitious proponent of liberal internationalism. The Maastricht Treaty, signed in 1992 and taking effect at the end of 1993, converted the European Communities (Coal and Steel, Atomic Energy, and Economic) into the European Union. The new entity took a further step toward European federalism, increasing the authority and the capacity of the EU organs relative to the member states and launching a project to replace national currencies with what became the euro. A drive to move power and legitimacy from national capitals to Brussels (actually Brussels, Strasbourg, and Luxembourg, the nominal homes of the Commission, Parliament, and Court of Justice, the three main organs of the European Union) began.

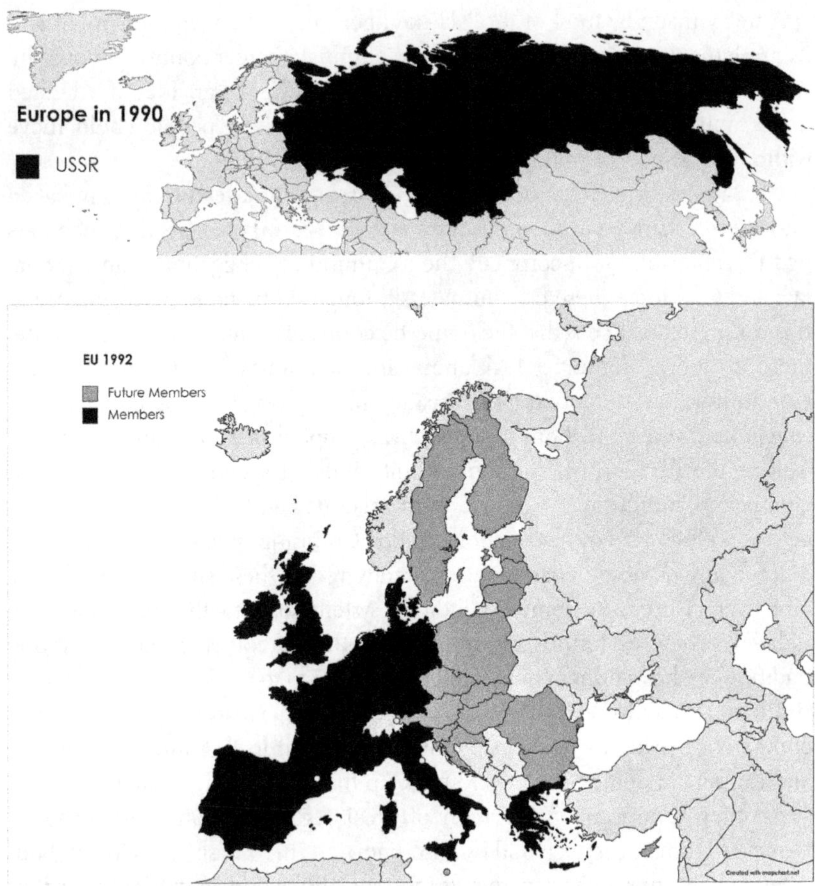

FIGURE 3.1 European integration. Source: "International Monetary Fund, 25 Years of Transition – Post-Communist Europe and the IMF" (2014), 3.

Shortly thereafter, the European Union brought in the three neutral states – Austria, Finland, and Sweden – that had served as a bridge between the West and the Soviet Union during the Cold War. Negotiations began to extend membership to former COMECON states as well as the three Baltic republics that had belonged to the Soviet Union until its collapse.

Figure 3.1 captures the transformation of the West and the East embodied in the European Union. Contrasting the continent in 1989 and 2012, it shows twenty-eight independent states in the west fusing into a single bloc, while in the east the Soviet Union and Yugoslavia, two large states, shattered into many. The implication was unification based on a common commitment to a winning formula and disintegration due to pathological politics, values, and societies.

A treaty made by most of the EU members, the Schengen Agreement and its implementing Convention, sought to eliminate border controls among the states. It went into effect in 1995 and expanded thereafter. Like the United States, much of Europe became a single space where people could move without a passport or putting their goods through customs.

For lawyers, the EU structure made more salient a feature already baked into the old European Communities. Under the original treaties, members had the obligation to incorporate their Community obligations into national law and to enforce these commitments through domestic legal organs. What this meant in practice is that the domestic courts of member countries had the duty to judge domestic legislation and administrative practice against Community law – not just the treaties themselves, but the entire *acquis communautaire*, regulations and directives adopted by Community organs as well as the decisions of the Community judicial system. Thus, under the European Communities Act 1972, British courts had to review parliamentary acts as well as government actions under Community law and to refuse to enforce any domestic enactment that transgressed these supranational rules. Not every European domestic judicial system took to this new power of judicial review as forthrightly as did the British courts, given the strong tradition on the continent of judicial subordination to parliamentary authority. But they all had to seem to do so. The Maastricht Treaty's expansion of EU competence made the duty of members to submit to EU authority broader, and the role of domestic courts to back up that duty all the greater.

Another European organization of great legal ambition, the European Court of Human Rights (ECtHR, also known as the Strasbourg Court), both extended its jurisdiction to the former socialist world and transformed its power by giving complainants direct access, dispensing with a bureaucratic structure that previously had selected cases for its disposition. The Court and its affiliated regional organization, the Council of Europe, took form in 1949 as part of the West's resistance to Soviet influence at the peak of the Cold War. The Council had a mandate to build and sustain liberal democracy and the rule of law on the continent, much of which had not known those institutions before World War II. The ECtHR backed up liberal democracy by policing the member states for their compliance with the European Convention on Human Rights (ECHR), an instrument informed by Anglo-American conceptions of due process, democracy, separation of powers, and the rule of law. The Convention and its Court, it was hoped, would deter either an embrace of Soviet-style institutions, as had just happened in the eastern part of the continent, or a return to the dark night of the 1930s.

The countries subject to ECtHR jurisdiction rose from twenty-two at the end of 1989 to forty at the end of 1999, all of the new members save Andorra coming from the former socialist world. The 1998 Protocol 11 to the ECHR abolished the Commission, an organ of the Council that had chosen what cases the Court would hear, and instead obliged the Court to hear all claims filed. Private persons thus would get direct access to the Court, rather than going through a body of state-selected officials. From this date forward, the Court took a more generous approach to its powers, expanding its interpretation of the Convention in several critical areas.

For its part, the United Kingdom adopted the Human Rights Act 1998, which incorporated the Convention (but not the case law of the ECtHR) directly into British law. This step reinforced and extended the power to review national law for conformity with EU law. It meant that something like US-style judicial review entered the British system. British judges now could block the enforcement of parliamentary laws to the extent that, in their view, the Convention required this and the enactment in question did not clearly and expressly mandate otherwise. Other European states reached similar outcomes. What limits might domestic law place on this power of judicial review became evident only in the new century's second decade. The workload of the ECtHR exploded. Claimants had filed 8,400 cases in 1999; in 2002 new filings had grown to 28,200.

NATO, yet another mostly-European international organization, both repurposed itself and grew during the 1990s. The United States and Canada formed NATO with ten European allies in 1949 as a means of holding off a perceived Soviet military threat. Article 5 of its founding treaty codifies its purpose: the members would consider an armed attack on any member as an attack against them all and each would assist the victim of an attack by taking "such action as it deems necessary, including the use of armed force." Although not stated in the treaty, the potential armed attack that the alliance anticipated would come from the Soviet Union and the subordinated states behind the Iron Curtain.

Symmetrically, the eastern states formalized the alliance that had existed de facto at the time of NATO's creation by making the 1955 Treaty of Friendship, Cooperation and Mutual Assistance (Warsaw Pact). Ironically, the Warsaw Pact saw its first use the following year when its members invaded Hungary, also a member, to put down its attempt to leave the alliance and free itself from Soviet overlordship. The Warsaw Pact reprised this role in Czechoslovakia in 1968 and threatened to do so again in Poland in 1980.

The Warsaw Pact dissolved itself in 1991, seemingly ending the reason for NATO to exist. At that point, however, NATO fell back on Article 2 of its treaty, which describes the parties as contributing to friendly international relations "by strengthening their free institutions, by bringing about a better understanding of the principles upon which these institutions are founded, and by promoting conditions of stability and well-being." What had been a military alliance became a platform for promoting the "Western values" that supposedly won the Cold War. Although the Bush administration had promised the Russians it would not enlarge NATO, the Clinton administration rethought the matter and enabled the Czech Republic, Hungary, and Poland to join. During the following decade, four more former Warsaw Pact members plus Albania and three former Soviet republics came in.[6]

The other great economic bloc besides Europe was North America. In 1988, the Reagan administration made a free trade agreement with Canada, the United States' most important economic partner, that included international-lawyer-friendly procedural innovations, conventional tariff-elimination commitments, and measures to boost trade in services and protect investments, in particular an investment protection regime modeled on the prevalent bilateral treaties. After years of corrupt autarky fueled by nationalist resentment of its overweening neighbor to the north, Mexico in 1988 selected Carlos Salinas de Gortari, a reformist and international economist, as President. Eager to use an international structure to reinforce Mexico's new direction, the Bush administration persuaded Canadian Prime Minister Brian Mulroney to extend the bilateral agreement he had championed to Mexico. The three leaders signed the North American Free Trade Agreement (NAFTA) in December 1992.

Unfortunately for Bush, he performed that function as a lame duck, in part because of NAFTA. H. Ross Perot, an eccentric billionaire and political novice, launched a third-party run for President that fall. Perot ran as a populist and focused his campaign on opposition to NAFTA. Consolidating the Canadian and US economies mostly reinforced existing cross-border cooperation between countries with complementary production functions and labor skills. Mexico, by contrast, swelled with low-skill, cheap-wage workers who could take on manufacturing work that no longer required the kinds of skilled workers that the United States had in abundance.

Perot's campaign reflected a changing economic environment. For more than twenty years, US manufacturing, or at least that part based on workers with little or no schooling past age eighteen, had lost ground to foreign producers. An uptick in immigration from Latin America bolstered by the 1986 Immigration Reform and Control Act made Latino identity more salient

[6] Mary E. Sarotte, Not One Inch: America, Russia, and the Making of a Post-Cold War Stalemate (2021).

among the aggrieved workers and their families, even if US production had yet to migrate south. Playing on these forces, Perot ran against Bush and captured nearly 19 percent of the popular vote. Bill Clinton, the Democratic nominee, also ran against NAFTA. Bush lost the election, and Clinton championed the deal he had attacked after Mexico agreed to a few cosmetic changes addressing labor and environmental issues.

At the time, opposition to NAFTA among thought leaders in the United States came largely from the moderate and far left. Liberal (in the US political sense) figures such as activist Ralph Nader, former California Governor Jerry Brown, Harvard law professors Laurence Tribe and Anne-Marie Slaughter, and most labor leaders attacked the agreement as giving in to the interests of multinational enterprises. After its adoption, they sponsored or supported litigation to overturn or undermine it. What many people failed to notice was the increasing political significance of Perot voters, people who combined economic insecurity – especially people in the automobile industry and other manufacturing sectors – with nativist resentment against the brown-skinned residents of Latin America. As US manufacturing moved south, Mexican nationals and Central Americans passing through Mexico moved north in ever greater numbers to take up work in construction and other service sectors that did not require English as a condition of employment. Cultural and economic resentments grew and reinforced each other.

HUMAN RIGHTS AND INTERNATIONAL LAW

Notwithstanding these clouds on the horizon, creation of new international organizations in the hope that they would become influential institutions not only proceeded apace, but extended beyond economic governance. As the democratic peace theory predicted and as the restructuring of the European Court of Human Rights indicated, many saw a connection between economic liberalism and human rights protection. Both projects saw law as the center of a flourishing society, supporting both economic freedom and personal autonomy as well as international peace and security. Together they embodied a diagnosis of what seemed most wrong about the Soviet model of socialism along with confidence that legal institutions offered the best response to the malady.

In the academy and civil society, people who mistrusted international economic governance because it unduly shrank the regulatory authority of states generally embraced upgrading the international infrastructure that held states accountable for their human rights commitments. Symmetrically, those who liked the use of international law to pry open closed economies often distrusted the deployment of international human rights law against states. This distrust rested in part in concerns about the prevailing method of applying international human right law, civil litigation brought by private plaintiffs.

A new alternative to private suits was public criminal prosecutions. Steps in this direction began when the UN Security Council created bespoke tribunals to mete out justice in the wake of atrocities. The first, the International Criminal Court for Yugoslavia, came into being in 1993. Like the Nuremberg Tribunal that served as its template, this body addressed genocide, torture, crimes against humanity, and grave war crimes committed in the course of the civil wars that followed the dissolution of Yugoslavia. The International Criminal Trial for Rwanda, created in 1994, dealt with the same offenses arising out of the Tutsi genocide in Rwanda. These tribunals, like Nuremberg, were confined to particular atrocities limited in space and time, but they indicated a broader impulse to use international bodies to enforce the mandates of international criminal law independent of individual states.

These experiments in internationally administered criminal justice gathered momentum as the decade progressed. The United States, long a champion of a permanent international criminal court, led the movement to realize this ambition. The Rome Statute, a treaty signed in 1998 that entered into force in 2002, created the ICC. Many in civil society and the academy celebrated this step, but the United States and most other military powers could not. They rejected the Court because of its autonomous control over its docket. Canada, Japan, South Korea, and most European, African, and Latin American states joined, but China, Egypt, India, Iran, Iraq, Israel, North Korea, Pakistan, Russia, Saudi Arabia, Syria, Thailand, Turkey, and the United States, world or regional powers most of which had used their militaries outside their territories within the last few decades, stayed out.

Previously the United Nations had created international criminal tribunals, beginning with those set up in Nuremberg and Tokyo at the end of World War II, where the state with primary jurisdiction over the perpetrators was unwilling or unable to impose its domestic law. The Rome Statute honored this principle of "complementarity" in the abstract but left it to the ICC prosecutors and judges to decide whether a state would properly investigate and deal with atrocities. The states that stayed out objected to this second-guessing of their prosecutorial judgments.[7]

7 Paul B. Stephan, *US Constitutionalism and International Law: What the Multilateralist Move Leaves Out*, 2 J. Int'l Crim. Just. 11 (2004).

For the three permanent members of the Security Council that rejected the Rome Statute, the other obstacle was the absence of Security Council supervision of the ICC's choices regarding whom to investigate and prosecute. The Rome Statute negotiators rejected a US proposal to that effect. Instead, the ICC determines its own jurisdiction subject only to a right of the Security Council to delay action for a year.

THE BRIEF RENAISSANCE OF THE UNITED NATIONS

Finally, the end of the Cold War seemed to revitalize another other legacy international institution – the United Nations itself. For strategic reasons, Iraqi dictator Saddam Hussein had enjoyed support from both the United States and the Soviet Union for much of his rule, notwithstanding his brutal, even psychopathic mode of governance. His annexation of Kuwait through a military invasion in the summer of 1990, however, offended the world at a time when the Soviet Union and the United States did not define their security interests in strict opposition to each other. The Security Council had not blessed an armed intervention in response to a threat to peace since 1950, when a Soviet boycott of the Council opened the door to a resolution authorizing a US-led coalition to repel North Korea's invasion of the South. Its 1966 licensing of British intervention against the racist state of Rhodesia doesn't really count, as the United Kingdom was not prepared to ride on this ticket. Forty years after Korea, Europe and the United States partnered with much of the world to repel the Iraqi invasion of Kuwait. The Soviet Union joined the resolution authorizing the use of force against Iraq, and China abstained.

Operation Desert Storm proved a remarkable success, meeting its goals with surprisingly few casualties on the coalition's side. Many public figures and academics saw this event as the beginning of a new world order based on comprehensive respect for the rule of law. International security would now belong to the international community as a whole, governed by the Security Council. The willingness of the United States in particular to work through the Council suggested that the end of the Cold War would not give rise to a single state hegemon, but rather would finally sustain a collective security system to which the postwar powers may have aspired in 1945 but had failed to bring off.

These beliefs certainly informed the Security Council's thinking when it established the initial criminal tribunals for Yugoslavia and Rwanda. As the decade progressed, however, new problems popped up. In spite of the International Criminal Tribunal, Serbia's leaders continued to carry out atrocities, now within the country's borders in its ethnically Albanian province of Kosovo. The United States and Europe wanted to deploy their militaries, preferably through bombing strikes that minimized risk to their personnel, to deter Serbia. China and Russia drew the line at what they saw as improper and illegal intervention in a state's internal affairs, no matter how horrible the atrocities.

Lacking permission from the appropriate international organ, NATO went ahead with its bombing campaign. The United States argued that the multilateral nature of the intervention rendered the operation, if not legal under international law, at least legitimate. China and Russia fumed but did not retaliate, even when a NATO plane dropped a bomb on China's Belgrade embassy. Rather, the episode showed that not all states the world over could swallow the implications of a new order of universal rule of law. This early sign of a fissure between the West, China, and Russia on the legal aspects of security proved prophetic.

MIGRATION

In a chapter on the growth of international organizations after the end of the Soviet Union, it is worth mentioning one aspect of the world economy that changed significantly without any help from international law. Before 1990, the lion's share of migration into the rich world involved people coming from other rich countries. Around that time, the composition of rich-world immigrants shifted. The end of restrictions on emigration imposed by the formerly socialist states led to significant movements of working-age people to the rich parts of Europe in particular, and to other destinations in the rich world to a lesser degree. Migration of people from other places in the South to rich countries matched this trend. Between 1990 and 2015, the foreign-born portion of the populations of Australia, Canada, and the United States roughly doubled, and for Europe roughly tripled, with people from the South making up much of the increase.[8]

This transformation of the labor markets of rich countries took place with no new international law or organizations, and indeed with almost no changes in the domestic law of the destination states. Enlargement of the European Union did affect immigration rights, as membership comes with migration privileges. Otherwise, states saw the current law, based on executive discretion over levels of enforcement, as adequate to meet the task. Unlike the other

[8] Giovanni Peri, *Immigrants, Productivity, and Labor Markets*, 30 J. ECON. PERSP. 3 (2016).

areas where states made treaties and institutions, for immigration the costs of an open political debate apparently exceeded the benefits of bolstering the liberal status quo.

SUMMING UP

Looking back, the international institution-building of the 1990s rivals and perhaps exceeds that of the years following World War II. The United Nations aside (admittedly, a big aside), the international organizations formed in the wake of the allied victory governed blocs rather than the entire world. The West had the IMF, the World Bank, the European regional organizations, and NATO. The Soviet bloc had COMECON to coordinate economic governance and the Warsaw Pact to handle security matters. True believers within the bloc might have believed, or at least pretended to believe, that the closely allied communist parties provided all the human rights protection that people needed, understanding the fundamental human right as participation in the construction of socialism.

What emerged in the 1990s, by contrast, were well-funded and powerful organizations with considerable sway around the world over international finance (the Fund), development policy (the Bank), and an expansive conception of free international trade (the WTO). Through ICSID, the Bank organized a comprehensive investor-protection regime that made further inroads into state regulatory autonomy. An international court that many states supported (although, notably, almost no states with significant outward-facing military capabilities) adjudicated individual responsibility for atrocities, and two courts in Europe (the Court of Justice of the European Union, known as the Luxembourg Court, and the Strasbourg Court) held sway over most of the region. NAFTA, although not as institutionally thick as the European Union, still took a large step toward integrating the North American economy and had its own legal organs, however understaffed and poorly housed compared to their European counterparts.

All of these international organizations promised surges in legal infrastructure, especially in the rich world. States adopted legislation and added bureaucratic elements to support their participation in these organizations. The members of the European Union bore the greatest burden, but other states also had to adapt to their new international responsibilities. An even greater effect, at least in terms of person hours and budgets, was in the nonstate sector, especially civil society and the academic community. Research institutes popped up and academic degree programs and academic journals emerged, all to study and, in important ways, propagate the influence of the new and improved international organizations. US law firms started opening Brussels offices so as to bring a new style of lobbying and litigating to the corridors of European power, as well as moving into emerging legal markets in the capitals of the former socialist world. Banks, accounting firms, and art dealers made corresponding moves as private wealth began to accumulate in these places.

The international institution-building represented a significant repurposing of the effort to remake formerly state-planned countries as liberal democratic exemplars. The first wave meant a transfer of skills and technical resources from the victors to the vanquished, a kind of Marshall Plan on a shoestring budget. The institutional move, by contrast, engaged the rich states as well as the poorer ones. Even though the terms of these deals reflected the values and competences of the rich world's experts, they did not rest on a broad political consensus within those states about how the new world order should work. Even during the triumphal 1990s, glimmerings of resistance and resentment occasionally broke through.

4

Cracks in the Foundation and System Shocks

Terror, the Great Recession, and the Arab Spring (2000–15)

The twin triumphs of liberal internationalism in the 1990s, the restructuring of the economic and political systems of the countries that had opposed liberal democracy and the shifting of law and power to international organizations, both global and regional, hid the faint hints that not all was well. In the United States, the battle over NAFTA turned out to be not a conclusive victory for free trade and investment mobility, but an opening skirmish in a battle over the world economy. The Asian financial crisis of 1997–98 exposed cracks in the consensus about wise financial management, in particular about unrestricted movement of foreign capital. The defeat of the OECD's MAI in the following year showed that important states thought better of submitting vital policy issues (here the protection of Francophone culture against the inroads of Anglophone imperialism) to the judgment of international lawyers. Thinkers on the left criticized the economic aspects of the new world order while embracing enhanced international enforcement of human rights; those on the right (a smaller, or at least quieter, group) did the opposite. Meanwhile NATO's Kosovo campaign signaled to aspiring revisionist states, China and Russia in particular, that the new world order might not work the same for everyone when bombs fell from the sky.

Still, as the new century dawned, history's arrow seemed to continue to point toward greater ordered liberty at the national level reinforced by entrenchment of liberalism internationally. The new Bush administration in the United States fully embraced free trade together with labor and capital mobility, just as the Clinton administration had in the 1990s. Even the Bush team's much criticized early foray into international human rights law, namely the unsigning of the Rome Statute, could be understood as supporting international law principles.

When the Rome Statute that created the ICC went into force in 2002, the Bush administration faced a dilemma. Clinton had signed the treaty near the end of his term while stating that the United States would not pursue ratification until the state parties had addressed US concerns about the ICC's self-judging jurisdiction. The Bush administration wanted to work with other states to fight terrorism and further open up the world economy but could not abide the threat that the court presented to the US military. Accordingly, Bush notified the United Nations that the United States saw no possibility of joining and intended to end the obligations that international law imposes on a treaty's signatory before ratification.

Rejecting the Clinton administration's pragmatic effort to have it both ways – reassuring domestic lawmakers that the United States would not join while holding out to the ICC's supporters the possibility of US participation – the Bush administration took the more transparent, if also brutal, path. It wanted a free hand to oppose ICC investigations and prosecutions it might view as hostile. It believed that customary international law would bar this opposition as long as the United States remained a signatory of the treaty, even without ratifying it. On the one hand, the Bush administration defended its decision as reflecting respect for US international obligations and a desire not to mislead. On the other hand, it necessarily rejected a kind of aspirational (what academics call constructivist) approach to international law, through which the making of promises that cannot be kept ends up overcoming the barriers that render honoring those promises impossible.[1]

Elsewhere in the world in 2000, the march to greater liberal internationalism seemed robust. The Blair government enthusiastically signed on to the program. Several former socialist states in Europe and the three Baltic ex-Soviet states were deep into accession negotiations with the European Union that would lead to their joining the club in 2004. Russia's new Putin administration seemed as open to the outside world as Yel'tsin's had been, and more competent in exercising its power. China joined the WTO at the end of 2001, seemingly cementing its integration into the world economy. The WTO also decided to begin the next "Round" of multilateral negotiations to further expand and bolster its authority. The only sour note was the site of the conference reaching this decision, Doha. Anti-globalist demonstrators had disrupted an earlier meeting in Seattle, leading the WTO to move its business to a small country with no qualms about suppressing public protests.

And yet the world was about to change. Long-term structural transformation often unfolds dimly, its nature and even existence hotly debated and the evidence mostly noisy. Startling things can happen, however, that uproot

[1] Ryan Goodman & Derek Jinks, Socializing States: Promoting Human Rights through International Law (2013).

beliefs and force people to grasp for new ways of making sense of the world. These events may not change the world themselves, but they locate a time and place where people come to recognize transformation. These system shocks serve as events around which conversations about change take place, whether they cause the change directly or simply expose what had been going on for some time beneath the surface of events.

THE FIRST SHOCK: 9/11 AND THE GLOBAL WAR ON TERROR

So it was with September 11, 2001. Images of hijacked airplanes wielded as terrorist weapons riveted the world. The spectacle of the collapse of the twin towers of the World Trade Center made for compelling television, however horrifying. By the end of that day, many people around the world had come to believe that something earth-shattering had happened and that life could not go on as before.

How to make sense of this event quickly became an issue. I found myself overseas at the time of the attack and two days later attended the opening ceremony of a law-and-economics conference at the University of Vienna. The president of the university expressed shock and dismay about the violence and compassion for the United States, but also worried about an excessive US reaction. *Le Monde* proclaimed that "we are all Americans" but also implored the country to reflect on its share of responsibility for the attack. The international lawyer Phillipe Sands, a visitor at NYU Law School (from where everyone could see the falling towers), spoke to similar effect at a convocation a few days later. The United States should not miss the chance to learn why it was so hated, he said. Implicit in these cautions was a hint that perhaps the end of the Cold War did not after all crown the United States and the rich West as the cutting edge of historical progress.

Such advice from foreign friends, however well-intended, did not go down well in the United States. Shock and sorrow quickly became anger coupled with a thirst for revenge. Perhaps wiser heads should have prevailed, and the Bush administration should have done more to temporize. When I returned to the United States a week after the terrorists struck, however, it seemed clear that many, perhaps most, of my compatriots demanded retribution on a scale that would exceed the initial attack in violence and compelling imagery. If the government had tried to ignore these impulses, it would have come under fire from almost every point of the political compass. In any event, the Bush administration avoided that particular risk, to say the least.

In one indirect way, the Bush administration took the 9/11 attack as a spur for building international cooperation based on law. Two months after the attack, it led the opening of the just mentioned Doha Round, meant to launch new negotiations to deepen the authority of the WTO while redressing its imbalance between the West and the global South. Part of the deal was acceding to China's admission. Great prosperity based on more liberal rules for the world economy, supervised through an international organization, would counter the resentments and fury that supposedly drove terrorism.

This nod toward the 1990s in the wake of 9/11 proved insufficient and ultimately a failure. The Doha Round never got anywhere and ground to a halt in 2008 during the world financial crisis. China reveled in its WTO membership but, as its role in the world economy grew, exposed the disconnect between traditional strategies for promoting an open world economy and the ability of a powerful authoritarian state with strong informal control over a large nominally private sector to game the system.[2] Meanwhile the US prosecution of its campaign against global terrorism divided it from its allies as well as its adversaries and trashed the ideal of a new world order based on UN control over international armed conflict.

The US military adventure in Afghanistan, concurrent with omnipresent manifestations of domestic security surveillance throughout the country, seemed inevitable at the time. Within three months of 9/11, US-led forces took control of Afghanistan's urban centers and drove the al-Qaeda leadership out of the country. Less than a year later, the United States created a Department of Homeland Security to consolidate and augment the scattered domestic security elements of the national government and to deliver funds and other assistance to local police forces around the country. Only a few unreconstructed liberals like me bleated that not being a homeland was exactly what had made the United States great. The unhappily named Patriot Act created new authorities for federal surveillance and data collection. The Justice Department articulated novel, poorly reasoned legal theories to insulate the executive from judicial review of national security choices that encompassed cruel and degrading interrogations and extraordinary electronic surveillance. The War on Terror had become institutionalized and well-funded.

Culturally, the vocabulary of war and revenge had unfortunate overtones. On whom should the United States seek revenge? The government focused on al-Qaeda and the Taliban regime that had hosted it. The proverbial person in the street cast a wider net, fueled by ignorance. For many people, not only in the United States, militant Islam was the enemy, and several important

2 Petros C. Mavroidis & Andre Sapir, China and the WTO: Why Multilateralism Still Matters (2021).

truths were often ignored: much of Islam is not militant, most followers of Islam are not Arabs, and many Arabs are not followers of Islam. A form of Islamophobia that took in all brown-skinned people from the Middle East as well as the Sahel and South Asia raised its ugly head. In Europe, the same malady blended in with fear and resentment of immigrants, many of whom also were brown-skinned people from those parts of the world. Most political leaders tried to tamp down this impulse, but it persisted. Before long other, more ruthless, politicians would exploit it.

THE FOREVER WAR TAKES ROOT

The worst fears of the people who cautioned the United States immediately after the 9/11 attack became reality when a US-led coalition invaded Iraq in March 2003. The United States and its allies justified Operation Enduring Freedom as necessary to end Iraq's program to assemble an arsenal of nuclear, chemical, and biological weapons (weapons of mass destruction or WMD) and supposed interest in passing them on to al-Qaeda. Less directly, leaders of the coalition gestured toward the Iraqi regime's widespread human rights violations as a justification for intervention.

These events were especially unfortunate for the international relations theorists that had promoted the idea of democratic peace only a decade earlier. It may be true that liberal democracies may not go to war against each other very often. But not every state gets to be a liberal democracy, and becoming one proved to be much more difficult than the theorists assumed. Even more importantly, the wars begun in 2001 and 2003 indicated that liberal democracies have a lower threshold for going to war against illiberal states than do other states. Liberal democracies, it turns out, will use force to defend an international order in which they believe and which, they also believe, validates their existence as states. So they deploy their militaries against states that do not pose a concrete, material threat to the state doing the deploying. Other kinds of states, it seems, are less likely to do this.

The US Congress approved an invasion of Iraq by an overwhelming bipartisan majority. The debate over Operation Enduring Freedom moved to international law. Its legality under the UN Charter turned on the meaning of several Security Council resolutions arising out of Operation Desert Storm, the Security-Council-approved campaign against Iraq to undo its invasion of Kuwait. In 1990, the Council had approved an armed attack on Iraq and, at the conclusion of hostilities the following year, imposed ongoing duties on Iraq to satisfy international efforts to thwart its WMD program. In 2002, Security Council Resolution 1441 had ordered "full and immediate compliance by Iraq" with its 1991 post-hostilities obligation not to develop WMD. The Resolution "determined" (an emphatic word in Security Council practice) that the Council would secure this compliance. For the United States and its allies, Resolution 1441's determination, when paired with the 1990 authorization of the use of force to hold Iraq to its international legal obligations, amounted to approval of further military action to fulfill the Security Council's demands. France and Germany, as well as China and Russia, maintained that Resolution 1441 did not say states were allowed "to use all necessary means." The Security Council uses this formula when it wishes to bless armed force by states in furtherance of its purposes. The absence of these words, they argued, meant that the ticket to invade had not been issued.

To a law outsider, these arguments might seem gossamer-thin distinctions and not enough on which to base terribly consequential decisions. Within law, this episode mirrors the Kosovo episode a few years earlier, but with more talk. The invasion's opponents could rightly claim that the Council never used the words that would have unambiguously approved a second war with Iraq, and that the coalition could not bootstrap the 1990 green light onto the current situation. The United States and its allies responded that the 1990 Resolution was an open license to hold Iraq to account for its flouting of the clear demands of the Security Council. The opponents of the invasion had a better-grounded argument formally, while the invaders could spin together their weak, but not preposterous, legal argument with their evident military superiority and the comfort that, as in Kosovo, no great power would interfere, however loud their protests.

The Bush administration hedged its bets, however, by not asking the American people to pay for either of its Asian wars. Rather than calling on the nation to join in a common sacrifice, it funded its military operations in Afghanistan and Iraq by borrowing from global capital markets, which as a practical matter meant China. The Johnson administration had prosecuted the last US land war in Asia – the one in Vietnam – by taking on debt rather than either taxing or cutting back on domestic programs. At that time, this choice led to inflation, an economic scourge that roiled the country for more than a decade. Bush took the same path, but at least so far the capital markets have not tested US financial viability. Instead, the lack of immediate pain has led each administration in this century take on new debt, stumbling along like a lost expedition fearing a cliff it knows exists but cannot find.

Vietnam, debacle that it was, did require one kind of common sacrifice. The draft meant that all young American men, whatever their station in life, had to worry about going off to fight in a miserable and pointless war. The system, to be sure, was stacked in favor of the talented and connected, with education deferments, access to the National Guard, and biddable doctors keeping the privileged out of danger. Every US president we have had who faced the Vietnam draft risk – Clinton, Bush, Trump, and Biden – managed to wiggle out of regular military service. Still, they and their families had to worry and call in favors. However unfair the system, every one of the right age and gender had a personal connection to the war, if only as a source of dread.

The US wars of the twenty-first century, by contrast, drew entirely on an all-volunteer force. One class of people – those for whom the knowledge economy held out only scant prospects – saw the military as better than any other options. For another class – those for whom four-year BA programs and graduate schools promised prosperity and status – military service offered a way to pay for school. The volunteers did not have families who rage at the government for forcibly taking their children and putting them in danger, as happened with the Vietnam war. This lowered the political threshold for going to war. It also reinforced the growing class divide that took over domestic politics in the 2010s.

Perhaps if it had turned out that Saddam Hussein not only aspired to get WMD but actually had some, people would look back on the invasion as a watershed that vindicated benign western leadership. Perhaps if the Iraqi people had embraced their conquerors (a most unusual event in history, to be sure), rather than mounting a sustained insurgency, more people could have reconciled themselves to the outcome. Perhaps if the US military had done a better job of deterring war crimes, in particular "cruel, inhumane, or degrading" treatment of captives (the legal standard under the Geneva Conventions), fewer people would have been shocked and disgusted by the ongoing campaign against the insurgency. As it was, these events stripped the invasion not only of whatever legality it might claim, but its basic legitimacy as well.

A technological revolution, a fruit of the knowledge economy, leveraged the backlash against the Iraq adventure. Desert Storm was the first major military campaign to unfold on global television, a medium over which a handful of broadcasters had curatorial powers. Enduring Freedom was the first to proceed in a world where many ground-level actors, especially ordinary soldiers, had smartphones with camera capacity. In effect, the new technology made everyone a potential broadcaster. Bored when not terrified by insurgent attacks, the custodians of the Abu Ghraib Prison documented their criminal mistreatment of their Iraqi prisoners and sent the pictures to friends and family (Figure 4.1). Once these horrible images escaped into the cybersphere, it was

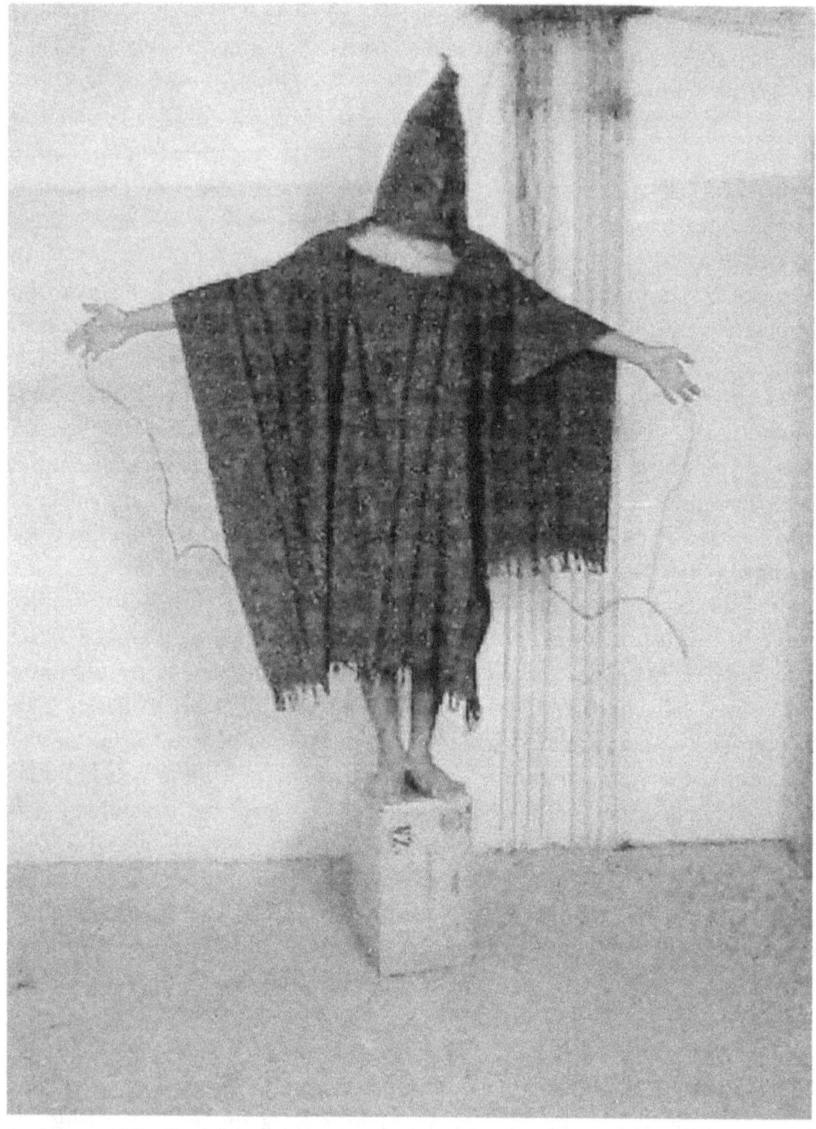

FIGURE 4.1 "The Hooded Man," Abu Ghraib 2003, 6 POLFOTO/AP.

not hard for the news media (this was before social media had displaced legacy news sources) to get hold of them and broadcast them on legacy networks. The pictures shaped the way the rest of the world saw the operation, making it harder for the coalition to justify its ongoing presence in Iraq and easier for adversaries to gain ground.

Stung by these setbacks, coalition partners Italy and Spain turned on the enterprise, as voters fired the politicians who had supported it. In October 2003, the Putin regime in Russia, taking advantage of the West's embarrassment and fissures, kicked off its program of renationalizing the country's dominant energy sector. It started by seizing Yukos, then the country's largest oil and gas company. A year later, it watched with dismay as Ukraine's Orange Revolution blocked Viktor Yanukovych, its chosen placeman, from taking power. This turned out to be the last time that Russia would tolerate any interference with its domination of its "near abroad."

A critical source of tension between Russia and the West was the ambitions of NATO. As Chapter 3 relates, this collective security alliance, which had lost its reason for existence when its adversaries had disappeared in 1991, discovered new meaning in its value-promotion mission and proceeded to incorporate eleven former adversary states. The members justified this expansion by asserting that its origin as a military organization should no longer matter with the end of any real threat of war in Europe. The military obligations imposed by Article 5 of the NATO Treaty, however, remained in force. As NATO grew, so did Russia's concerns and, from 2008 on, its willingness to deploy its armed forces to deter further enlargement. First in Georgia, and then six years later in Ukraine, Russia responded to the aspirations of former Soviet states to join NATO with much the same kind of force that the Warsaw Pact had wielded in Budapest in 1956 and Prague in 1968.

Yet more challenges arose. The Coalition Provisional Authority that governed occupied Iraq wound itself down in June 2004 and transferred the rudiments of sovereignty back to Iraqis that had passed through anti-Ba'athist screening. The large coalition military footprint, however, endured and the invaders continued to wield effective power in the country. Turmoil ensued. Most directly, the ongoing troop presence inspired an insurgency, which led the coalition to repurpose the occupation from liberation to counterinsurgency.

Making sense of these events is not easy. Western military operations in Afghanistan, and then Iraq, shifted terrorist targeting away from the US mainland. Terrorists instead attacked European states, straining trans-Atlantic relations. Spain suffered the 3/11 attack, a wave of terror bombings, days before the 2004 general election. Voters turned on the incumbent center-right government, and the new Zapatero administration quickly pulled its forces out of Iraq. London sustained a terrorist attack in July 2005, although the Blair government survived and remained the Bush administration's staunchest international partner. The blood that previously had flowed in New York, Washington, DC, and Shanksville stained European capitals and threatened more and greater violence.

Conflicts over the anti-terror campaign partly reflected the way the United States prosecuted it, partly the different and often opposing strategic interests of the United States and its European partners. Security measures at home coupled with attacks abroad led to greater anxiety, not confidence and security. The new communications media made it easier to expose the uglier aspects of both. During the 2010s, Julian Assange and Edward Snowden got hold of and then broadcast huge digital files documenting the excesses and brutalities of the security state and its many uses of force. Confronted with this evidence of what mass surveillance and a war look like, many in the West flinched.

EMIGRANTS AS RESPONSE AND THREAT

The so-called Global War on Terror also made the issue of Islamic identity more fraught in European and US politics. Finding themselves living in a battlefield, noncombatants increasingly turned to emigration as a way out. As of 2020, the various campaigns against al-Qaeda and ISIS had displaced, internally or through emigration, as many as 38 million people from Afghanistan, Iraq, Libya, Pakistan, Syria, and Yemen, a figure equivalent to 8 percent of the entire population of the European Union.

Emigration led to immigration, with knock-on effects. Many people fleeing Iraq found themselves warehoused in refugee camps in the Middle East. Europe represented the closest part of the rich world for those with the means and resolve to get out of the camps. Most European leaders at first embraced these immigrants, many skilled and embedded within families, as a sensible way to plug their own demographic gaps while reducing tension in the Middle East. To their surprise, a large portion of their incumbent population saw things differently.

Early evidence of the disconnect between the technocrats and politicians that ran the European Union and the people of the member states came from an effort to bestow a constitution on the Union. Since 1952, international treaties had functioned as the basic laws of the enterprise, first the European Coal and Steel Community, then from 1957 the European Communities and, from 1993, the European Union. To a lawyer, these treaties did everything that a constitution normally does for a state – organize the structure through assignment of capacities; specify checking mechanisms, veto points, and voting rules; and articulate the aspirations that inspired the organization in hopes of making it an institution. The EU bureaucracy, set up as its Commission, and the leaders of the member states, acting as its Council, decided early in the century that they wanted something more.

They sought an international agreement called a constitution that would not just update the existing treaties, but anoint the entity as an imminent state itself, something moving toward a federation with its own polity, citizenship, and culture. After a drafting process presided over by Valery Giscard d'Estaing, a former French President and one of the great and the good of the European project, the European Union submitted the instrument for approval by its members.

All the members signed the constitution treaty in October 2004, but then things got dicey. Some states, notably Germany, regarded the constitution as just another treaty subject to approval by the Bundestag (its legislature) and the *Bundesverfassungsgericht* (its constitutional court). Others, including France, Ireland, Luxembourg, the Netherlands, Spain, Portugal, and the United Kingdom, decided that the aspirational element required direct democracy and organized referenda. Spain, the first to vote, approved the constitution, but a majority of voters in France and then the Netherlands rejected it. Although Luxembourg joined Spain in approval, rejection by two of the original six members signaled that the process was doomed. No one expected the British to embrace the pact.

Faced with these setbacks, EU leaders halted the effort to make a constitution and returned two years later with a new proposal. The Lisbon Treaty, signed in December 2007 and entering into force two years later, did essentially everything the constitution did, but without the pretensions. Only Ireland, as required by its constitution, submitted the new treaty to a referendum. Its electorate initially rejected the instrument, leading to further negotiations and concessions. A second Irish referendum in 2009 enabled the Treaty to enter into force later that year.

What should we make of this foray into symbolic European unification? It seems evident that as late as 2004 leaders in Europe saw an ever closer union as a realistic project. Perhaps they believed that this was the only path that would allow Europe to remain a global power, balancing and playing off the United States and China. To do this, they needed to create a popular sense of a common European culture, something that could displace increasingly irrelevant national identities and, for many, the tragic histories that had formed them. Substituting the Lisbon Treaty for the constitution meant that they could still advance the project, as long as they did not give the people a vote or speak too openly about where they saw themselves heading. The need for this switch, however, looks with hindsight like a warning signal. What the leaders wanted and what the voters would tolerate were growing apart. By the end of 2009, when Lisbon became law, the fault lines had become clearer and more dangerous.

THE SECOND SHOCK: THE GREAT RECESSION

As anti-immigrant politics took form in Europe, the United States teetered on the edge of its own precipice. Since the beginning of the century it had taken on two costly military missions while cutting taxes. The economy nevertheless boomed. The decision made in the 1990s to draw from the seemingly bottomless well of Chinese investment capital continued to bear fruit.[3] Asset prices – financial instruments and housing – surged until they didn't.

In 2007, a bubble in US housing mortgages burst. Distress passed throughout the financial system. Banks and regulators alike had rejected the possibility that housing prices could collapse simultaneously in all markets across the country, an assumption that proved fatal. By October 2008, the financial crisis escalated into a global recession that invited comparison with the Great Depression of the 1930s. It became known as the Great Recession. People in Hong Kong awoke to unaccustomed clear air as manufacturing in neighboring Shenzhen ground to a halt. Some banks and other financial intermediaries failed, others were restructured, and around the world stock markets, domestic and international sales of goods and services, and employment shrank.

In the United States, the unemployment rate doubled between December 2007 and October 2009 and gross domestic product (GDP) fell by 4.3 percent. The European sovereign debt crisis, which started in 2008, persevered past the peak of the US recession. It reached its zenith in 2010–12. Global GDP declined 2.9 percent in 2009.

The Great Recession was if anything a more pervasive global shock than 9/11. No one missed out, although some suffered more than others. A few countries, notably Iceland and Ireland, went through a complete financial meltdown but came out the other end without terrible consequences. Others, especially the southern EU tier of Portugal, Italy, Greece, and Spain (which wits in the press called the PIGS), suffered sustained and severe economic harm.

The government debt of the PIGS (money owed by the state, not its subjects) well exceeded their nationwide product, as measured by GDP. Bank regulators in the European Union had encouraged loans to these countries by treating them as risk-free, even though their debt paid a premium over that of, say, Germany. Creditors trusted the authorities to make good on an implied assurance about the creditworthiness of these problematic countries and kept lending in the face of growing evidence of their financial incontinence.

[3] Niall Ferguson & Moritz Schularick, *"Chimerica" and the Global Asset Market Boom*, 10 INT'L FIN. 215 (2007).

Greece and Portugal were sufficiently small economies that a write-down of their public debt would not by itself endanger any international banks. Italy and Spain, however, were big fish with the capacity to wreck a good part of the international financial system. The debtors in Iceland and Ireland had been largely private, and the creditors had sufficiently diversified loan portfolios to survive defaults on those debts. Iceland and Ireland also had flexible and diversified economies that could survive surprise and stress. The PIGS, in contrast, largely found themselves behind the knowledge-economy curve compared to the richer members of the European Union. Accordingly, their prospects for economic expansion as a means to grow out of their debts seemed bleak.

The PIGS's financial problems had political as well as economic consequences. They had to submit to a demoralizing virtual receivership under the auspices of the European financial institutions and the IMF. Given the German backbone of the European financial system, considerable Teutonophobia and dissipation of the political consensus supporting the European Union ensued.

Around the world, the Great Recession exacerbated the divide between the prosperous and the insecure and pushed democratic politics toward poles rather than consensus. In the United States, people who had prospered under the knowledge economy faced only fleeting pain. Those already falling behind suffered life-changing challenges. One-fourth of American families lost at least 75 percent of their wealth, and more than half of all families lost at least 25 percent of their wealth. The largest losses fell disproportionally on lower income, less educated, and minority households.[4] Elsewhere, similarly uneven distribution of pain and insecurity occurred. In the PIGS, constraints imposed by the international financial institutions blocked efforts to ramp up the social safety net to meet the needs of the newly unemployed and displaced.

From one perspective, many who suffered under the Great Recession could trace their miseries to their own improvidence. These nations, states, and people, the argument went, needed to embrace their suffering as a valuable life lesson that points to a course correction. Governments, this critique maintained, heightened the likelihood of financial crisis through their history of bailing out institutions that took on too much risk. In the United States, this was called a "Fed Put" (an option right to sell improvident loans to the government at an above-market price). Only by eliminating this moral hazard

[4] Fabian T. Pfeffer, Sheldon Danzinger & Robert F. Schoeni, *Wealth Disparities before and after the Great Recession*, 650 ANN. AM. ASS'N POL. & SOC. SCI. 98 (Nov. 2013).

could governments look to the financial sector to stave off future crises. If policymakers did not want to repeat this debacle, the argument went, they had to convincingly convey the message that such bailouts would not occur in the future. They could do so only by making the failure of banks such as Lehman Brothers the norm, not a puzzling exception.[5]

Germany exemplified this attitude. It took the lead in organizing the response of the European financial institutions, in partnership with the IMF, to the plight of the PIGS. The German government insisted that the debtor states show contrition and a willingness to reform as a condition of receiving any help to manage their burdens. No one should expect a Bundesbank put, either directly or, at least the Germans believed, from the ECB.

Most people, however, did not take such an austere view of the crisis. They focused instead on the seeming recklessness of creditors. They believed that the big banks and other financial institutions, rather than husbanding credit to safeguard against disaster, pushed loans onto unwitting customers to pump up their profits. When hopes met reality, this narrative went, government intervention saved the improvident lenders, but not the retail borrowers whom the lenders had encouraged to take on more debt than they could realistically sustain. To add insult to injury, in most places the leaders of the financial institutions exited the industry with large rewards, and no prosecutor was able to prove that any had committed criminal fraud. There arose in the popular imagination a belief that bosses had made out like bandits, that the crisis had exposed the financial engineers as a bunch of deluded Dr. Frankensteins, and that the politicians had looked after the bosses while leaving average folk to fend for themselves.

Many have written much to support or attack these competing narratives. Fights over the origins of the crisis and the lessons to be learned still rage on. For my purposes, it matters more that a large portion of the public around the world considered the Great Recession a product of the hubris of experts and the corruption of government, not as a teachable moment about risk and the inexorable persistence of the downside. Just as 9/11 and the ensuing forever wars cast a shadow on peace, the Great Recession put prosperity in doubt. With these anxieties, the pall on the liberal internationalist project grew broader and darker.

The Obama administration seemed at first an antidote to this malaise. Obama's election by itself justified a Peace Prize, apparently on the

5 Paul G. Mahoney, Wasting a Crisis: Why Securities Regulation Fails (2015).

assumption that he would undo the injuries that the liberal world order had suffered under George W. Bush. He came to office in 2009 with the Great Recession at full tide but, within a year, the US economy (unlike Europe's) seemed on the mend. The capture and killing of Osama bin Laden in May 2011 burnished his popular image and seemed to provide a bookend to the War on Terror. Whether from luck or wisdom, the administration seemed to be leading the country back to virtue and fulfillment after a decade of wrong turns.

THE THIRD SHOCK: THE ARAB SPRING AS A CAUTIONARY TALE

Also in 2011, hopes for liberal internationalism based on bottom-up people power armed with new technology and infused with liberal ideals first blossomed, then withered. In December 2010, Mohamed Bouazizi, a Tunisian street vendor tormented by corrupt local authorities, set himself on fire. Mass protests followed, largely organized through cellphones and social media. Things reached the point where the long-time oligarchy had to abandon power. That opened the way for a Constituent Assembly to remake the nation's governance, supposedly on liberal democratic lines. Thus began the Arab Spring.

Similar resentments and structural problems – corrupt authoritarian governments, widespread mismatches between education and life prospects, stagnant economies – plagued almost all the countries in North Africa and the Middle East. Inspired by the events in Tunisia, people throughout the region took to the streets. In Libya, Egypt, and Yemen, demonstrators drove out long-term, seemingly untouchable leaders. Elsewhere, the Arab street rallied and the incumbents responded with a mixture of violence and nominal reform.

The popular uprising relied heavily on the fruits of the knowledge economy to mobilize people. During the heady early days, liberals and technological utopians saw these events as a late fulfillment of the promise of 1989. The Arab world had missed out on the triumph of liberal democracy and open economies that had swept over Central and Eastern Europe and Latin America twenty years earlier. The invasion of Iraq had made things worse. Now that technology had empowered the people by cutting out curators and making self-organization cheap and easy, the natural tendency toward freedom and equality could manifest itself in the overthrow of corrupt autocrats. Arabs as much as anyone had the right to live in liberal democracies. With years of further technological innovation, they now were able to take charge of their lives.

These hopes quickly collapsed. The reasonably peaceful and stable transition that Tunisia pulled off happened nowhere else. Egypt dallied with democratic governance that brought the Muslim Brotherhood to power, but the military exploited the resulting chaos to install one of their own, General al-Sisi, as a brutal autocrat. In Libya, a Security Council resolution authorizing outside intervention boomeranged against the West. Acting on what China and Russia considered an overly broad reading of the mandate, the United States spurred on militia and gangs that captured and murdered Muammar Gaddafi, the longstanding dictator. This intervention, however, failed to establish even minimal security. Libya never got past the initial chaos and for a decade now has remained a failed state. Perhaps the worst outcome, however, unfolded in Syria.

Bashar al-Assad, the dynastic leader of Syria, embodies everything that the Arab Spring rose up against. Corrupt and ineffectual, he relies mainly on violence and cronyism to hold on to power. His family belongs to the Alawites, a minority sect within Shi'a Islam, which complicated his relationship with a majority Sunni nation. At the dawn of the Arab Spring, people in Syria mobilized. Following in his ruthless father's footsteps, he attacked the demonstrations with armed force, slaughtering thousands. Civil war ensued. At that point, everything seemed to go wrong.

Syria became a proxy battlefield for outsiders, a tragic echo of the Spanish Civil War that had served as a dry run for the looming calamity of World War II. Iran and Russia backed Assad and escalated their support as the conflict unfolded. Turkey intervened to suppress radical Kurdish forces that, it feared, could use gains in Syria to turn against it. Da'esh, a militant Islamicist group inspired by al-Qaeda, exploited the chaos to gain control of stretches of Syria and Iraq. Its terror and murderous repression attracted a small but still alarming number of adherents from the West while motivating international powers to intervene to eliminate the threat. Burned by what they saw as US fecklessness in Libya, China and Russia refused to allow the Security Council to organize or approve the response. In the fall of 2014, the United States put together Operation Current Resolve, a coalition that bridged European and regional states. Largely limited to aerial support of fighters on the ground, the coalition struggled to pick and choose among the Assad regime's adversaries, the most immediately effective of whom drew on the ideology, if not the resources, of radically militant Islam.

Ultimately, Syria, its supporters, and the western interveners ended Da'esh as a de facto state but left it able to mount an effective insurgency. Assad held on to power, at a terrible cost to Syria. The interveners remain in place. The principal effect on the rest of the world was yet another wave of emigrants.

German Chancellor Angela Merkel's attempt to open the European Union to these people produced an emphatic backlash both in her own country and in the rest of Europe. The resulting fight exposed fissures in the European Union and arguably pushed forward the end of Merkel's career.

Looking back a decade later, the Arab Spring provides as clear an endpoint as any to the liberal self-confidence that flourished after 1989. Breakthroughs in communications technologies would allow people to connect with each other and thwart the grey men, in uniform and out, whose crude threats had kept them apart and disappointed. They also would expose corruption and fraud. Liberated from state oppression, people would embrace markets as the embodiment of democracy, self-actualization, and striving for a better life. Freedom would ring. No ideology, no theory of history, could take over from liberal democracy, which had prevailed against all others.

At first, the Arab Spring recapitulated 1989. A generation had passed and communications infrastructure had advanced beyond what anyone could have imagined at the time of the Berlin Wall's fall. Phones first became mobile, and then smart. The internet appeared, and then took off. Social media came into its own. The resistance to the region's autocrats exploited these resources to draw on deep resentments that bottom-up self-organization could easily mobilize. Dynamic emulation propelled street demonstrations and strikes.

Taking to the streets worked to oust or disturb existing power structures but failed as a means of wielding power after the ruptures happened. Liberation did not morph into liberal self-rule. Disorder opened the door to violent repression. The men with the guns returned, as the people fighting for liberal self-governance fell to violence, exhaustion, and disillusionment.[6]

THE GLOBAL CRISIS ON THE HORIZON

Here I offer a snapshot of the world as it seemed at the start of 2015. The United States had pulled out of the Great Recession. Sectors of the economy, especially those associated with technology, finance, medicine, law, higher education, and other high-value-added services, thrived. But new pockets of misery, different from historic poverty, had appeared. In that year, people started talking about deaths of despair.

Elsewhere, signs of instability popped up. The United Kingdom had just survived a secession referendum in Scotland but faced an upcoming

6 Zeynep Tufekci, Twitter and Tear Gas: The Power and Fragility of Networked Protest (2017).

parliamentary election with an increasingly frayed coalition government and a deepening split within the Conservative Party over EU membership. In Europe, the ongoing economic crisis in the PIGS had brought outsider political parties to power in Greece and Italy and disrupted longstanding settlements between center-left and center-right political establishments in much of the rest of the European Union. Many of the former Soviet satellites, shocked by the Russian seizure of Crimea (more on this in the next chapter) and dismayed by the ineffectual EU response, began to reconsider their commitment to the ideals and obligations that had seemed so powerful in 1989. President Putin enjoyed unprecedented popularity in Russia in the wake of that seizure, notwithstanding (if not because of) the West's sanctions. Xi Jinping, a year and a half into his first term as China's President, had just consummated an anti-corruption campaign that had taken out his greatest rivals and seemed poised to consolidate personal power like no other Chinese leader in the twenty-first century. Narendra Modi, a Hindu nationalist whose supposed responsibility for a massacre of Muslims had dogged his career, had recently become Prime Minister of India. Dilma Rousseff, leader of the center-left Workers' Party, had just won reelection as Brazil's president but battled against corruption charges. South African President Jacob Zuma was halfway through a tenure marked by flagrant corruption and contempt for the rule of law. The Middle East was aflame. Nicolás Maduro had risen to power in Venezuela, even as his corruption and incompetence made his continued hold on the presidency seem unimaginable.

At that moment, the only unambiguous rebuke to the post-Cold War status quo had been Russia's attack on Ukraine. Each of these situations, however, undermined liberal internationalism with potentially dire consequences. Growing cultural and economic inequality in the United States threatened the nation's capacity to cope with problems over the horizon. The rise of nationalist politicians in Europe and the large emerging powers called the BRICS indicated a lack of confidence in international entrenchment and cooperation. The consolidation of one-man power in China introduced a new stage in its competition with the West.

Each of these problems threatened a global regime that embraced liberal principles and relied on international institutions as a safeguard. None had yet graduated to the status of a crisis. Their accumulation, however, indicated a growing insecurity in the world that the events of the 1990s had shaped and inspired. And the system shocks of the century's first decade, the War on Terror and the Great Recession as well as the terrible aftermath of the Arab Spring, confirmed people in their fears.

5

Crises Come in Waves

National Populism, the Poisoning of Cyberspace, a New Cold War, and the Pandemic (2015–21)

We know 2015's looming problems were serious because of what happened since. This does not mean that reasonably astute people should have seen all this coming. Speaking for myself, I spent much of 2015 traveling around the world, teaching in Australia, China, and France as well as lawyering in Germany, the Netherlands, and the United Kingdom. Everywhere old friends and new acquaintances asked about Trump's chances for the presidency. I assured them all that he had none, that American politics would reject him like a healthy immune system would repel a virus. Good thing I don't hold myself out as an expert on American politics or immunology.

What seems clear today is that this cascade of crises poses an immediate threat to the global order constructed on the back of the collapse of communism. These events have different aspects – political, technological, geopolitical, and epidemiological. Yet their emergence now reveals a pattern, even with all due concessions to the randomness and contingency that make up history. It was not inevitable that the world economy and the global international order would face the particular challenges that they confront today. But, the next section of this book will argue, deep currents driving the world economy undercut the international structures built during the 1990s and compromise the attitudes and assumptions – if you will, the ideology – that sustain them. These forces brought us to where we are, even if no one could have foreseen exactly where we ended up.

This chapter tells the story of the twenty-first century's turn from system shocks to crises. It begins with the emergence of national populism in the domestic politics of many states. The trend is complicated, because there exist as many forms of national populism as there are nations. But enough commonality exists to tell a coherent, even if incomplete, story. It continues with an account of the other developments that exacerbate national populism, namely the pollution and increasing danger of cyberspace, an incipient Cold War, potential hot ones, and the global COVID-19 pandemic.

NATIONAL POPULISM

After the British referendum on Brexit and the Trump election – the most visible and disruptive eruptions of national populism – scholars and pundits tried to account for the sudden emergence of tribal and populist politics.[1] As I understand it, national populism represents both a cluster of beliefs about identity and politics and a mass movement inspired by, expressing, and reshaping those beliefs. It emphasizes a communal identity based on exclusion and drawn from an understanding (often an invention) of nationhood, itself a loose notion of varying degrees of inclusion, specificity, and historic validity. It also draws on a sense of shared grievances that, in the present moment, target managerial, educational, and cultural élites, with some invention involved in labeling those élites. It distrusts traditional means of interpreting the world – in particular, the so-called mainstream media – as dishonest and corrupt. It emphasizes the group over the individual and subordination to just authority over radical skepticism.

National populism does not easily fit into the received political categories of right and left; if we want to use historical labels, the best is romantic, in the sense of Rousseau, Byron, and de Staël. It is in large part what psychoanalyst Erik Erikson called a negative identity, defined more by opposition and resentment than a clear sense of an achievable project that binds those who pursue it.[2] Its followers embrace some forms of technology, especially social media, but they distrust science because of what they see as élite capture and corruption. To the extent that science is about withholding and revising conclusions pending evidence and analysis, national populism will have none of it.

The United States has a long tradition of national populism, perhaps older and more episodically ascendant than in most parts of the world. Modern historians such as Richard Hofstadter (*Anti-intellectualism in American Life* and *The Paranoid Style in American Politics*) and C. Vann Woodward (*The Strange Career of Jim Crow* and his biography of Georgia's Tom Watson)

[1] Jan-Werner Müller, What Is Populism? (2016); Pippa Norris & Ronald Inglehart, Cultural Backlash: Trump, Brexit, and Authoritarian Populism (2019); Mark Tushnet & Bojan Bugarič, Power to the People: Constitutionalism in the Age of Populism (2021).

[2] Erik Erikson, Childhood and Society, 241–43, 261 (2d ed. 1963).

devoted much of their careers to the subject. Andrew Jackson, the seventh president, epitomizes the tradition. William Jennings Bryan and Watson carried forward the populist legacy in the wake of the Civil War and the unfolding of the Industrial Revolution. Woodrow Wilson, a nationalist, adopted the slogan of America first and promoted racial segregation, but could not be considered a populist due to his faith in scientific administration and technocratic rule. Huey Long exemplified the national-populist response to the Great Depression. Among more recent presidential candidates, Richard Gephardt and Patrick Buchanan presented themselves as adversaries of the status quo who would look to native traditions and resources to counter the fallen ways of the contemporary world, its corrupt élites, and the undue influence of foreigners. Donald Trump, who proposed to "make America great again" and to put America first (Woodrow Wilson's old slogan, but without any love for experts), managed to gain the White House by embracing national populism more effectively than any US political leader since Jackson.

In England, Boris Johnson seems as good a national populist as any, showing how a toff can work with the plebs. In France, Marine Le Pen outperformed her father politically by appealing to a sense of national identity that rejects immigrants and the European Union. She gained 38 percent of the vote in the second round of the 2017 election and 42 percent in 2022, far exceeding her father's 18 percent in 2002. She, along with the far left opposition, command a majority of the legislature after the June 2022 election. Italy's Brothers of Italy and two other populist parties, expected to form a government after the September 2022 election, also rely on a kind of national identity to oppose immigrants and the European Union. Poland's Law and Justice Party and Hungary's Fidesz, both currently in power, exemplify national populism. Of the major European states, only Germany lacks a national populist party that seems a credible contender for power in the near term, although its Alternative for Germany (AfD) was the fifth most successful vote-getter in the 2021 Bundestag elections with more than 10 percent of the vote. I suspect that Germany's terrible embrace of its form of national populism from 1933 to 1945 led to a residual immunity not found in most other countries.

Outside of the rich West, applying the concept of national populism requires flexibility due to compounding factors that complicate the story. Consider Putin's Russia, Xi's China, Modi's India, Bolsonaro's Brazil, Andrés Manuel Lóbrador's Mexico, Duterte's Philippines, and Erdogan's Turkey. Each has a politics that revolves around a strong leader with a populist style. They claim that liberal internationalism is hostile to their national interests, that liberal democracy and the rule of law are ploys to hobble their efforts to realize their nation's cultural and historic destinies, that their nations are enjoying a renaissance after one kind of imposition or another by the rich West, and that appeals to these destinies bolstered by attacks on nonconforming minorities (Muslims, Caucasians, and liberals in Russia, non-Han people in China, Muslims and Christians in India, westernized élites and sexual minorities in Brazil, secularized élites and Kurds in Turkey, East Asians, and Muslims in the Philippines, and gringos in Mexico) provide a basis for popular support. Populism works differently, of course, in a long-term democracy such as India, fragile democracies such as Brazil, Mexico, Turkey, and the Philippines, a seriously compromised democracy such as Russia, and an autocracy like China. Contrasts in history and culture determine what counts as nationalism. But, using psychoanalytic terms, each country's populism relies heavily on an "other" to define its "self." Each leader sees an advantage in standing up to the rich West and privileging the masses at the expense of outliers. None looks back to the 1990s as a golden age.

I do not mean to suggest that these various manifestations of national populism share a well-developed and coherent ideology or political agenda. Nor did romanticism during its heyday in the late eighteenth and early nineteenth century. Because national populism emphasizes and exaggerates the peculiarities of each nation, the differences may seem more striking than the commonalities. Like Tolstoy's unhappy families, each nation is national populist in its own way. Rather, the point is that in a large part of the world, in both the rich West and the revisionist South, national encounters with the world economy led to popular resistance, which a growing cohort of opportunistic political leaders successfully exploit. The precise grounds for the resistance and the arguments used to tap into popular unrest vary among states, but the twin realities of disenchantment and of growing gaps between the people and incumbent élites hold true around the world.

POLITICAL TURMOIL

The next section of this book provides an explanation for populism in the rich world, especially the United States. Here I describe what the rise of national populism looks like in the world's richest and most powerful countries. Power and prosperity brought its own discontents, with both greater economic and social divisions within the country and new technologies that amplified those divisions. A preexisting cultural and political tradition that drew on a particular national identity helped but cannot account for the extent of the phenomenon.

Generalizing greatly, in the United States since the 1970s each of the two political parties contained anti-élite strands, but neither made that tendency the foreground of its image. Democrats attacked big business and old money, stood up for Main Street over Wall Street, and held themselves out as the party of the common person. For people of a certain age, Spiro Agnew's attack on nattering nabobs of negativism, understood as a broadside against the *New York Times*, CBS, and Harvard, triggers a wry memory. Objectively, Nixon achieved significant inroads among the Democratic Party's blue-collar base. Congressman Richard Gephardt, running for the Democratic presidential nomination in 1988, made an attack on trade liberalization a central part of his campaign. Pat Buchanan did the same in the 1992 Republic primaries and added a layer of tribalism (his adversaries called it racism) to the mix. Each were squashed in turn, however, by George H. W. Bush and Bill Clinton, Yale men who embraced free trade, global finance, the international rule of law, and a robust aspiration to bless the world with American values and institutions. The elder Bush and Clinton embodied all that contemporary US national populism opposes and even despises.

Obama's election first promised an end to the twin debacles of the global War on Terror and the Great Recession. Yet it faced strong pushback in spite of its successes. The 2010 midterm election saw the Republicans retake the House of Representatives and, perhaps more importantly, the rise of an outsider movement within the Republicans called the Tea Party. The 2014 midterm saw the defeat of House Majority Leader Eric Cantor, an establishment Republican, and the Republican recapture of the Senate. These unsettling events transitioned from noise to signal in 2016, when Donald Trump, much to almost everyone's surprise (including Trump's, I suspect), won the presidency.

Making sense of Trump's victory has bedeviled many analysts, and no firm, empirically based judgment enjoys consensus support. A prominent account credits racial resentment as a significant factor, even though Trump harvested support from many who had voted for Obama.[3] Data collected by Harvard economist Dani Rodrik are suggestive, even though not conclusive. Put simply, the racist hypothesis accounts for a substantial portion of the composition of the Trump electorate, but class-based hostility to economic trends provides a more powerful explanation for switches in voter preferences from Democrat to Trump. In simple and tentative terms, it seems as if racism explains a significant portion of votes for Republican presidential candidates over time, but economic grievances tell us more about why Trump's share of

[3] Jacob S. Hacker & Paul Pierson, Let Them Eat Tweets: How the Right Rules in an Age of Extreme Inequality (2020); Isabel Wilkerson, Caste: The Origins of Our Discontents (2020); Pippa Norris & Ronald Inglehart, *supra* note 1.

the electorate went up in the states that mattered for the electoral college, compared to McCain and Romney (the Republican nominees in 2008 and 2012). Economics, in other words, drove Trump's *delta* (the rate of change in his support), even if it does not account for the absolute size of his vote.[4]

At the end of the day, the historical significance of the 2016 election lies less in who prevailed than in the manifestation of a large and powerful national populist movement able to affect significant policy choices in the world's richest and most powerful country. Even if Hillary Clinton had prevailed that year, a Republican party controlling both houses of Congress and forced to live with a large national populist faction doubtless would have made her life miserable. I suspect that a Republican-controlled House of Representatives would have ginned up an impeachment in 2017 or 2018, much as befell her husband in 1997.

On the one hand, Trump was unable to implement much of the national populist agenda as law. During the two years that Republicans enjoyed a majority in Congress, their signature legislative accomplishment was a package of tax cuts that, given the incidence of the federal income tax, necessarily benefited the wealthiest taxpayers, not the victims of economic dislocation. Congress did nothing about immigration, Trump's most mooted issue, and found itself unable to repeal the Affordable Care Act, Obama's signature legislative achievement and therefore Trump's primary target. On the other hand, Trump, much like Obama before him, responded to a truculent Congress by wielding executive authority in areas that mattered to his supporters, including immigration and health insurance.

In retrospect, perhaps the most enduring legacy of his often shambolic tenure will be the manner of his leaving. His reality-bending claims of election fraud and the violence they provoked traumatized his adversaries as they energized a substantial portion of his supporters. The no-hope impeachments during office may serve as a template for partisan conflict going forward. Meanwhile baseless but dangerous disputes over elections threaten to become part of the expected background of US politics. Each of these developments, going forward, threatens the viability of American representative democracy.

For international law, Trump's national populism worked more as a series of threats than a concrete trashing of international commitments. Perhaps his administration's most significant accomplishment, as Chapter 11 relates, was to consummate a threat previously made by its predecessor to disassemble the WTO's Appellate Body. This permanent court no longer functions and the

4 Dani Rodrik, *Why Does Globalization Fuel Populism? Economics, Culture, and the Rise of Right-Wing Populism*, 13 Ann. Rev. Econ. 133 (2021).

Biden administration has not yet chosen to restore it. The Trump administration also forced the renegotiation of NAFTA and the US–Korean Free Trade Agreement, although the resulting changes seem more cosmetic than structural. Its invocation of the national security exception to the Uruguay Round Agreements joined other states in a destabilizing strategy that poses a significant threat to those Agreements, as Chapter 11 also describes. But Trump did not leave NATO or the United Nations, as his rhetoric hinted might happen, or undermine the international financial institutions, which continued to do their work as they saw fit.

National populism in the United Kingdom may lack the manic quality of the US variant, but it has brought about deeper institutional change. The focus of British anti-establishment politics was the European Union. The British form of representative democracy generally avoids plebiscites. Voters select members of parliament, but neither the head of state nor the head of government. In the face of this tradition, Prime Minister Cameron, seeking to cabin the national populist faction in the Conservative Party, promised as part of his platform in the 2015 election a referendum on continued British membership in the European Union. Much to his surprise, in June 2016 a majority of the UK electorate backed Brexit. Cameron fell on his sword and, after an interval with Theresa May and her diffidence toward Brexit, the Tories embraced Boris Johnson, the noisiest national populist in the party's leadership, as Prime Minister. After protracted negotiations with the European Union and two Supreme Court cases on parliament's role in the process, the United Kingdom and the European Union reached a withdrawal agreement in the fall of 2019. The British people immediately rewarded Johnson with an overwhelming electoral victory. The United Kingdom and the European Union officially parted ways on January 31, 2020, just before the start of the COVID-19 pandemic.

The process has only begun, so it will take years to assess the impact of Brexit. Over the short run, the Johnson government's handling of COVID-19 vaccinations seems better than the European Union's and strengthened popular support for the leave option. On the other side of the ledger are the shortages in many basic goods and worries about a lack of fuel for the winter of 2022–23. Whether these problems represent the natural and long-term harms of Brexit or only the short-term effect of restarting the economy after COVID-19 remains unknowable for now. The costs incurred in sanctioning Russia for its invasion of Ukraine further complicates the story.

At the outer (but still plausible) range of possible outcomes, Brexit might accelerate the breakup of the European Union, the United Kingdom, or both. EU leaders and bureaucrats fear that national populists in the PIGS, France, and the former socialist countries, bolstered by the UK example, might also take their nations out of the Union. The Scots, who voted to stay, make noises about a new referendum to leave the United Kingdom so that Scotland can gain admission to the European Union. Northern Ireland, which also voted to stay, can reverse Brexit for itself through a merger with the Republic of Ireland. These outcomes, were they to unfold, would have profound consequences for a remnant England and Wales.

Two similarities between US and UK national populism stick out. First, each has a plutocrat as its face, both products of élite education (Johnson more than Trump, but the latter technically an Ivy Leaguer) and beneficiaries of inherited wealth (Trump more than Johnson, but both did well in the birth lottery). Privilege apparently does not make it hard to mobilize the masses, as long as the mobilizer says the right things and sends the right signals.

Second, the voting patterns in Trump's two elections and in the Brexit referendum show distinct geographical patterns that map on to significant economic divides. Trump's votes came largely from outside the great cities that serve as nodes of the knowledge economy, as Chapter 8 discusses in detail. Brexit support came from everywhere in England and Wales except London and the prosperous counties to its south and southwest, reflecting a division between the main beneficiaries of the knowledge economy and the rest of the country.

The story of national populism in parts of Central and Eastern Europe reflects different historical and economic forces than that of the United States and United Kingdom, but the accounts converge with regimes hostile to liberal internationalism generally and international organizations in particular.[5] The evolution of Hungary's Fidesz and its leader Viktor Orbán is noteworthy. They started out in the 1980s as liberal critics of the incumbent communist regime. In the mid-1990s, stuck in opposition, they rebranded as conventionally conservative and formed their first government in 1998. After another stint in the political wilderness between 2002 and 2010, they again remade themselves, this time as populists appealing to national pride, Christian values, hostility to outsiders such as Jews and Romani, and opposition to immigrants and the European Union. The realignment seems to have worked. Fidesz won three further elections since returning to power in 2010, including an overwhelming triumph in 2022. National populists elsewhere in the world come to Budapest to kiss Orbán's ring.

5 Ivan Krastev & Stephen Holmes, The Light That Failed (2019).

The Liberty and Justice Party in Poland overlaps with Fidesz in its general anti-liberal stance but has a different history and somewhat different politics. It taps into Poland's strong Catholic-nationalist tradition that throughout modern history has resisted individualism and free markets. It has come closer to the brink than Hungary in conflicts with the European Union, although both countries got into hot water over restructurings of the judiciary intended to defang independent constitutional courts. The European Court of Human Rights attacked both countries' measures as a breach of their duty to provide a disinterested tribunal, but it has not found a means to reverse the changes. EU organs, while expressing concern, also failed to take effective action, much to the dismay of civil society groups and academics.

The Luxembourg Court also attacked Poland's judicial reforms, as Chapter 12 discusses in detail. Two decisions in 2019 condemned the restructuring of its Supreme Court and lower courts, but Poland refused to change anything. The Commission sought sanctions in 2021, but the Court only requested that Poland comply with its rulings. The Commission also brought an additional claim based on another Polish law allowing a new organ of the Supreme Court to punish judges for what the organ determines to be flouting of the law. The Luxembourg Court in September 2021 ordered Poland not to apply disciplinary measures while the litigation was pending (equivalent to a preliminary injunction in US law) and in October imposed a fine of €1 million a day for noncompliance with its order.[6] Meanwhile, Poland's Constitutional Court ruled that the provisions on which the EU case rests violate Poland's Constitution and therefore lack legal effect.[7]

Outside the rich West, opposition to the liberal principles of the 1990s and rising nationalism dominates. The meaning of both nationalism and populism varies considerably in these places. Especially in authoritarian states and those with illiberal democracies, populism functions more as a device used by political élites to rally support, and less as an independent force that constrains political leaders. Still, even this form of populism contrasts with the Marxism–Leninism that élites in the socialist bloc previously used to justify their power. Populism implies a popular will, while Marxism–Leninism appeals to objective forces that reveal themselves through (supposedly) careful study and rigorous analysis best done by the élites. One is for the masses, the other for highbrows.

6 Case No. C-204/21, *Commission* v. *Poland* (Oct. 27, 2021) (order of the Vice-President of the Court).

7 Assessment of the Conformity to the Polish Constitution of Selected Provisions of the Treaty on European Union, Ref. No. K 3/21 (Oct. 7, 2021).

Under Article 6 of the old Soviet Constitution, the party organs were the bodies that, "armed with Marxism–Leninism, … [impart] a planned, systematic and theoretically substantiated character to [the Soviet people's] struggle for the victory of communism." Russian Foreign Minister Sergey Lavrov's formulation of the nonwestern take on populism shows how the élite and the people changed roles. He recently asserted:

> Russians have always demonstrated maturity, a sense of self-respect, dignity and national pride, and the ability to think independently, especially during hard times, while remaining open to the rest of the world, but only on an equal, mutually beneficial footing. Once we put the confusion and mayhem of the 1990s behind us, these values became the bedrock of Russia's foreign policy concept in the 21st century. The people of Russia can decide on how they view the actions by their government without getting any prompts from abroad.[8]

Lavrov makes explicit the role of the people of Russia as drivers of history. At least rhetorically, the organs have become servants of the people, not carriers of higher political consciousness that guide popular attitudes based on a profound theoretical insight. Today, Lavrov claims, the organs follow the people's lead.

As Lavrov's remarks indicate, Russian disenchantment with the West became manifest under Putin. The annexation of Crimea dashed all hopes of resets and other ways of bringing the country back into the liberal international fold. That adventure greatly boosted Putin's domestic support. Western sanctions only hardened the Russian position, rewarding Russian leaders for their truculence. A Russian threat of countersanctions forced one liberal international organization, the Council of Europe, to drop its penalties. His 2022 invasion of Ukraine has raised the stakes, including Russia's expulsion from the Council, and may yet bring about his fall. But a bitter, grinding conflict that tests western unity more as the costs of sanctions rise also seems possible.

Whether "populism" captures the political basis of Putin's support is debatable. Since the 2018 presidential election, which the tiny band of Russian liberals attacked as rigged, the regime has increased repression, including the jailing of opposition figures and the criminalization of resistance activities. These measures grew broader and more severe as domestic dissent to the Ukraine war popped up. Constitutional amendments adopted in 2020 forbid

8 Sergey Lavrov, *The Law, Rights, and the Rules*, Ministry of Foreign Affairs of the Russian Federation, No. 1301, June 28, 2021, www.mid.ru/en/foreign_policy/news/-/asset_publisher/cKNonkJE02Bw/content/id/4801890.

calls to revise Russian borders, which implementing legislation treats as a form of terrorism. Generally, politics in Russia focus on which group and personality best exemplifies the "people" for whom populism advocates; avowed liberals poll in the single digits.[9]

The 2020 constitutional amendments also codify changes in Russia's approach to international law and foreign relations. They root this approach in a conception of a protracted global conflict, in which Russia leads one of the opposing sides. They also commit Russia to the protection of ethnic Russians living outside the border of the Russian state, implicitly by bringing the motherland to them. They repudiate talk of western values, which they equate with imperial domination.

China also stretches the concept of national populism. Categorizing China's position as populist requires adjusting for the absence of formal democratic politics. The regime both encourages Han nationalism as a means of attacking its perceived adversaries and reins it in when it becomes too boisterous. Nationalism manifests itself directly in the treatment of non-Han minorities such as the Tibetans and Uyghurs and serves generally as a source of legitimacy for the regime. Although nominally a Marxist–Leninist state, China has resurrected Confucianism and Chinese culture and history as the basic norms that justify its project. Dialectical materialism, the essence of the ideology that once pervaded the country, no longer does much work.

After thirty years of chasing foreign investment and pursuing deeper integration into the global economy, China under Xi now uses its economic power as an international political instrument. The belt-and-road initiative and infrastructure projects throughout the global South indicate its aspirations. New international institutions it has created leverage its influence. Its Asian Infrastructure Development Bank, founded in 2016, now has 103 state members and provides an alternative to the World Bank. China responded to the US campaign against the WTO's Appellate Body by partnering with the European Union to create an alternative appellate structure. Conceptually, its take on international law has remained consistent since its turn toward international integration after the end of the Cultural Revolution, but the distinct features came into sharper contrast under Xi. The regime's ambitious claim about its rights over the South China Sea and its steps to advance that claim, particularly by converting rocks into islands, highlight its approach. As the West and Russia find themselves embroiled in a growing conflict, China has greater room to chart its course.

[9] Sebastian Hoppe, *Sovereigntism vs. Anti-corruption Messianism: A Salient Post-Soviet Cleavage of Populist Mobilization*, 38 Post-Sov. Affairs 251 (2022).

Brazil, India, Mexico, the Philippines, and Turkey, once embracing the world economy while shoring up their domestic democracies, either elect charismatic populist leaders (Brazil in 2018, India in 2014, Mexico in 2018, and the Philippines in 2016 and 2022) or lurch toward authoritarianism in the wake of a failed coup (Turkey in 2016). Distinct stories apply to each of these large and important states, but a common theme also emerges. Domestic political dynamics led each to reconsider its relationship with the international system as a whole and particularly with the world economy. They do not act as direct adversaries of the West in the way that China and Russia do, but their collective drift reinforces the notion that liberal internationalism has lost much ground around the world.

CONNECTIVITY TURNS AGAINST US

The connectivity revolution had its origins in breakthroughs in computing going back to World War II, but the last thirty years brought about extraordinary things. Netscape Navigator, the first widely available web browser, radically democratized access to the internet when it appeared in 1994. Presenting data visually and mixing in sounds and images transformed connectivity by broadening the appeal of the online experience. Web utopianism exploded, even though it soon became clear that, by volume and money value, the internet's largest contribution to modern life was its distribution of pornography. The ubiquity of smartphones in the first decade of the twenty-first century and the development of cloud computing, social media, and the Internet of Things in the following decade means that a vast array of activities – political, economic, cultural, and structural – take place online in much of the world, not only the rich West.

People embraced this technology because it was smarter, faster, and in many ways more democratic. Poor farmers in the South could use their smartphones both to get price information that guided how they planned their crops and to cut out costly intermediaries when marketing their products. At least for a while, politically marginalized people could hurdle barriers to take to the streets and seize power. Vast resources opened up to people doing their own research, breaking down hierarchies of knowledge and authority. Access to services – housing, food, travel, housework – became more flexible and cheaper. The new technology seemed to make free markets both freer and better.

Technological innovation, however, is both dynamic and amoral. Recall the invention of the cotton gin, a breakthrough that greatly lowered the costs of producing cotton to feed Manchester's mills and thus made cloth cheaper and more widely available, but also greatly increased the profits of enslavers, and therefore the returns from enslaving people. The twenty-first century's connectivity revolution has had at least three unforeseen (although perhaps foreseeable) bad consequences. It has made it easier for both public authorities and private actors to turn transparency on its head by increasing their access to and control over information generated by bottom-up action, political and otherwise. By undermining knowledge hierarchies, it has disrupted traditional means of holding the powerful to account and substituted an anarchic and often compartmented world too often awash in virtue signaling, fake news, and misinformation. Because connectivity typically produces what economists call positive returns to scale – firms enjoy higher profits the more they produce, due to both lower marginal costs and increased product value resulting from network effects – these industries naturally evolve into monopolies. Chapter 6 discusses these effects in detail.

China's Great Firewall provides a vivid example of how cyber freedom turned on its head. As people moved their lives online, an authoritarian government both monitored and censored information flows. A few states take the crude but ephemerally effective step of shutting down nationwide internet access during crises. Others simply used existing technology to mobilize repression. In Myanmar, for example, the regime used Facebook to incite mass violence against a reviled minority, the Rohingya.

Private firms in the technology industry presented their own threats. Motivated by profit rather than a wish to exercise political power, they pursue advertising revenues and mass data collection in ways that do not necessarily elevate public welfare. Both strategies aspire to manipulate people for their own, typically profit-seeking, ends. Nudging consumer choices may seem less malignant than diminishing people as political actors, and the jury is out as to the effectiveness of current industry efforts. Both projects, however, impair agency and promote alienation. They sow distrust even if they don't meet their primary objectives.

Compromises of US national security information by Edward Snowden, Chelsea Manning, and Julian Assange, as well as the Chinese hack into the US Office of Personnel Management database in 2015, showed the world its great cyber power's inability to protect its most important secrets. Over the last seven years, the malignant use of connectivity by state actors and criminal gangs, sometimes acting on their own and sometimes as partners, exploded. During the 2016 US presidential election, a Russian intelligence service gained access to emails belonging to the Democratic National Committee and then leaked those that might harm the Democrats' cause. Similar operations apparently took place in Europe in connection with the Brexit referendum and various parliamentary elections. Cyberattacks against Estonia in 2007 and Ukraine in 2017 are believed to be Russian actions against former Soviet states that it regarded as asserting too much independence. Attribution, of course, remains controversial. The existence of the risk and attendant insecurity, however, is not.

As more activity went online, the possibilities for exploitation of the attendant vulnerabilities increased. Over the last few years, ransomware coevolved with crypto-currencies as a way of scaling up the conversion of unauthorized access to information systems into monetary rewards. There are reasons to believe that, even if intelligence services did not directly carry out these operations, people within those services either moonlighted as criminals or sold their know-how to private actors who carried out these crimes. The compromise of health systems around the rich world and the Colonial oil pipeline in the United States made the general public aware that something bad is going on.

These attacks continued to escalate and disrupted private lives as well as public functions. In October 2021, a cyber operation attributed to Israel stopped the distribution of gasoline to Iranian consumers for almost two weeks. Iran retaliated by hacking a dating site for people with unconventional sexual preferences and then released on social media the embarrassing information it stole. Cyberwar increasingly becomes a way states can harm the general population, not simply harass each other.

The broad point is that information insecurity, the inevitable downside of a connected world, has produced significant harms to large numbers of people in their daily lives and promises to get worse. Disenchantment with an important component of liberal internationalism, a promise of greater prosperity and personal fulfillment through information technology, inevitably follows.

GEOPOLITICAL ANXIETIES AND A NEW COLD WAR

An important piece of the liberal-internationalist post-Cold War settlement was lowering the risk of war from great power competition. China and Russia, people in the West believed, would accept the logic of the new world order, especially free trade and investment bolstered by the international rule of law, as the foundation of their international relations. *Wandel durch Handel* (change through trade) was the German slogan, but everyone in the West seemed to buy it. Everyone, the liberals thought, saw that prosperity depended on peace and that for most regimes, existential threats no longer existed. Even rogue states would learn from the lesson of the first Gulf War and forswear aggression.

In the first decade of the present century, liberals could dismiss signs to the contrary as inconclusive. Russia posed a threat to regional stability, but an optimist could write off its invasion of Georgia in 2008 as provoked by the inept Georgian leadership and in any event of only local consequence. China used its new membership in the WTO as both a sword and a shield. It relied on WTO rules to open up foreign markets to its low-priced manufactures while taking advantage of gaps in those rules to block retaliation for its export-promoting strategies. Yet it invested heavily in expertise in international economic law, seeming to signal a commitment to the liberal vision of international economics, whatever its shortcomings as to political liberalism.

By the second decade, it had become clear that things were not going as hoped. The 2012 ascendancy of Xi Jinping to the leadership of China began a new, more revisionist phase in China's approach to the rest of the world. Its belt-and-road initiative pointed to a more organized and emphatic effort to extend China's economic power as a means of geopolitical influence. Its assertion of sovereignty over the South China Sea rested on dubious legal claims and sketchy geoforming of rocks into islands. Russia did in Crimea what it had declined to do in Transnistria, Abkhazia, or South Ossetia – conquer and annex. North Korea extended its nuclear armory while acquiring long-range missiles to deliver its bombs. Iran got closer to becoming a nuclear power while using military assets to deepen its influence in Iraq, Lebanon, and Syria. Regional conflicts in the Middle East, South Asia, and the Horn of Africa became more violent and entailed greater humanitarian casualties. The roster of failed states and the extent of territory under the sway of terrorist groups grew throughout the decade.

The collapse of the western adventure in Afghanistan put an exclamation point to the process of apparent western decline. The United States and its allies invested trillions of dollars and many lives to remake Afghanistan as a modern state with some liberal resonance. All went to naught. Although China and Russia reasonably may fear a failed state on their borders, the imperative of discrediting the West mattered more to them. They did not help the Taliban, but nor did they expend any treasure or honor to prevent them from taking Kabul. Pakistan, China's close ally, backed the Taliban and may yet reap the whirlwind. The lurking but terrifying challenge for the West rests in Russia's invasion of Ukraine and China's capacity to conquer Taiwan. Both threaten to expose a lack of resilience and capacity to act collectively.

Armed conflict aside, a particularly troubling aspect of the new great-power competition is the targeting by revisionist states of social capital in the incumbent states. As Chapter 6 discusses more fully, social scientists use the term social capital to describe the practices, institutions, and structures that multiply the value of private investments, just as conventional investment multiplies its owner's income. A significant part of social capital is social trust, an I-know-it-when-I-see-it quality that lowers the cost of planning for the future. If we can take people at their word, we can rely on their representations, express and implicit, without taking the costly precautions that plague those who live in low-social-trust societies. Put simply, the ability to count on others is a socially produced quality that makes people's lives better.

Most great powers export propaganda to embellish their images and to disparage their adversaries. The United States invested heavily in the battle of ideas during the Cold War, both overtly and covertly. Over the last five years or so, however, adversaries of the West, China and Russia in particular, increased the tempo of information warfare that does not attack the West's institutions and culture so much as incite distrust generally. These interventions sought not to persuade, but to promote information nihilism, an across-the-board doubt about the credibility of all.[10] The growing divisions in the rich world provided plenty of targets, which these efforts fully exploited. Some campaigns took place through overt outlets such as Sputnik and Russia Today, but increasingly Russian organs used false accounts on social media to stir up conflicts and grievances. China does much the same. For instance, it deflected international concern over tennis star Peng Shuai, who disappeared after accusing a top leader of rape, by exploiting social media to invent new narratives.

COVID-19

Even before the pandemic, growing socioeconomic divergence had significant effects on well-being. In the rich world, which has the best morbidity and mortality data as well as the most reliable measurements of socioeconomic variables, the evidence is powerful. Consider a recent study of life expectancy in Glasgow, a rich world city with a substantial mix of better-off and relatively deprived people.[11] Glasgow saw a significant increase in the life-expectancy gap between the most and least deprived deciles of Glaswegians between 2000 and 2019. This gap grew by 3 years for women and 9.1 years for men. As Chapter 8 discusses, the data collected and analyzed by Princeton

[10] Fiona Hill, *The Kremlin's Strange Victory*, FOREIGN AFFAIRS (Nov./Dec. 2021); THOMAS RID, ACTIVE MEASURES: THE SECRET HISTORY OF DISINFORMATION AND POLITICAL WARFARE (2020).

[11] Bruce White, Mairi Young & Katharine Timpson, Health in a Changing City: Glasgow 2021, www.gcph.co.uk/assets/0000/8225/Health_in_a_changing_city_Glasgow_2021_-_report.pdf.

economists Anne Case and Angus Deaton on class divides, morbidity, and mortality in the rich world, first published in 2015 and made available to general audiences in their 2020 book *Deaths of Despair and the Future of Capitalism*, confirm this picture on the macro level.

Then came the pandemic. Anyone with a sense of history could have anticipated that the great increase in human movement that followed the end of the Cold War would have public health consequences. The global influenza pandemic of 1918–19 came on the heels of unprecedented upheavals of populations due to World War I. The emergence of new strains of lethal pathogens combined with increasing contacts among people with different disease histories, and hence different immune defenses, makes rapidly spreading pandemics more likely. The 2003 SARS outbreak and the 2009 H1N1 pandemic signaled the risk associated with greater and more rapid personal contacts around the world, even though they did not become world-scale catastrophes. Epidemiologists understood that something worse would emerge eventually. They failed, however, to convince policymakers around the world to take concrete precautions, such as stockpiling of medical supplies and the development of shovel-ready quarantine programs.

This is not the place to revisit the general problem of low-probability, great-harm risks and the tendency of societies to invest too much or too little in precautions. The point is that in the fall of 2019 the scope of high-speed, high-volume human contacts throughout the world, fueled by the growing knowledge economy, made the spread of a lethal, highly communicable virus shockingly easy. The time and nature of the first incidents, and particularly whether the virus originated in an animal-to-human or human-to-human transmission, remain hotly contested. What seems clear enough is that SARS-2-CoV made its way from China to Europe and the United States in sufficient numbers by the end of 2019 to set in motion the global COVID-19 pandemic of 2020–21.

The immediate cost of the pandemic was lost lives, long-term disabilities, and economic dislocation. For more than a year, the global economy ground down, if not to a halt, then to a shuffle. The United Nations guessed a drop in global GDP of $4 trillion attributable to the pandemic, a number that represents 6 percent of global GDP in 2019. We will not have reliable estimates of excess deaths and economic losses for several years, as the data must mature and withstand analysis.

Whatever the extent of the quantifiable losses, the intangible costs of the pandemic – demoralization, aggravation of social divides, and loss of social trust – are at least as significant. Sometimes in the past, quantifiable losses led to quick rebounds, as happened after the 1918–19 pandemic. Our present pandemic, however, had hugely uneven effects across class and place in the knowledge economy, producing deeper if harder-to-measure harms to many, especially those who thought themselves entitled to prosperity and security.

A few data illustrate the gap. Ashish Jha, Dean of Brown's School of Public Health at the time, in May 2021 compared the COVID-19 vaccination rates and socioeconomic measurements for Newton and Springfield, Massachusetts. Newton had vaccinated 99 percent of people over thirty and 64 percent of children aged 12–15; for the same categories Springfield had vaccinated 64 and 12 percent. In Newton 79 percent of the population had bachelor's degrees and overall the city had an average per capita income of $73,000, Springfield's figures were 19 percent and $21,000. Also, 8 percent of Newton's population was Black or Latino, compared to 60 percent for Springfield. The well-educated, affluent, and White population got protection, once available, at a substantially greater rate than less educated, poor, and minority people, even within a single state's health system.

Even before vaccines became available, education and class dictated both danger and resiliency. First, the ability to work at low risk of infection during the first stage of the pandemic turned on the nature of the job. Knowledge workers using remote conferencing technology did fine; people who had to work face-to-face and hands-on, such as those employed in manufacturing, health care, and basic services like building maintenance and transportation, did not. Second, people in the rich West, and especially the well-educated, prosperous portions of that population, had better access to vaccines compared to the rest of the world. Third, the beneficiaries of the knowledge economy generally had better options for investing in their children's knowledge-economy futures compared to those who depended solely on state-provided schooling, especially where education went online. Parents who valued education, often knowledge workers who themselves had enjoyed better educational opportunities, devoted more of their own time to supplementing their children's schooling as well as hiring tutors and other substitutes. An education gap resulted that will aggravate already great divides between the privileged and the rest in the rich West for years to come.[12]

Add to these general trends two other things that played out during the pandemic. First, segments of the knowledge economy, especially those providing the infrastructure for connectivity, thrived. Firms supporting remote connections during lockdown and the delivery of tangible goods to

[12] Nicholas A. Christakis, Apollo's Arrow: The Profound and Enduring Impact of Coronavirus on the Way We Live (2020); Adam Tooze, Shutdown: How Covid Shook the World's Economy (2021).

quarantined households had significant abnormal positive returns. Their stockholders fared brilliantly. Second, the social and psychic burdens of the pandemic manifested themselves in higher crime rates and, in the liberal democracies, more expressive and dysfunctional politics. Greater awareness in the rich world of institutional racism and abuse in police practices met growing apprehension about violence, further fracturing politics in many places, not least the United States.

Throughout the crisis, international institutions performed badly. The World Health Organization, the UN agency with direct responsibility for addressing pandemics, gave out inconsistent advice during the first months of the pandemic, and, in the eyes of its critics, showed excessive deference to powerful states, China in particular. Its botched and allegedly corrupt investigation into the origins of the pandemic did its reputation no good. Its defenders say that WHO was designed to be ineffectual and should not be criticized for its failure of leadership. This may be true but is not an argument that generally builds confidence in international organizations.

The world trading system, the WTO in particular, failed to discourage states from hoarding medical equipment and vaccines for fighting the disease at the most severe points of attack. Even as COVID-19 exposed the vulnerabilities of a deeply interconnected world civilization, countries reacted with eat-me-last measures. The international institutions meant to enable global cooperation failed to respond.

* * *

The crises that have overtaken liberal internationalism over the last five years feed off each other. National populism and connectivity dysfunction obviously do so, and class-based gaps in morbidity and mortality stoke the fires of social division and political breakdown. The increasing number and severity of geopolitical conflicts fuels distrust in national security élites while inducing the weaponization of connectivity. These trends point to an international system confronting great, perhaps existential, challenges.

Unrestrained optimism about the potential of liberal internationalism that ran throughout the 1990s now founders in the face of today's cascade of crises. The battle between liberal democracy and Marxism–Leninism seemed an unconditional victory for the former. The supposed victors saw the task facing the world as spreading liberal-democratic experience and values as extensively and rapidly as possible, with the construction of international institutions premised on the international rule of law reinforcing this work. Thirty years on, much of this project has come undone.

PART II

The Knowledge Economy

World Conquest and Creative Destruction

This part explains why so much of the world committed to liberal internationalism as much as it did and what then undermined these commitments. In important ways, economic forces drove these events. The compelling background story is the rise of the knowledge economy.

Knowledge always has played a role in how people make things, and economists for more than a century have built knowledge into their models of how economies remake themselves. What distinguishes the last fifty years from earlier economic transformations is the increasing importance of knowledge, and therefore knowledge workers, as both a factor of production and a product. We now live in an era where the knowledge worker – a person of talent and skill who continually reinvents how we make things and what we make – dominates.

The paradox of the knowledge economy is that it creates great things for humanity as a whole, but it also drives inequality, dislocation, and resentment. It divides the world between great global cities, where knowledge workers and unskilled immigrants gather to make better lives for themselves, and economic hinterlands, which become ever more backward as the knowledge economy grows. The knowledge economy thrives on liberal internationalism, but implementing that agenda increases the misery and resentment of those whom the knowledge economy bypasses and brands as losers. Conflict between urban centers and the hinterlands ensues, and the accomplishments of liberal internationalism come under fire. The battle explains the arc of events from the supposed triumph of 1989 to the many crises of the present day.

6

Knowledge, Technological Innovation, and Wealth

I started working on Soviet politics and economics in the 1970s and first went to the Soviet Union in 1982, when Brezhnev still reigned. As my visits multiplied, my early impression became clearer and stronger. The country prized education and culture and its people did great science in the laboratory. Notwithstanding the risible ideology and the great pressure for outward conformity, it had a rich intellectual scene, even though people could find the cutting edge only around kitchen tables rather than in print, at lecterns, and on stages. Yet the material culture of even leading parts of society seemed fifty years behind the United States. A factory in Irkutsk and the top hospital in Kishinev, both showcases in which our Soviet hosts took pride, seemed like movie sets from films about the Great Depression. The gap between knowledge in universities and research institutes and the knowledge employed in production was glaring and enormous.

The numbers that economists come up with have lots of shortcomings, but still indicate something. Using the World Bank's data, GDP per capita for the Russian Federation was (in current dollars) $3,777 in 1988 compared to $21,417 for the United States. Nor did this GDP gap hide a better quality of life and greater happiness in Russia. In 1985, life expectancy there plummeted to levels seen in the more impoverished parts of Central America, while hidden structures of privilege and corruption, not expressed in formal prices, imposed grossly unequal access to goods and services, including staples such as housing and medical services, and long-term life opportunities, such as élite education. Notwithstanding Nobel laureate Paul Samuelson's assertion in the most widely used introductory economics textbook of the day that the Soviet Union would overtake the United States in GDP by 1990, in many ways the gap had widened.[1]

[1] Paul A. Samuelson, Economics: An Introductory Analysis 828–31 (5th ed. 1961).

The country's knowledge backwardness had affected its core industry, oil and gas. Energy exports had given the Soviet Union considerable economic and political clout during the 1960s and 1970s, even more than arms sales. Yet by the end of the 1970s it confronted the near prospect of declining production. It had used up some fields too early because out-of-date production techniques failed to keep ground water out of the underground deposits. Large quantities of oil and gas lay offshore in the Far East, but its engineers had not mastered the deep-water drilling technology that the international firms had developed to exploit such fields. The technological gap was stripping the country of its most valuable international economic resource.[2]

The launch of reforms in the mid-1980s reflected the leadership's growing appreciation of the knowledge gap with the West, made vivid by the 1986 Chernobyl disaster. These included initially small steps to open up the Soviet Union to the world economy. I took this as a cue to retool my own skills. Already a tenured full professor, I became a neophyte scholar in the legal foundations of international business, trade, and investment. Economists and legal scholars had convincing explanations about how Soviet-style central planning suppressed the spread of knowledge within its economy.[3] What I learned from my new studies was how much the liberal world economy of the late twentieth century relied on knowledge as a factor of production, and how much law in the West supported the production, distribution, and sale of knowledge-related goods and services.

The economic model that prevailed in the self-described socialist world rewarded the creation of knowledge almost entirely through government bounties or bestowal of prestige and deference. Either way, bureaucrats wielding power without exposure to the economic outcomes of their decisions made the choices about whom to reward. In the West, investors in knowledge could look to markets to test the value of their projects. These markets were themselves the product of political choices and social structures. Often far from perfect competition prevailed. As a first rough cut, however, it was clear that the West's approach to the production and use of knowledge in the economy was far superior to the Soviet model.

In this chapter, I approach the knowledge economy in several steps. First, I describe what it is, even though a rigorous definition remains elusive. Second, I map out an informal economic theory of knowledge, based largely on the insights of Gary Becker, Paul Romer, Robert Lucas, and Paul

[2] Marshall I. Goldman, Petrostate: Putin, Power, and the New Russia 33–54 (2008).

[3] John H. Moore, *Agency Costs, Technological Change, and Soviet Central Planning*, 24 J. L. & Econ. 189 (1981).

Krugman. This account emphasizes the ability of investments in knowledge to scale, that is to overcome the traditional rule of diminishing returns, and therefore to promote uncompetitive markets. Third, I discuss the complex interactions between the knowledge economy and social capital. Fourth, I consider the international dimensions of the knowledge economy, particularly its preference for larger, and ultimately global, markets. Fifth, I explain how the knowledge economy promotes economic inequality by making the smart better off and the slow poorer, drawing down social capital as it does so. I depict an economic transformation with worldwide effects that does enormous good but contains the seeds of its own destruction.

A few words about the limits of economic theory are necessary here. Most practitioners rely on simple models about human behavior and decision-making. So constrained, the theory still does a good job of describing how particular choices can lead to specified material outcomes. It thus offers a useful account of the material incentives that decision-makers, from individuals to firms to governments, face when they choose.

Only a hopeless reductionist would insist that incentives dictate outcomes. Most people, including the best economists, recognize that people face a swarm of forces – cognitive, cultural, social, and historical – that shape their choices and the way others interpret and react to those choices. Identifying economic incentives, as I do here, helps to understand and predict human behavior, but equating incentives with outcomes would be a foolish mistake. I unpack the theory here because I haven't seen other work joining an economic account of the knowledge economy with the building crises that the world faces today. This account demands consideration, but it does not answer all the questions or exclude other stories. That it is helpful, I think, suffices.

WHAT IS THE KNOWLEDGE ECONOMY?

We do not have a good definition of knowledge for economic purposes. Traditional categories of production inputs such as labor and capital are not up to the task. As the 1992 Nobel laureate Gary Becker demonstrated, labor encompasses human capital – the combination of knowledge traits (skills, experience, certifications, and connections) that makes one person's work more valuable than another's.[4] Similarly, knowledge can augment the value of financial capital, as the ability to assess risks and opportunities improves. Robert Solow's great 1957 article that established the importance of "technical

4 Gary S. Becker, Human Capital: A Theoretical and Empirical Analysis with Special Reference to Education (3d ed. 1994).

change" as a factor of production, contributing to the case for his Nobel Prize thirty years later, contains a revealing disclaimer: "I am using the phrase 'technical change' as short-hand expression for *any kind of shift* in the production function."[5] At the dawn of the economic transformation driven by the knowledge economy, Solow understood that the US production function was changing in ways that traditional understandings of contributions from workers and financiers could not capture but that were tremendously important. He was humble enough not to try to reduce these changes to pat constructs.

Sixty-five years on, we still struggle to define exactly what the knowledge economy includes. Knowledge is that which distinguishes sand from semiconductors, but that observation has more poetry than rigor. Harvard Professor Roberto Unger, a radical visionary drawing on the Marxist tradition, talks about the knowledge economy as "the most advanced practice of production." He observes:

> In one sense, it is the practice of production that is closest to the mind, and especially to the part of our mental life that we call the imagination. In another sense, this most mindful practice is the one that, among all available forms of economic activity, most intimately and continuously connects our experiments in using and transforming nature and our experiments in cooperation.[6]

This seems right but doesn't help us much in deciding what counts as "advanced," "the mind," or "imagination." Still, it advances the ball and deserves unpacking.

First, Unger indicates that knowledge bolsters not only our ability to do things in and to the material world, but also, and as importantly, our ability as humans to work with others in the social world. Second, he suggests that knowledge involves the passing on of the content of one mind to others. It is thus a social practice dependent on communication. Better communication may mean more knowledge, although not always. The relationship need not be linear and, beyond a few basic factors such as speed, storage, organization, and signal-to-noise ratio, we may have difficulty deciding what we mean by "better."

Nor can we treat knowledge as the same thing as information, even if the two enjoy a close relationship. Knowledge includes skills at processing information, such as pattern recognition and the development of useful heuristics. In Bayesian terms, knowledge enables people to do a better job of setting and updating priors, that is our working assumptions about reality. As those of us in

5 Robert M. Solow, *Technical Change and the Aggregate Production Function*, 39 Rev. Econ. & Stat. 312, 312 (1957) (emphasis added).

6 Roberto Mangabeira Unger, The Knowledge Economy 4 (2019).

the academic world recognize all too often, knowing more does not necessarily mean knowing better. But sometimes we can learn to know better as we know more.

Unger uses the term "imagination" to indicate that the mind does something with information. This seems indisputable, but I struggle to see imagination as anything more than a placeholder, not unlike Solow's "technical change." The processes within the mind that convert information into knowledge remain largely opaque. In the artificial-intelligence world, we think of information as accumulated data, and knowledge as what comes out after we run algorithms on those databases. In that world, people see the data-to-algorithm process as a black box. So it is with imagination. We know it's there and indispensable, but the Spinal Tap rule applies: "There is such a fine line between stupid and clever."

These points do not give us an easy-to-measure concept that economists can use to determine the value of knowledge as a factor of production. As the human capital literature teaches us, distinguishing investment (human capital formation, as through élite education) from consumption (partying, hooking up, sports entertainment bundled into the product) can be challenging. Sorting out knowledge from luck (more precisely, factors that we do not understand) as causes of outcomes is also very hard.

Measurement difficulty, however, does not mean invalidity. We can observe knowledge even if definitional challenges preclude the use of quantitative tools to explain it. As a law professor who only borrows from economics, I feel free to give up on rigor when necessary to get at something important.

At the outset, I want to avoid a narrow conception of knowledge as an economic force. Terms such as "technical change" (Solow's language) and "technological innovation" (that of Paul Romer, the economist whose work in this field brought him a Nobel in 2018) suggest to some readers the kind of things that scientists and engineers do. Think of people who wear white lab coats at work. Looking only at the last twenty-five years, you might think that the knowledge revolution mostly means coding and microchips.

Some scholars believe that patents serve as a decent proxy for the use of knowledge in economic activity.[7] This move yields valuable results but remains incomplete. On the one hand, patenting need not equate with economically useful invention. Michigan State economist Lisa Cook's research into post-Stalin Soviet practice in obtaining foreign patents shows as much. The Soviet Union used these patents to obtain hard-currency

[7] Ufuk Akcigit, John Grigsby, Tom Nicholas & Stefanie Stantcheva, *Taxation and Innovation in the Twentieth Century*, 137 Q. J. ECON. 329 (2022).

revenues, not to reward inventors, and mostly obtained only modest licensing fees.[8] On the other hand, economically significant knowledge reveals itself in many places. Some innovations may not even strike us as technological except in a very loose sense and by no means could be patented. Yet they can involve leaps of imagination combined with rigorous research and produce momentous results.

Consider, for example, the rise of containerized shipping. The idea of shipping cargo in containers existed in the 1920s, but at the time carriers rarely used specialized storage units to enable multimodal transportation – trucking, rail, and ships. In the mid-1950s Malcolm McLean, founder of a family trucking company based in North Carolina, assessed the possibilities presented by a new national transportation network based on interstate highways coupled with war-surplus ships available cheaply for reengineering. He imagined how, in these circumstances, containers could radically reduce the costs of transferring cargo between modes of transport and so revolutionize the commercial carriage of goods on sea and land. The techniques he developed caught on in the industry and became standards (Figure 6.1).[9]

Calculating how much these insights, based on business management as much as engineering, lowered the costs of commerce over the last seventy-five years is difficult to calculate. We know that this particular innovation created a significant surplus for shippers, carriers, and customers to divide, but how big was it? On the one hand, the containers as well as the carriers (ships, trains, trucks) are physical structures that we might value based on their cost of manufacture or their arms-length sales prices. The initial concept and its deployment rested on more trial-and-error knowledge than laboratory work, but no less important for that. Breakthroughs in information technology (both software and hardware) further enhanced the value of containerized shipping by making it easier to organize and track the containers and their contents. The parallel development of just-in-time inventory management, a business strategy (conceptual knowledge) originating in postwar Japan as a way to cope with its lost industrial capacity, complemented these innovations to produce even greater cost savings.

8 Lisa D. Cook, *A Green Light for Red Patents? Evidence from Soviet Experiments with the Market and Invention, 1959 to 1991* (Aug. 2012). The paper does not make clear whether the author understood that during most of the period under study, a state agency collected hard-currency royalties and remitted to the patentees only modest ruble amounts based on an artificial conversion rate.

9 Marc Levinson, The Box: How the Shipping Container Made the World Smaller and the World Economy Bigger (2d ed. 2015); Marc Levinson, Outside the Box: How Globalization Changed from Moving Stuff to Spreading Ideas (2020).

FIGURE 6.1 Shipping container. Source. Photograph by Ian Taylor on Unsplash.

Even without a clear definition and measurement of the knowledge economy, its importance and remarkable expansion seems evident. We can put this growth in the context of the overall world economy, about which we do have decent data. What these reveal are three things. First, the world makes more stuff, specifically goods and services that people want to buy. In that sense, we can say that the world economy has grown enormously. Second, the share of the world economy devoted to international transactions, defined as exports of goods and services, has also grown. Data on investment (capital flows) confirms this pattern, although it shows greater volatility than do the trade numbers. Third, economic inequality increased considerably in both the rich world and, remarkably, the becoming-rich world.

These are the data on growth, drawing on World Bank sources: world GDP per capita rose from $5,549 in 1990, to $8,014 in 2000, to $12,907 in 2010, and to $17,109, more than tripling over thirty years (all figures adjusted to exclude inflation). For China and the United States, respectively, the numbers are $1,424 and $40,411 in 1990, $3,452 and $50,125 in 2000, $8,886 and $54,315 in 2010, and $16,411 and $60,236 in 2020 (Figures 6.2 and 6.3). This amounts to a more than tenfold increase for China and 50 percent for the United States. China's relative success reflects how new were its economic reforms in 1990 and poor it had been before them.

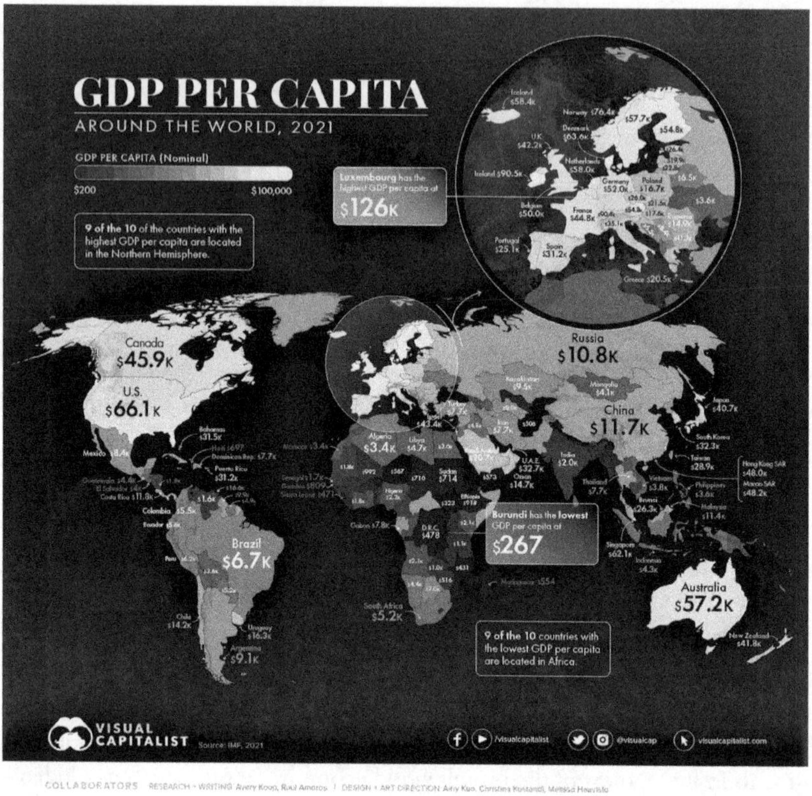

FIGURE 6.2 GDP per capita, IMF, 2021. Source: Visual Capitalist.

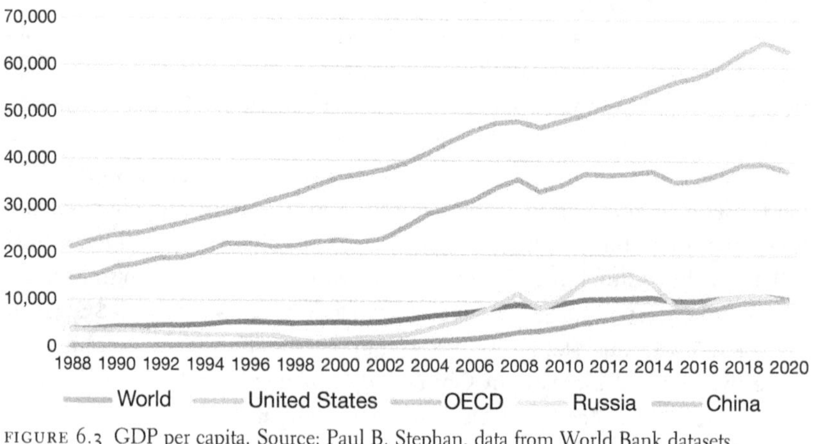

FIGURE 6.3 GDP per capita. Source: Paul B. Stephan, data from World Bank datasets.

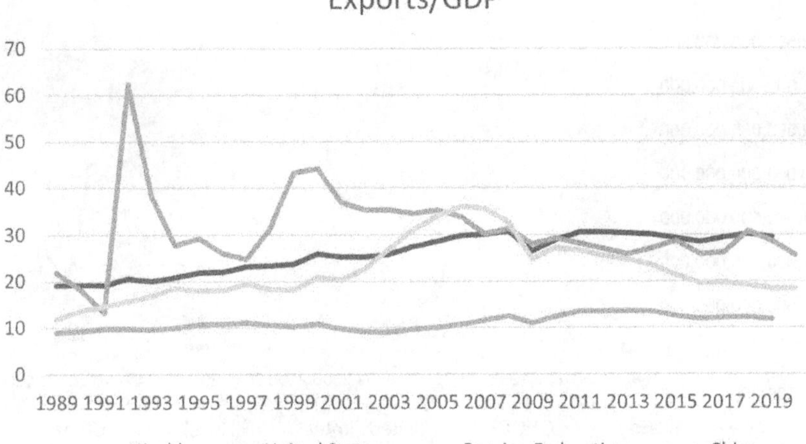

FIGURE 6.4 Exports/GDP. Source: Paul B. Stephan, data from World Bank datasets.

Consider next exports as a portion of GDP. These figures get at the relative importance of the international economy. For the world as a whole, all exports must be imported somewhere, so exports and imports should be equal. In 1980, countries exported 18.8 percent of all their products, as measured by value, 19.2 percent in 1990, 26 percent in 2000, 28.9 percent in 2010, and 29.5 percent in 2019, the last year for which the WTO has published data. The comparable figures for China and the United States are 5.9 and 8.2 percent, 13.6 and 9.3 percent, 20.9 and 10.7 percent, 26.6 and 13.6 percent, and 18.5 and 11.7 percent (Figure 6.4). The figures for both the world and the two largest economies peaked in 2014 and began to decline as the cascade of crises described in the last chapter got underway.

Cross-border investment flows provide another lens on the international economy. They represent bets that moving production offshore will produce higher returns than domestic projects. Because investors look to the future for those returns, the level of cross-border investment reveals useful information about what people with skin in the game expect from future international transactions. World outflows of foreign direct investment (investments meant to give the investor an active stake in their management) were $55,924,205,803 in 1980, $277,902,904,616 in 1990, $1,403,568,606,562 in 2000, $1,785,237,384,630 in 2010, and $758,311,301,822 in 2019, after reaching a peak of $2,198,530,367,270 in 2015 (Figure 6.5).

Data on global income inequality is less comprehensive for the world as a whole but good for the United States. A simple, indeed crude, way of

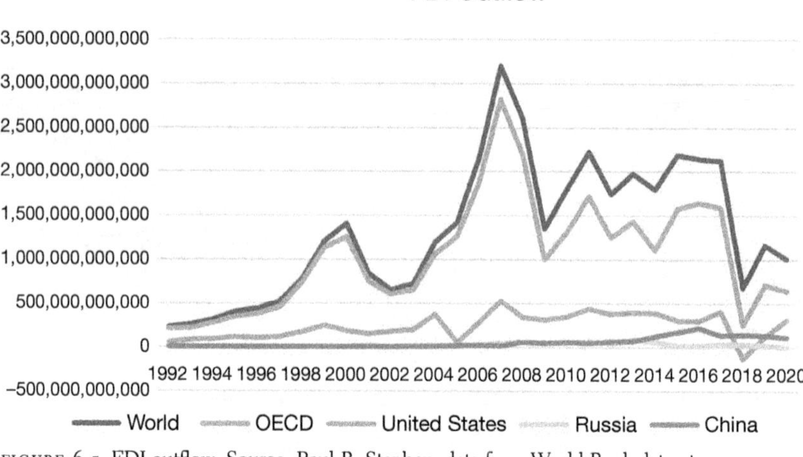

FIGURE 6.5 FDI outflow. Source: Paul B. Stephan, data from World Bank datasets.

measuring inequality is the Gini index, which measures the distribution of income within a set group. It rises from 0 at complete equality to 1 when one person in a society has all the income. Based on US census data, the index has risen steadily, from 0.357 in 1970, 0.367 in 1980, 0.406 in 1990, 0.442 in 2000, 0.456 in 2010, to 0.465 in 2020. World Bank per-country estimates have significant gaps and rest on less reliable data, but their guesses are probably better than others out there. According to the Bank, the numbers for the United Kingdom are 0.337 in 1969, 0.284 in 1979, 0.359 in 1991, 0.384 in 2000, 0.344 in 2010, and 0.381 in 2017. Periods of Labour rule coincide with temporary declines, but otherwise income inequality tracked that of the United States, although at a lower overall level. Figure 6.6 shows changes in the index for several countries of interest.

It would be great if we had data for China, but the Bank understandably concluded that what it has is not good enough. Casual observation, however, suggests that China's transformation has brought about profound material inequality. On the one hand, there exists decent evidence that China over the last forty years has managed largely to eliminate the most extreme kind of poverty, a great advance in human welfare. On the other hand, the persistence of the Hukou system – a regime of residence permits that allow people to come to the cities from the countryside to work in low-skill jobs only if they surrender most civil, economic, and social rights – points to a persistent chasm between those who benefit most from the knowledge economy and the bulk of the country's vast population.

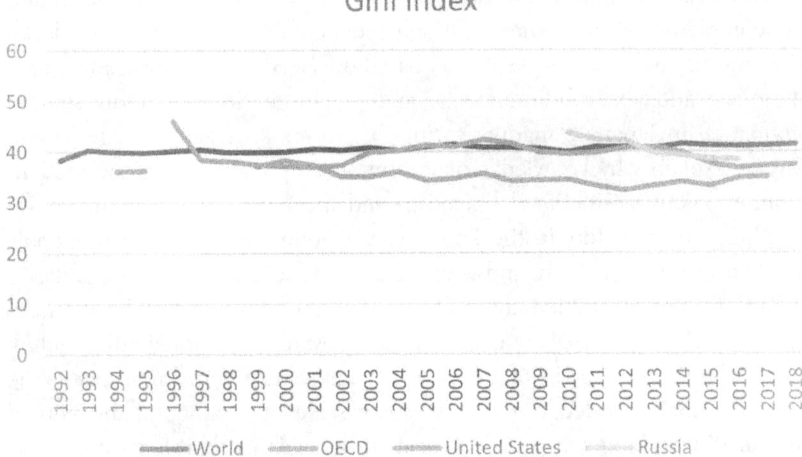

FIGURE 6.6 Gini index. Source: Paul B. Stephan, data from World Bank datasets.

As a regular visitor to Shenzhen over the last twelve years, I see this gap in places like convenience stores. In the University City neighborhood where I work, large construction projects abound. The construction workers live under challenging conditions in barracks or tents alongside the projects. The students, products of rigorously meritocratic selection, do not live in the kinds of luxurious dorms that US undergraduates know and love, but their amenities are much better than those of the workers. The workers and students stand in line together at the stores, but buy different things, wear different clothes, and project radically different hopes for the future. This juxtaposition of physical proximity and social distance must keep the Chinese political leadership up at night.

Combining the gross and clunky, but still powerful, global statistical evidence with impressions of this sort, many observers infer that whatever is driving economic growth has something to do with inequality. I turn to economic theory to find explanations as to why growth of the knowledge economy *might* drive income equality. The theoretical story shows that it is not crazy to believe that this relationship exists. Until we get systematic and comprehensive data that rules out other explanations, we cannot say that we know for sure.

AN ECONOMIC THEORY OF KNOWLEDGE AND THE PROMISE OF EXCLUDABILITY

To get at the theoretical story, consider again the containerization example. It illustrates two facets of the knowledge economy, *scalability* and *synergies*. Once McLean and his colleagues figured out how to do containerization, the entire global shipping industry followed. This is scaling. Containerization also complemented two other seemingly independent knowledge-based developments, the information revolution based on speed of communication, ease of storage and accessibility of data, and the just-in-time inventory strategy originating in Japanese manufacturing. These are synergies. Scalability and synergy explain why knowledge plays such an important role in the modern economy, why international liberalism and the knowledge economy thrive together, why investors in the knowledge economy tend to reap monopoly profits over the short term, and why these gains fuel economic inequality.

Paul Romer assembled the basic elements of this theory. Its premises include costly creation accompanied by low-cost reproduction, partial excludability (limits on access) of the fruits of knowledge investments, and the possibility that knowledge investments can scale in defiance of the normal rule of diminishing returns. Scaling in turn leads to short-term monopoly profits, until either government regulation or further improvements in knowledge render the investment obsolete.

First, Romer observes that knowledge entails low-cost reproduction. Copying normally takes less time and effort than creating.[10] An insight, once tested, became easily replicable. Take containerization as an example. No natural barriers prevented its extension to the entire transport industry. McLean's company, having originated the practice, had a technological lead due to its familiarity with the process and freedom to tinker with it. Nothing, however, kept other companies from copying or hiring the company's employees to learn how to do containerization better.

To say that an activity lends itself to scaling means that it becomes more valuable – its profitability increases – as production grows. Economists call this positive returns to scale. Romer provides the framework for understanding the connection between knowledge and profit, and in particular how knowledge, compared to other factors of production, can bring about positive returns to scale. Building on Solow's work, he proposes a distinction between knowledge, a quality that functions socially, and human capital, skills and other economically valuable qualities that belong to particular individuals. Human capital, like physical capital, is both rivalrous and excludable. Knowledge is not rivalrous but can be made excludable.

I use rivalry and excludability here in their economic sense. To say that choices are rivalrous means that a person can do one only by forgoing the

[10] Paul M. Romer, *Origins of Endogenous Growth*, 8 J. ECON. PERSP. 3 (1994); Paul M. Romer, *Endogenous Technological Change*, 98 J. POL. ECON. S71 (1990); Paul M. Romer, *Increasing Returns and Long-Term Growth*, 94 J. POL. ECON. 1002 (1986).

other. To say that a good is excludable means that people can control who gets access to it and thus exclude unwanted users. In the case of human capital, people blessed with skills face natural limits, such as time and energy, on how to direct their talents. Any particular application of human capital requires passing up other applications. This is what rivalrous means. The beautiful genius can work as a model or creator, but still can do only one thing at a time.[11] Human capital is also excludable because the possessor, a person, may refuse to work on particular projects. It has a limited useful life because all people face a natural boundary on how long they can work. Death, disease, imprisonment, cancellation, or other events take human capital out of the market with no way to transfer it to others.

Knowledge, as Romer describes it, survives individuals, even if societies as a whole can lose it (think of the Ming Dynasty's abandonment of distant navigation in the fifteenth century).[12] It is largely nonrivalrous, because the act of drawing on knowledge does not get in the way of others using the same knowledge. Technological developments have enhanced the nonrivalrous nature of knowledge by lowering the cost of duplication of sources so as to enable more users to learn simultaneously. As the world moved from manuscripts to printing presses to digitalization, the cost of copying texts (in the broadest sense of the word) plummeted.

Transmission of knowledge lends itself to some excludability, however, either through laws (intellectual property, business secrets, duties of loyalty imposed on agents) or mechanisms (passwords or similar means of controlling access and frustrating copying). In spite of successful exclusion mechanisms, however, spillover effects typically persist. Excludability mostly works only up to a point.

Partial excludability is Romer's key insight. It explains why people will invest in knowledge creation. Recall that public goods are neither rivalrous nor excludable. Because investors cannot capture any direct return from creating public goods, only the state or equivalent collective actors will provide a satisfactory level of them. Previous theorists assumed that knowledge had these qualities and therefore depended on collective providers. Romer showed that because of partial excludability, private actors have an incentive to invest in knowledge creation, knowing they may harvest benefits from deploying knowledge that they need not share (all that much) with others. This opened a window on investment in knowledge for private gain.

[11] Richard Rhodes, Hedy's Folly: The Life and Breakthrough Inventions of Hedy Lamarr, the Most Beautiful Woman in the World (2011).

[12] David Abulafia, The Boundless Sea: A Human History of the Oceans 260–71 (2019).

KNOWLEDGE AND MONOPOLIES: THE PROMISE OF SCALING

Critical to my argument is Romer's observations that knowledge investments lend themselves to monopolistic returns. Patents illustrate one way in which this works. Under patent law, the state intentionally grants short-term monopolies to exploit discoveries. Romer points out that there exist many other ways to limit competition through controlling access to knowledge. But for these exclusion mechanisms, investors would have a much weaker economic incentive to create knowledge.

Under conditions of perfect competition, where marginal return equals marginal cost, the marginal return on knowledge would equal the marginal cost of enforcing excludability. We know that investors do better than that. The only possibility that makes sense is the prospect of supercompetitive profits (a return greater than marginal cost) during the investment's useful life. These profits in turn motivate new investment in projects that pursue similar payoffs.

An explanation of how knowledge investments lend themselves to monopolies relies on competition theory. Monopolies (imperfect competition, to use economics jargon) occur for many reasons, but some businesses develop into "natural" monopolies that require no collusion among competing producers. Where the emergence of multiple producers leads to wasteful duplication, organizing production to eliminate this waste benefits society.

A good example of a natural monopoly is a transportation network. In the US Northeast during the nineteenth century, railroad companies built separate networks, leading to wasteful duplication. At the end of the nineteenth century, J. P. Morgan rationalized this system. He formed Northern Securities, a holding company that bought the firms that owned the tracks, and then closed duplicative tracks and infrastructure. Monopoly pricing resulted, provoking the government to regulate through antitrust proceedings. The courts compelled the breaking up of Northern Securities.[13] They did not, however, require the restoring of redundant tracks and services. Morgan's rationalization of the railroad industry benefited society as a whole, even if the accompanying monopoly profits were neither inevitable nor necessarily desirable.

An important kind of natural monopoly is one created through network effects. Network effects exist when the value of an endeavor grows with the number of users. These arise in many knowledge-based products, such as communications systems or operating software for computers. William

[13] *Northern Securities* v. *United States*, 193 US 197 (1904).

Nordhaus, who shared the 2018 Nobel with Romer, observed early on that knowledge investments have network effects.[14]

To think about network effects concretely, recall a bygone era when people could talk to each other at a distance only by using a physical, hard-wired telephone network. In the early days, the available networks did not link up with each other, so users could reach only people who had access to the same network. Eventually people figured out that the value of the network scaled – its profits increased with size. The more people using a particular network, the more valuable belonging to that network would be. Ultimately the world moved to one big network, reachable by all. The World Wide Web's great breakthrough in the early 1990s epitomizes standardization based on inclusion, the consummation of network effects.

One might object that the internet seems a lousy example, because it doesn't charge for access (although users pay third parties to go online, with price linked to quality) and one person's use does not affect others, bandwidth considerations aside. It is thus both nonrivalrous and nonexcludable – in other words, a public good. Indeed, public funding, especially through the US Department of Defense's Advanced Research Projects Agency (DARPA), provided much of its seed investment.

But since the 1990s, private investment has poured into internet-based projects, exactly because entrepreneurs found out how to build excludability into their products so that they can trade internet access for value. Some of the returns on these projects are transparent – think of subscription-based access to websites. Others are indirect. Many businesses sell users' mindspace to advertisers. Social media and search engines gather data from their users, which when accumulated and organized can become very valuable. The bargain is evident, even if not transparent: we let you play in our playground, and you let us harvest the data you make as you play. The World Wide Web thus provides compelling evidence of knowledge creation driven by the prospect of monopoly rents derived from network effects.

A possible reaction to this insight is that knowledge production must be bad if it leads to monopolies. Monopolies deny us the benefits of free competition, namely lower prices, better products, and robust competition to weed out slackers. This is why most rich states set up institutions and policies to suppress them.

The rejoinder is twofold. First, if a monopoly sticks because it represents the most productive way of making something (think of AT&T before the internet),

[14] William D. Nordhaus, Invention, Growth, and Welfare: A Theoretical Treatment of Technological Change 58–59 (1969).

government can limit the most obvious cost (sustained monopoly superprofits) through price regulation (think of the Federal Communications Commission and state regulators). Second, even where regulation fails, technological innovation can defeat knowledge-derived monopolies. A few prominent law professors, including Columbia's Lina Kahn (on leave to chair the Federal Trade Commission), maintain that monopolies can gain enough political power from their economic success to block government regulation. If so, we might break up firms that provide the economic benefits of concentrated production, thereby staving off political dysfunction.[15] Where technological change can oust monopolies, however, we don't need to make that tradeoff. Motivated by a desire to supplant the monopolists, others can aspire to create new knowledge to drive successor projects. Eventually they succeed.[16]

I am old enough to remember when sensible people thought that Microsoft's operating system, MS-DOS, gave it an insurmountable advantage in the market for personal computers. A single operating system lowered the costs of developing apps, thus driving consumers towards MS-DOS so as to get access to the best apps. Then along came the cloud, making personal workstations, if not irrelevant, much less important to personal computing. Joseph Schumpeter popularized the insight, even if he was not the first to have it: the innovation process leads to temporary monopolies that fall prey to further innovation. This is the cost of creative destruction in advanced capitalism.[17]

The containerization story offers examples of creative destruction at both ends of the technology's life cycle. McLean's innovation led in the late 1950s and early 1960s to enormous growth in harbor-related work in New Jersey, especially Newark and Port Elizabeth, to the benefit of McLean's shipping companies. The New York Port Authority used loans and licenses to support the expansion of existing capacity and the building of new facilities in the Newark Bay. These facilities eliminated costly transit of cargo by train or truck across Manhattan to the East River and made renovation of the outmoded and worn-out docks along the East River unnecessary. Workers and businesses associated with harboring in Manhattan and Brooklyn, those in wholesaling and warehousing as well as dockworkers, paid the price.

The second phase of creative destruction came at the end of the 1960s with the withdrawal of McLean's companies, and US shipping lines generally,

[15] Tim Wu, The Curse of Bigness: Antitrust in the New Gilded Age (2018); Tim Wu, The Master Switch: The Rise and Fall of Information Empires (2010); Lina M. Kahn, *Amazon's Antitrust Paradox*, 126 Yale L.J. 710 (2017).

[16] W. Brian Arthur, The Nature of Technology: What It Is and How It Evolves (2009).

[17] Joseph A. Schumpeter, Capitalism, Socialism, and Democracy 81–92 (3d ed. 1950).

from the industry. In 1969, after the peak of the shipping boom driven by the US war in Vietnam, McLean sold off SeaLand, the entity he had created for containerized shipping. Ultimately Maersk, a Danish shipping giant, acquired it. Protectionist US legislation that barred foreign firms from the domestic market, including the valuable routes to and from Puerto Rico that SeaLand dominated, undercut SeaLand's incentive to match its foreign peers in adaptation and innovation. Lack of competitive pressure drew down the knowledge component of the firm's activities. A failure to innovate changed its services from a knowledge-based product to a mere commodity. As a result, the US industry nearly disappeared and European and East Asian companies achieved their present dominance in containerized shipping.

These stories of waves of technology and organizational skills overtaking each other do not undermine the fundamental point: knowledge scales. Not all investments in knowledge pay off, but those that do fuel projects that grow, often achieving market dominance for a while. Monopoly superprofits result – perhaps short-term but potentially massive while they last. The investments succeed often enough in the advanced modern economy to encourage more and greater investment. Enlarging the scope of the economy increases the incentive to make more knowledge. And a large part of the returns from these investments go to those who have the power to exclude others from access to the knowledge. Both income and wealth flow to those with power over knowledge, increasing economic inequality as a side effect.

SYNERGIES, LOCALITY, AND THE KNOWLEDGE ECONOMY

Closely related to scaling are opportunities derived from synergies. As noted already, not all returns from investments in knowledge go to entitlement holders (those who control the means of exclusion). In Romer's model as well as in observed practice, spillovers happen. These spillovers give people who can take advantage of them a reason to stay close to knowledge creation even when they lack direct access to it. This is the synergistic dimension of knowledge. Projects to create knowledge have outcomes that the investors do not necessarily anticipate but that attract other knowledge investments.

One way of confirming this theory-based conjecture is to look at the movement of knowledge workers. Conventional economics holds that a good's scarcity, keeping all other things equal, increases demand, which causes a price rise. Capital, if a factor in producing that good and free to move, will migrate toward scarcity. If this dynamic were to apply to human capital, we would expect knowledge workers to spread out to find places where others with their skills are scarce. Yet, as 1995 Nobel laureate Robert Lucas observed, we see the opposite: knowledge workers cluster rather than distance.[18]

Romer has a persuasive explanation for this observation. Under his model, the formation of knowledge depends on the stock of available human capital. Increasing access to human capital thus results in more knowledge. Knowledge workers can invest in knowledge-creation projects, inasmuch as they supply their skills (human capital) to these projects and not others. One way to lower the cost of an investment is to use knowledge created by others that spills over exclusion barriers. Harvesting spillover knowledge thus is an element of investing in knowledge creation.

Note that I say "element of," not "substitute for." There is a rich literature on what economists call first-mover disadvantages – the downside of being the first to create knowledge for a project. Why don't all knowledge workers wait for someone else to create and then exploit the spillovers? What we think we know is that converting knowledge into economic benefits requires both basic insights into a technology and knowing how to convert these concepts into products that people want.

Again, containerization illustrates both – the basic insight of studying the logistics of cargo containers and the reduction of that knowledge to practical applications. Once that practice became manifest, others copied. In the interval, McLean's companies enjoyed over a decade of extraordinary profits. In most cases, copying without creation leaves the copiers playing catch-up, with fewer opportunities to develop projects with short-term monopoly profits. The nimble entrepreneur that can find the right mix of creation and copying does well. First-movers can collect supercompetitive profits for some time, even if not forever.

As Romer observes, one way to increase the stock of human capital available for producing knowledge is to make it easier for knowledge workers to collaborate. Spillover effects explain why. Notwithstanding covenants not to compete and legal protection of trade secrets, workers talk to their peers, sometimes face-to-face, sometimes in chat rooms and other online media, and sometimes through publications. Knowledge workers seek each other out exactly because they are exceptionally capable of exploiting these spillovers. Physical proximity is not the only way to get access to these spillovers, but it has its advantages.

[18] Robert E. Lucas, Jr., *On the Mechanics of Economic Development*, 22 J. Monetary Econ. 3 (1988).

An observer might look at remote work during the pandemic and conclude that online connectivity has overtaken clustered, connected knowledge work. Although the jury remains out, I doubt it. Just as cold fusion has been only twenty years away for the last fifty years, so replacing direct human contact with electrons and bytes seems more like science fiction, not the next big thing. As an educator, my experience with online teaching suggests lost nuance, feedback, and connection. I believe that locality will be with us for some time and remain the core of the knowledge economy. Hence the connection between spillovers and locality will persist.

Hypothetically, a society can increase the stock of human capital available for knowledge creation through across-the-board investing in education and training. Where spillover effects exist, however, an alternative and less costly strategy is lowering the barriers that keep knowledge workers from joining up with their peers. These barriers include legal rules such as covenants not to compete as well as restrictions on migration across national boundaries. Governments that suppress these barriers smooth the path for greater human capital accumulation.[19]

Opportunities for scaling and synergy thus drive investments in knowledge. Successful investments in turn fuel the growth of the knowledge economy. Not all investments pay off, because not all knowledge makes it easier to provide people with things that they want. What the last half-century or so has seen, however, are enough successes to transform both how we work and what we consume.

INTERNATIONAL DIMENSIONS

The knowledge economy loves international economic liberalism, as I discuss at length in the next chapter. Both scaling and synergies increase with the size of the market. More markets means larger markets. From the sales side, a larger market allows a monopolist to increase the territorial scope of, and therefore the revenues from, its monopoly. From the producer side, ramping up collaboration by knowledge workers increases the synergies from knowledge, making it easier to build more monopolies in other areas.[20]

[19] Ronald J. Gilson, *The Legal Infrastructure of High Technology Industrial Districts: Silicon Valley, Route 128, and Covenants Not To Compete*, 74 N.Y.U. L. Rev. 575 (1999).

[20] Elhanan Helpman & Paul Krugman, Market Structure and Foreign Trade: Increasing Returns, Imperfect Competition, and the International Economy (1985); Paul R. Krugman, *Increasing Returns, Monopolistic Competition, and International Trade*, 9 J. Int'l Econ. 469 (1979).

An important example of international scaling is branded goods. Brands have value to the extent they convey reliable information about product quality as well as letting the consumer signal things that others will understand, such as coolness. The ubiquity of international brands on local high streets around the world seems the face of the new global economy. Many saw the opening of the first McDonald's in Moscow in January 1990 – the triumph of a brand – as a watershed in liberal internationalism's vanquishing of the Soviet system.

Sales of branded consumer goods make vivid how universal the world economy has become. But the ubiquity of branded products is only part of the story. Another way of understanding knowledge's contribution to the world economy is through the lens of supply chains. Knowledge-based products, from aircraft to smartphones, use components made around the world. Producers at each stage of the supply chain must meet tight quality standards for the assembly to work. Managers of the supply chain, typically the firm in charge of delivering the assembled good to buyers, rely heavily on data generation and rapid communication both to drive current work and to adjust the supply chain in light of current performance and future challenges.

Smartphones are a good example. Their different makes are mostly branded goods, largely a product of the twenty-first century, that enjoy nearly universal adoption. Estimates of the number of subscriptions run at 6 billion, with 85 percent of US adults having at least one and nearly 3 billion people around the world possessing a device. Unlike many branded goods, they function not only as a means of consumption but, for many, an investment in pursuit of profit. From investment bankers searching for the next deal to back-country farmers in Kenya keeping track of market movements, people use smartphones to do their work faster and better. Their apps perform tasks that would have been unimaginable not long ago.

Smartphones are physical products sold globally that draw on knowledge in their design and production and in turn support knowledge-based enterprises in international markets. The method of their production – the supply chain – is also international. By value, a bit more than a fifth of the components of an iPhone 12 comes from the United States, as compared to more than a quarter from South Korea and more than 30 percent from China, Japan, and Taiwan. The residual share, mostly European, is slightly larger than the US share (Figure 6.7). Each supplier of components uses knowledge to contribute to the product.

A smartphone could be made with only domestic components. Surely, though, it would be costly – perhaps as much, relatively, as automobiles before Henry Ford's assembly-line innovation. They would be playthings for

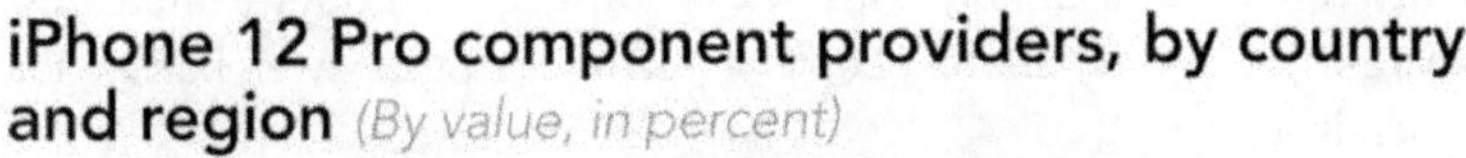

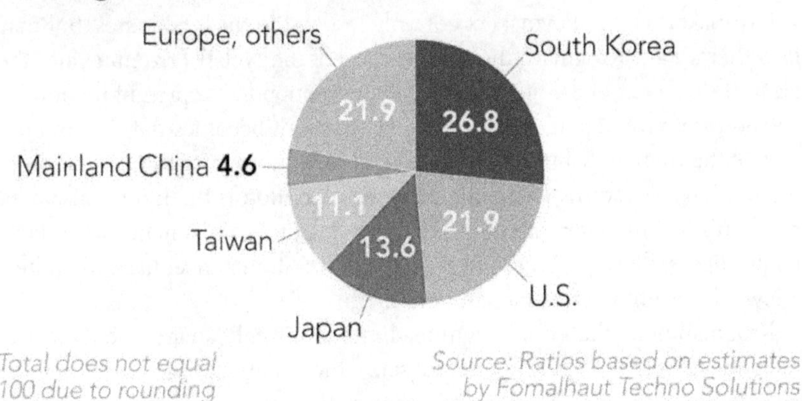

FIGURE 6.7 iPhone 12 components. Source: Fomalhaut Techno Solutions.

the rich rather than a staple for billions. The transnationally distributed supply chain that make them relies on discrete clusters of human capital for knowledge exchange. This system works only because both the components and knowledge workers can cross borders easily.

Smartphones are highly salient but are only a small portion of the global knowledge economy. In 2019, international sales of services – industries such as communications, education, engineering, finance, and law – amounted to $6.23 trillion, according to WTO figures. Not all services qualify as knowledge products, but it seems fair to guess that the portion of their value attributable to knowledge is greater than that for physical objects such as agricultural commodities, oil and gas, and metal ores. In comparison, the total volume of smartphone sales for that year was estimated at $404 billion. The service industries developed their own version of supply chains. They increasingly established separate but connected offices, each with its own specialists. International banks, accountants, engineers, and law firms opening new outposts around the world exemplify supply-chain production of services.

Expectations of the rewards from international transactions have a political effect. These prospects give knowledge investors a powerful reason to push for greater freedom to move factors of production – goods, services, capital, and knowledge workers – and products – goods and services for which people will pay – across borders. As these freedoms accumulate – tariff and nontariff barriers to goods decline, restrictions on the sale of services by outsiders loosen up, regulation of capital flows relaxes, and obstacles to migration disappear –

investment in knowledge, and thus the knowledge economy, increases. This dynamic gives even more people a reason to push even harder for further liberalization.

Lawmakers and policymakers not only respond to these pressures, but may lead them. Paul Krugman, the 2008 winner of the Nobel Prize, provides the clearest statement of the argument.[21] Where monopolies represent the lowest-cost form of production, the issue for government becomes not the suppression of the monopoly but rather coming up with ways to capture a portion of the monopoly's returns for public purposes. Taxation is the most transparent mechanism, but others abound. For this reason, governments want local knowledge spillovers. Accordingly, states have strong incentives to induce knowledge-economy firms to come to them.

Krugman notes that some might read into this insight an argument for state selection of national champions to seize the commanding heights of the knowledge economy. He responds that states have a bad track record in choosing technological champions. The evidence of the thirty-five years since he wrote that confirms the point. The world is dotted with places that governments designated as tech centers and innovation incubation hubs, none of which has justified the cost of creating it.

Krugman's broader point is that when states dismantle barriers to trade, migration, and investment, a task well within their capacity, good things can happen. The likelihood that local firms will become global powers goes up, even though states cannot predict which particular firms will make the leap. Accordingly, governments may welcome private-sector pressure to advance liberal economic internationalism.

This is what theory predicts. The evidence, with all appropriate disclaimers for noise and contingency, confirms the prediction. Chapters 2 and 3 document the willingness of most states to embrace these policies from the end of the 1980s until the onset of the great crises in the late 2010s. The case for building a liberal international economy seemed so clear that most opponents found themselves on the periphery, dismissed mostly as uninformed or ill-willed cranks. Some of these critics, however, turned out to have been Cassandras, prescient even though ignored. They saw, as most did not, the fundamental problems with the knowledge economy, namely the erosion of social capital and increasingly painful economic inequality through sudden dislocation of people and communities.

[21] Paul R. Krugman, *Is Free Trade Passé?* 1 J. Econ. Persp. 131 (1987).

SOCIAL CAPITAL AND THE PARADOX OF THE KNOWLEDGE ECONOMY

So far, I have described theoretical accounts that explain why the knowledge economy did as well as it has over the past few decades. A confounding factor is what social scientists call social capital. Roughly speaking, social capital represents the sum of a society's social networks that support and sustain human interaction. High levels of social capital attract investments in knowledge. Paradoxically, the knowledge economy also draws down social capital even as it uses it to grow. The draw-down comes from two natural consequences of a successful knowledge economy: individual dislocation as economic changes drive people to new places to work and live, and a loss of connection and trust as the composition of communities change. Chapter 8 describes how dislocation works. Here I review the theoretical arguments that predict and explain these outcomes.

Romer points to one connection between knowledge and social capital. Economic theory generally predicts that, all things being equal, a person's willingness to invest in a project that produces returns in the future depends on the discount factor, the number that describes the present value of future money and represents the inverse of the discount rate.[22] While money in hand is always more valuable than money received in the future, the difference shrinks as the discount factor goes up. Romer supposes that societies with higher discount factors should produce more knowledge, as knowledge entails a costly present investment in the hope of future rewards.

What Romer did not make explicit, but what research into social capital indicates, is that increases in social capital raise a society's discount factor. Freedom from corruption, protection of property rights, and confidence in institutions all bolster social stability and reduce the fear that hopes will be dashed and rewards stolen. Conversely, interventions that lower social capital

[22] Economists prefer the discount factor because of its elegance and ease of use mathematically; noneconomists tend to prefer the discount rate, which looks like the commonplace interest rate. Thus people understand that inflation erodes value, and that one way of expressing inflation is through higher interest rates, which produces higher discount rates. The more heavily discounted a future sum is, the less valuable it is. The discount factor, by contrast, is the answer to the question, by what fraction do you have to multiply a future sum to express its present value? The higher the discount factor, the more valuable the future sum. With apologies to the non-mathy, the equation that relates the discount factor (ω) to the discount rate (r) is: $\omega = \frac{1}{1+r}$, with both variables ranging between zero and one and the time period between the present and the future receipt held constant.

decrease the discount factor, making investments in knowledge riskier and, in an economic sense, less rational.

What, then, is social capital? The concept has enjoyed much attention in this century. It is a metaphor, much like the human capital idea, that describes a class of intangible investments that produce returns for both individuals and society as a whole. It comprises features such as stable and reliable governmental institutions, the rule of law, and social trust.

Harvard political scientist Robert Putnam, who brought social capital into the public eye with his best-seller *Bowling Alone* in 2000, quotes L. J. Hanifan, an early twentieth-century educational theorist: social capital comprises qualities that "count for most in the daily lives of people: namely good will, fellowship, sympathy, and social intercourse among the individuals and families who make up a social unit." Social scientists working in the second half of the twentieth century, including urban theorist Jane Jacobs, Harvard economist Glenn Loury, French social theorist Pierre Bourdieu, and Chicago sociologist James Coleman, independently invoked the concept.[23] Their work established that societies have different levels of social capital, just as they do physical capital (e.g., streets, highways, trains, navigable rivers, broadband, and Wi-Fi), and that the level of this capital affects the quality of life in that society. As Putnam puts it:

> Whereas physical capital refers to physical objects and human capital to properties of individuals, social capital refers to connections among individuals – social networks and the norms of reciprocity and trustworthiness that arise from them. In that sense social capital is closely related to what some have called "civic virtue." The difference is that "social capital" calls attention to the fact that civic virtue is most powerful when embedded in a dense network of reciprocal social relations. A society of many virtuous but isolated individuals is not necessarily rich in social capital.[24]

People can build their own social capital, which belongs to them in much the way that human capital does. Networking does exactly this, by cultivating friendships in élite schools or in professional or civic organizations. Not only the privileged network: recent immigrants to the rich world can draw on social networks based on old-country ties to cushion their landing and to find chances for fulfillment.[25]

[23] Robert D. Putnam, Bowling Alone: The Collapse and Revival of American Community 19–20 (2000).

[24] *Id.* at 19.

[25] E.E.O.C. v. *Consolidated Service Systems*, 989 F.2d 233 (7th Cir. 1993).

The building of social capital through private groups matters, but so too does activity at the level of an entire society. Social capital here functions as a public good. Independent of individual clubs, congregations, teams, and the like, a society acquires general qualities that either promote or undermine social trust and willingness to cooperate. Pervasive corruption, unsafe streets, and hate in its many ugly forms indicate a society with low social capital, a place where people must spend enormous time and energy on high alert for threats. Faced with these disincentives, people forgo potentially valuable projects because the obstacles seem so great. Conversely, good government, public safety, and stable institutions encourage people to cooperate with each other and to invest in the future.

The social capital concept can help explain why some states transform themselves for the good of their people, and others fail.[26] The best work remains anecdotal rather than econometric, with formal models not fully developed. Economists who had worked on post-socialist restructuring projects, seeking to explain why so many failed, turned to the quality of institutions as a condition for economic success.[27] This research indicates that inheritance, including geographical location, matters a lot.

A growing body of work documents the locality as well as the variability of social trust. A massive cross-cultural study of outcomes of experiments using the public goods game produced powerful results. Participants in the game could punish other participants. Those who otherwise displayed qualities indicating higher social trust confined punishment to persons who behaved uncooperatively in the game, while low-social-trust players punished everyone. These outcomes differed significantly among sixteen locations, with statistically significant numbers of experiments in each location.[28] This evidence indicates that low social trust is self-propagating.

University of Hamburg economist Stefan Voigt explains these differences in terms of the distinction between formal and informal institutions. The first are artifacts of politics and law; those adopted in the post-socialist world in the

[26] Daron Acemoglu & James Robinson, Why Nations Fail: The Origins of Power, Prosperity and Poverty (2012); Daron Acemoglu & James Robinson, The Narrow Corridor: States, Societies, and the Fate of Liberty (2019).

[27] Rafael La Porta & Andrei Shleifer, *Informality and Development*, 28 J. Econ. Persp. 109 (2014); Rafael La Porta, Florencio Lopez-de-Silanes & Andrei Shleifer, *The Economic Consequences of Legal Origins*, 46 J. Econ. Lit. 285 (2008); Edward L. Glaeser, Rafael La Porta, Florencio Lopez-de-Silanes & Andrei Shleifer, *Do Institutions Cause Growth?* 9 J. Econ. Growth 271 (2004); Paul G. Mahoney, *The Common Law and Economic Growth: Hayek Might Be Right*, 30 J. Leg. Stud. 503 (2001).

[28] Benedikt Herrmann, Christian Thöni & Simon Gächter, *Antisocial Punishment across Societies*, 329 Science 1362 (2008).

1990s exemplify the category. The latter rests on social capital. A society's social capital affects how people relate to formal institutions and in particular whether they seek to reinforce or bypass them:

> For a long time, property rights and contracting institutions had been assumed to be perfect and the enforcement of contracts as essentially costless. Institutional economists showed that these assumptions were naïve at best, but possibly also dangerous if they were at the basis of policy-making. The policy implication of recognizing the relevance of transaction costs seemed straightforward and can [be] succinctly summarized in "get the institutions right." Many times, this imperative was, however, confined to "get the formal institutions right."[29]

The takeaway, a reflection on all the investment in new formal institutions described in Chapter 2, is that those seeking to reform societies must treat social capital as an independent variable that dictates what changes in formal institutions will or will not work. A failure to do this in the 1990s explains why so many of the reforms came up short.

Learning not to take social capital for granted when undertaking reform is a critical first step. Still, we need to learn more about what societies can do to change social capital as such. In this century, we have discovered the effects of its drawing down. Accumulating social capital, by contrast, remains more of an art than a science.

DRAWING DOWN SOCIAL CAPITAL

The misinformation campaigns that have become a familiar part of cyber life over the last five years illustrate deliberate attacks on social cohesion. COVID-19 measures provide another. Immigration illustrates both sides, lowering social trust and cooperation but also providing a pathway over time to greater resilience and flourishing.

Chapter 5 discusses the use of cyberspace as an instrument for degrading social capital. Unlike traditional psychological warfare and clandestine operations that seek to push a society in one direction or another – say, for Trump or Brexit and against Macron and the European Union – the more recent campaigns promote distrust as an end in itself. Publicity for crazy theories – Microsoft chips smuggled into people through COVID-19 vaccines, anyone? – reflects not a desire to persuade, but rather a purpose of destroying trust and belief itself.

[29] Stefan Voigt, Determinants of Social Norms (July 20, 2022), https://papers.ssrn.com/sol3/papers.cfm?abstract_id=4157924.

No one planned COVID-19 as an experiment in social cohesion, but such it has become. Quarantines, masks, burrowing away in isolated vacation homes, and other forms of social distancing essential for stopping the spread of the pandemic have the collateral effect of feeding anxiety and distrust. The eye contact we lose when we go remote, and the drop in expressive facial cognition we suffer with masks, takes its toll, even apart from the highly rational fear of infection and suffering. In the United States first and foremost, but also in much of the rich world, COVID-19 has cost societies not just material well-being, but social trust and solidarity.

In low-social-capital societies such as Russia, quarantine and vaccine resistance did result in open conflict because distrust of authority dominates. Fights over quarantines and masking pop up in places that historically enjoyed higher social capital. One side publicly signals its compliance with public health mandates with masks, isolation, and proudly displayed vaccine passports, not infrequently going beyond public health requirements as a means of doubling down on virtue. The other shows its contempt for authority by going maskless, gathering in crowded indoor places, and rejecting vaccines, sometimes noisily. Stressed out by the months of disruption and loss – social if not always economic or physical – people on both sides hate each other. The maskers think the unmasked show contempt not just for authority but for the lives of others and revel in *Schadenfreude* when COVID-19 takes them; the unmasked think that the masked bolsters the power of expert élites whose corruption and self-regard have disserved society as a whole. To think that the problem will go away once one side is liquidated, whether through benign reeducation or the relentlessness of the disease, is naïve.

Immigration provides another context for studying social capital. Putnam presents good evidence that reinforces a widespread intuition: social diversity in a population shaped by the arrival of immigrants contributes to flourishing and resilience. Many instruments, from Nobel prizes to per capita GDP, indicate that societies with greater ethnic and cultural diversity do better than homogenous ones. What Putnam's research also demonstrates, however, is that integrating immigrants into an incumbent society draws down social capital even as it creates a possibility for future social growth.[30]

Drawing on surveys administered alongside the 2000 census, Putnam looks at county-level data measuring diversity across multiple variables. He combines that with data measuring propensity for cooperation and trust. They consistently indicate negative correlation between diversity attributable to

30 Robert Putnam, E Pluribus Unum: *Diversity and Community in the Twenty-First Century: The 2006 Johan Skytte Prize Lecture*, 30 SCAND. POL. STUD. 137 (2007).

immigration and the level of cooperation and trust. The losses in social capital do not reflect polarization: members of one group do not increase their trust in people within the group with which they identify. Rather, changes in group diversity increase distrust with respect to everyone. Research by two of Putnam's economist colleagues, Alberto Alesina and Ed Glaeser, provides indirect confirmation of this observation. They show a strong correlation between levels of state spending on social solidarity and support, on the one hand, and ethnic homogeneity, on the other.[31]

Putnam reconciles the seeming paradox between the macro – immigrant-based diversity as a source of social prosperity and accomplishment – and the micro – loss of trust as a response to increases in local diversity – by arguing that adaptation occurs but is costly. A learning process allows members of a society disrupted by immigration-driven change to rebuild social networks, often successfully. These adaptations take time and are not inevitable. Societies overwhelmed by immigration can suffer enduring losses in social capital, as the immigrant neighborhoods called *banlieues* that surround Paris exemplify. Putnam argues, though, that immigration presents an opportunity as well as a challenge, if properly managed: "My argument here is that in the short run there is a tradeoff between diversity and community, but that over time wise policies (public and private) can ameliorate that tradeoff."[32]

Immigration prompted by the rise of the knowledge economy explains a lot of the recent interest in social capital. People who are not knowledge workers – that is, people who do not possess much human capital – still migrate to find better jobs, even though the spillover effect does not draw them. Higher levels of social capital can multiply the value of skills even for people that do not have many. As Dani Rodrik puts it: "In reality, a key reason why poor countries are poor is precisely that they have poor institutions: they suffer from corruption, inadequate property-rights protection and contract enforcement, political instability, low levels of infrastructure and public goods provision, and so on."[33] A dish-washer in my home town, a university community in the mid-Atlantic region of the United States, gets a greater return on labor than does a farmworker in Guatemala; a worker doing construction in Shenzhen thrives compared to a farmer in Hunan; and a dish-washer in a restaurant in Bari, Puglia, does better than a worker just across the Adriatic in Bar, Montenegro,

[31] Alberto Alesina & Edward L. Glaeser, Fighting Poverty in the US and Europe: A World of Difference (2004).

[32] Robert Putnam, *supra* note 30, at 164.

[33] Dani Rodrik, *Is Global Equality the Enemy of National Equality?* 105 Rivista di Politica Economica 7 (No. 10–12 2018).

and much better than those next door to Bar in Albania. Studies estimate that wholesale reduction of the barriers to the movement of low-human-capital workers to high-social-capital markets can generate huge economic surpluses.[34]

As the examples of disinformation, COVID-19 responses, and spikes in immigration illustrate, social capital may dissipate. We know that physical capital, say a factory, depreciates over time due to wear and tear as well as the outdating of its technology. Social capital can do the same. The last decade has shown that societies thought to represent best practices in strong institutions and high trust, such as the United States and the United Kingdom, can decline through political and social conflict. Places such as Australia and Germany give hints of heading in the same direction. Adversaries such as Russia target social trust as a vulnerability of these states.

THE KNOWLEDGE ECONOMY, INEQUALITY, AND JUSTICE

Some of the ramifications of the knowledge economy's take-off were not as foreseeable as others. Economic growth driven by more use of knowledge as a factor of production seems like a good thing. We end up with more stuff – goods and services – that we want. Recall the profound differences in satisfaction and life prospects between Russia and the United States at the end of the 1980s. A large part of these differences, I am convinced, were due to different approaches to knowledge in the economy.

The knowledge economy, through material interest more than moral generosity, also supports an attractive kind of equality. In people, what the knowledge economy values to the exclusion of all else is the ability to get and make knowledge. Any social arrangement that stands in the way of the smart and gifted finding their best life within the knowledge economy must give way, if that economy is to work properly. Because states compete with each other to achieve economic success, international competition over knowledge workers drives those states away from old-fashioned prejudices that keep gifted people from realizing their best selves.

Evidence of this effect abounds. Singapore relaxed its measures suppressing gay culture to remove an impediment to attracting talented workers. As my colleague David Law puts it, "human rights attract human capital."[35] The

34 Michael A. Clemens, Claudio E. Montenegro & Lant Pritchett, *The Place Premium: Bounding the Price Equivalent of Migration Barriers*, 101 Rev. Econ. & Stat. 201 (2019). *But see* George J. Borjas, *Immigration and Globalization: A Review Essay*, 53 J. Econ. Lit. 961 (2015).

35 David S. Law, *Globalization and the Future of Constitutional Rights*, 102 Nw. U. L. Rev. 1277, 1333 (2008).

"wokeness" of capitalist giants, the technology firms in particular, may well be enlightened but also reflects the demands of the market for knowledge workers.

What emerges from this dynamic is a commitment to a concept of equality as freedom from senseless discrimination. It attacks public and private use of attributes that societies wield to oppress – race, ethnicity, religion, sex, gender, sexual orientation. I will call this concept liberal equality to indicate its link to liberal internationalism.

I do not mean to suggest that liberal equality rests on selfish economic interest. Profound normative arguments support this principle, independent of how it affects economic outcomes. My point is simply that liberal equality, in addition to invoking deep principles of moral and historic justice, complements the goal of maximizing the economic returns from the increasingly dominant form of economic production that we call the knowledge economy.

To say that the knowledge economy is on the side of the battle for liberal equality does not mean that the triumph of the principle is inevitable. Whatever progress some societies have achieved in the past decade – a matter of deep controversy – no one can claim that irrational prejudices that demean people and frustrate basic human flourishing do not remain powerful forces in much, perhaps all, of the world. The incentives generated by the knowledge economy provide no guarantee of ultimate victory. My argument is only that these incentives exist and demand our attention, even if other forces push in the opposite direction.

Accordingly, a big part of the liberal international project, however unrealized, is suppression of these kinds of discrimination. Consider those who argued, and still argue, that the West's intervention in Afghanistan was necessary to protect women from a cruel form of patriarchy. Many people who believe global capitalism to be generally repugnant find themselves making common cause with this particular facet of the knowledge economy.

Equality, however, admits multiple meanings, at least one of which has a very different relationship to the knowledge economy than liberal equality. Consider economic equality, the idea that all participants in a society merit roughly equal access to the goods and services that society produces. A society might realize this kind of equality by abolishing price rationing of significant goods and services so as to make ability to pay irrelevant.

Over the last century most experiments to do that failed. Getting rid of price rationing always led to other ways of allocating scarce goods and services. In most places, including the Soviet Union and China as well as the smaller states that embraced their model, those ways included informal distribution based on influence and patronage as well as corruption, sharpening the division between winners and losers rather than narrowing the gap.

A more feasible strategy instead might limit disparities in economic power so that all members of a society have a roughly equal chance of obtaining those goods and services that are necessary for living a decent life. Debates rage about how to do this. In the past, politicians successfully responded to attacks on new modes of production by those most harmed by the innovations. Leaders from the center-right such as the Liberal minister Churchill or the German Reich's Bismarck anticipated these grievances with social insurance and other ameliorative policies.

Ultimately, the pursuit of economic equality focuses on output – returns from economic activity – rather than the inputs that the liberal equality principle addresses. It means saying that certain disparities in economic status cannot be tolerated, no matter how free from violations of liberal equality the process of distributing income and acquiring wealth may be. Importantly, a world where talent reigns, unobstructed by brutal prejudice, violates economic equality to the extent that the talented are rewarded much more than the less gifted.

Because we live in a world where liberal equality remains an aspiration rather than a reality, a committed liberal might see little practical conflict between these principles. We have plenty of evidence that at the present moment many differences in economic status reflect historic violations of liberal equality. But as we contemplate the future of the knowledge economy, the potential for conflict grows. Imagine a workplace, access to which depends entirely on talent, defined in a way that fully implements liberal equality. Also suppose that the knowledge economy delivers exceptional rewards to those in that workplace, based on the normal operation of market forces as to its product. Should we reward that workplace for satisfying liberal equality or punish it for the exceptional returns to its workers?

Recall that the knowledge economy pursues and promotes uncompetitive outcomes – short-to-mid-term monopolies – for investors. These investors, mostly knowledge workers (and more so under conditions of full liberal equality), gain greater payoffs than the normal returns paid to ordinary workers and suppliers of financial capital. These disparities in outcomes contribute to growing economic inequality. Even if the knowledge economy doesn't do all the work, it seems hard to ignore that economic inequality is a natural consequence of greater investment in and reliance on knowledge as a factor of production.

The wealth-inequality data confirm this prediction. Investors in knowledge, especially knowledge workers, enjoy great rewards as a result of their contributions to (the economic conception of) global well-being. Regulatory interventions and technological upheavals cap those rewards, but the trend toward greater economic inequality persists.[36]

THE COSTS OF CREATIVE DESTRUCTION

The extraordinary returns from success in the knowledge economy are only a part of the economic equality conundrum. The knowledge economy creates losers as well as winners. Just as those who succeed in the knowledge economy get above-average returns, those displaced by that economy see losses.

That the knowledge economy has not floated all boats seems manifest. Recall how containerization ruined New York's shipping economy. After World War II, Manhattan and Brooklyn provided a home for docks as well as many firms – wholesalers, longshoremen, stevedores – that serviced, and needed proximity to, the docks. Containerization radically reduced the amount of labor needed to transfer goods from one form of carriage to another. It became cost effective for trucks and trains to exchange cargo coming from or going by rail or truck to or from the Mid-Atlantic, South, and Midwest with ships docked in New Jersey, eliminating the expense of transiting Manhattan to the docks on the East River. As a result, work associated with the East River docks collapsed during the 1960s.

Collective action organized by trade unions failed to prevent this outcome. The unions accepted a deal that guaranteed job security and other benefits to incumbent workers in return for freedom for the carriers to implement the new carriage technologies. The concession to the carriers ensured that new workers would not replace the incumbents. The incumbents' protections softened the blow of the industry's decline, but only for a fixed group that shrank over time. The businesses that serviced the docks got nothing, and people who otherwise would have worked in them in the future had to find other, less rewarding jobs.

Imagine this pattern played out in thousands of industries in thousands of places to the cost of millions of firms and workers. Also consider a general phenomenon observed by economists since at least the 1950s: growth in one sector can starve a competing sector of resources. Unbalanced growth occurs when different sectors compete for the same limited set of inputs, such as labor

[36] Daron Acemoglu & Pascual Restrepo, *Tasks, Automation, and the Rise in U.S. Wage Inequality*, 90 Econometrica 1973 (2022); Anton Korinek & Joseph E. Stiglitz, *Artificial Intelligence and Its Implications for Income Distribution and Unemployment*, in The Economics of Artificial Intelligence: An Agenda 349 (Ajay K. Agrawal, Joshua Gans & Avi Goldfarb eds., 2019).

and capital. The sector that can find more profitable uses for those inputs will bid up their prices, shrinking the profit margin of the competing sector.

An Anglo-Polish economist, Tadeusz Rybczynski, had worked out the analytics of unbalanced growth within the domestic economy in the 1950s.[37] International effects can exacerbate the problem. To the extent the growth sector exports more than the competing sector, the shift in production will also strengthen the local currency and thus suppress exports of the products of the competing sector.[38] Journalists coined the term "Dutch disease" to describe how the North Sea oil boom of the 1960s and 1970s raised the cost of labor and other inputs on which the Dutch manufacturing sector depended. The boom in energy ravaged Dutch manufacturing. The cost of land, workers, contractors, and capital went up, while surging energy export revenues increased the value of the Dutch currency and thus made it harder for everyone else to export.

The issue is not as simple as knowledge versus manufacturing. Knowledge does not stand on its own, but rather becomes part of the process of production, even when production results in physical objects (manufactured goods). The knowledge component of containerization affected the design of carriers (trucks, trains, and ships) and containers, all physical objects. The resulting cost savings from transport expanded the market for manufactured goods by lowering the cost of delivering them. Greater knowledge does not end manufacturing as such, but rather drives manufacturers to employ more knowledge workers and fewer workers with low or average human capital.

A relevant example is the US steel industry. Overall, this sector has declined significantly, leaving rust belts in its wake. Much the same has happened in the United Kingdom and the European Union. Yet a boutique US industry continues to thrive, focusing on highly engineered, customer-specific products. As with containerization in shipping, contemporary steel production sheds workers with low and average human capital in favor of knowledge workers that master design, automation, and organization. In a sense, US steelmaking has become as much a knowledge-industry producer as a kind of manufacturing, however it counts in national statistics.

Luxembourg provides an example of a different response to obsolescence in the steel industry. That country joined the European Coal and Steel Community in 1952 because its economy depended heavily on steel, but the industry's decline was already evident. A small state, it could move more

37 Tadeusz M. Rybczynski, *Factor Endowment and Relative Commodity Prices*, 22 ECONOMICA 336 (1955).

38 Paul Krugman, *The Narrow Moving Band, the Dutch Disease, and the Competitive Consequences of Mrs. Thatcher*, 27 J. DEV. ECON. 41 (1987).

nimbly than its larger neighbors. Beginning in the 1960s, Luxembourg developed a banking industry that competed with Switzerland for business by providing strong customer-secrecy protection along with high social capital. Within a decade, steel manufacturing had disappeared and its financial industry dominated the economy, as it still does.

Admittedly, I paint with broad strokes. Still, the point is clear enough: the knowledge economy, the source of great wealth creation and growth in human capacity over many decades, also disrupts the status quo. This effect perpetuates deep divisions in society and strips meaning and pride from the lives of many people around the world. The divisions are especially salient in the rich world, where people with the most to lose from the backwash of the knowledge economy live.

* * *

The rise of the knowledge economy underlies the transformation of work, production, and consumption over the last fifty years. Its capacity to scale explains both its appetite for international markets and commitment to talent over outdated social norms. At the same time, it also frays social solidarity, both by dislocating people through creative destruction and feeding economic inequality.

People who thrive in the knowledge economy have profoundly different views as to what the future holds and how to shape it from those the knowledge economy leaves behind. The next two chapters compare these views and ties them to economic forces. First, I consider what the winners want. Then I look at how the losers respond.

7

Law and the Knowledge Economy

What the Winners Want

This chapter shows how the knowledge economy motivates those who succeed within it to push for the particular projects of liberal internationalism. Knowledge workers, the firms that employ them, and the states that tie their fate to the knowledge economy benefit from free movement of goods, services, firms, capital, and people. They also value liberal equality, which makes them better off as well as better.

The chapter first lays out a political-economy story that explains why people in the knowledge economy embrace the several projects – free trade, investment protection and greater freedom for multinational enterprises to operate, antidiscrimination and human rights, and open immigration – that make up the contemporary liberal internationalist agenda. It then looks at why the beneficiaries of the knowledge economy use law generally, and international law in particular, as a means of designing and implementing the projects that reward them. Finally it traces the postwar implementation of the liberal internationalist agenda, emphasizing an acceleration in the bite of international law in the latter part of the twentieth century. As the knowledge economy grew in importance, the projects of liberal internationalism developed more quickly and became more ambitious.

THE POLITICS OF THE KNOWLEDGE ECONOMY

I have already indicated that liberal internationalism pursues open borders for inputs and outputs of production, pushes governments toward uniform regulatory standards, and opposes arbitrary discrimination that thwarts people of talent from realizing their full potential. What needs to be established is the connection between the knowledge economy and these objectives. The field of political economy provides that link.

Political economy explores the way that economic incentives affect politics. It posits that one of the things that motivates people in politics is the pursuit of their material well-being. It does not assert that this factor alone explains how and why social choices turn out as they do. It does insist that people's perceptions of how they will benefit shape what they seek from politics. There is vast evidence that political choices do not always reflect the material interests, objectively understood, of the people making those choices. But there is also plenty of evidence that people can smuggle their material interests into their values and self-construction so that they can regard as estimable actions that also make them better off.

A direct connection exists between the material interests of knowledge workers and the liberal internationalist agenda. Implementing that agenda results in increasing both the size and profits of the knowledge economy, and thus the returns to knowledge workers. It does so through both demand- and supply-side effects. Because of scaling, the sector's profits (and not just revenues) go up as markets for its products expand. Accordingly, people in the knowledge economy push for greater access to markets around the world, which increases demand for knowledge products.

At the same time, the making of knowledge products often entails distributed, modular processes – that is to say, supply chains. These chains use knowledge workers at every stage. Measures that facilitate matching knowledge workers to places in this chain increase the supply of knowledge available for production. Lowering barriers to immigration and making irrational discrimination against talented people more costly do this. In economic terms, lowering the cost of production translates into a greater supply of the products.

For both demand- and supply-side reasons, then, the knowledge economy does well under liberal internationalism. Firms and people in that economy benefit from that agenda, giving them strong incentives to embrace it. They find it easy to identify with the good things it does (or that they think it does), reducing global poverty, disease, and misery as well as enabling people trapped in the worst places on earth to find homes and fulfillment in better places. Those who do well in the knowledge economy especially find attractive the principle of liberal equality, which valorizes exactly the qualities of ability and diligence to which they attribute their success.

LAW'S ROLE IN LIBERAL INTERNATIONALISM

In its pure form, liberal internationalism prescribes that states must, to the fullest extent possible, open their borders to commercial transactions, firms, capital, and workers. As part of this object, it calls on states to reduce the regulatory burden on these endeavors to those necessary to implement essential national policies such as national security, public welfare, safety, and environmental sustainability. Just as importantly, the policy prescription includes an end to all impediments to the realization of human talent. Mandates for greater openness and liberty work across many dimensions. They frequently look to law generally as a means of fulfilling their demands, and especially to international law.

The drive for greater international economic openness and the liberation of human economic potential easily, perhaps even necessarily, translates into a push for rules and rule enforcement. Liberal internationalism and law go together. First, law characteristically embraces a position of abstract neutrality or impartiality, expressed in the dictum that the law is no respecter of persons. This principle, applied internationally, makes it easier to address people and what they do without using categories such as nationality, gender, class, religion, and ethnicity. It does not take status for granted, but rather treats people as capable of making their own status. It does not ignore history and culture and the limits they impose on people's choices but looks for ways to break these shackles.

Second, law in general provides useful information about the consequences of contemplated action. It aspires to bridge the present and the future by making it more likely that, if certain events or circumstances happen, specific outcomes will ensue. If I sell my goods across a national border, law will reassure me that the potential tax bill will be *x*, and not *2x*. This reassurance encourages people to deal with strangers, which is at the heart of all international activity. If I buy something from a seller in a foreign land, or borrow money from a foreign lender, or buy land, build a factory, and grow a business abroad, law tells me something about what I am entitled to expect from the strangers at the other end of these transactions. Other institutions, including high levels of social capital, might do the same thing, but law (sometimes) can substitute for them.

Third, international law helps people get around local variations in law that undermine the status-independent and informative features of law. In many parts of the world, law is about empowering the state or particular groups, not the interests of the individual. Critics of liberalism regard this as good. From the perspective of the antiliberal right, affirming authority is what law does, and submitting to authority is what gives meaning and value to life. For the antiliberal left, advancing progressive projects means sorting out who are on the right and wrong sides of history. Law, they maintain, cannot be impartial between progress and reaction.

Where liberalism prevails, as it did in the international sphere during the 1990s, it looks to international law to overcome variations in national approaches to legality. It urges the creation of international rules that can override, or at least complicate, national law. Substituting international law for local law amounts to pushing back against illiberal national law that thwarts the objectives of the knowledge economy.

Using international law this way works, however, only if it has consequences. With international law, enforcement poses special problems. Very few international officials can reward or punish. Direct enforcement prevails in only a few small pockets. I describe them here to contrast direct enforcement with the means that international law more frequently uses to make its commands consequential.

A rare example of an independent organization enforcing a kind of international law (at least a body of law not under the direct control of any state) is the International Committee for Assigned Names and Numbers (ICANN). This nonprofit corporation, a creature of US law with worldwide representation and governance, runs the domain-name system that assigns internet addresses (always numeric) to particular words, typically proper names or catchphrases. ICANN uses an arbitration process to settle disputes about what numbers go with what names, and wields a powerful enforcement mechanism, namely automatic reassignment of the name in dispute. As it controls how the internet associates names with numbers, it automatically implements the decisions that its arbitral organs reach.

The IMF and the World Bank do something similar. These international organizations can withhold resources and validation from states that violate their rules. To the extent that truculent states lack other sources of financial capital, they must either suffer or bend to the international financial institutions' will. Perhaps for this reason, the trend in the South during this century has been to find alternative sources of revenue that free states from these institutions.

Most international organizations lack anything like direct law-enforcement power. Instead, law works, to the extent it does, through indirect social pressure based on a shared culture and commitment to certain values. The organizations remain at constant risk of becoming irrelevant and thus impotent.[1]

Consider as an example the international investment regime that grew up over the last forty years. The modern treaties give foreign investors the right to

[1] Robert E. Scott & Paul B. Stephan, The Limits of Leviathan: Contract Theory and the Enforcement of International Law (2006).

bring suits against host states when the host state fails to honor its treaty obligations. The host state will have a BIT with the investors' home state. Either that treaty or a different instrument such as the Bank's ICSID Convention will offer an arbitration tribunal and procedural rules. Under all of these treaties, the arbitral tribunals can only order money compensation. They cannot invalidate whatever the host state did that breached the treaty and require that state to restore the status quo ante.

Getting money compensation from a state requires using national law to compel payment. This is extremely hard for many reasons. Outside of war, states do not seize the property of other states (or anyone else) unless that property can be found in the seizing state's territory. States rarely directly own property in other states, but rather use state-owned entities (banks, businesses, airlines, and the like) as the nominal owner. States where the property can be found (think of a ship or aircraft) rarely look through these entities to the ultimate owner. The few items of property that states do directly own abroad – principal examples are embassies, purchased but not-yet-delivered military equipment, bank accounts used by central banks to clear international currency transactions – almost always enjoy special protection under the host state's laws. As a result, if a losing state doesn't pay a treaty-based arbitral award, the person owed the money can do little under national law to convert the award (a debt) into money (payment).

Yet states often honor these awards. They do so for transactional and reputational reasons. Nonpayment can lead to retaliation in other areas. For example, the Kirchner government in Argentina broke many treaty obligations during the early years of this century in response to its financial problems. Its actions led to many international arbitral awards, which it steadfastly refused to pay. In response, lenders and investors going forward insisted on a large premium as the cost of doing business in that country. Finally the voters repudiated the Kirchners, the new Macri administration settled the claims, and commerce and capital returned for a while. Even Kazakhstan, a country whose political leadership has nothing to fear from its voters, paid an international arbitral award it had originally ignored because its failure to abide by its international legal obligations hurt its candidacy for the WTO.

Even when countries do not get a transactional payoff from (belatedly) honoring their treaty-based debts, as Argentina and Kazakhstan did, they may care about their reputation as a law abider. They may anticipate the boycotts that would occur if they acquired a bad reputation, from a poor credit rating to the drying up of new investment. Other states may hold off from cooperating with them on important projects, such as managing a river that flows through several countries or maintaining a military alliance. Being known as a law abider may get a country into clubs (international institutions) that bestow cachet or provide tangible benefits, such as credit and technical or development assistance.

The connection between obeying the law and transactional and reputational benefits exists, however, only if there is a consensus about the value of the rule of law. That consensus depends on widespread satisfaction with the content of the law and, perhaps even more significantly, confidence in the values and practices of the international lawmakers and law enforcers. A large part of the liberal internationalist project, then, entails bolstering the reputation of and encouraging deference to the international institutions that supervise and implement the international rule of law.

To see how law worked to implement the liberal internationalist agenda, I review briefly the evolution of international economic law from the era of European imperialism to the end of the twentieth century. The story connects the evolution of the legal regimes, and the increasing internationalization of the relevant law, to the emergence of the knowledge economy. What started as the principle of free trade became law for multinational enterprises increasingly taken up in knowledge production and the making of knowledge products. The law reflected and supported these developments.

LIBERAL INTERNATIONAL LAW AND FREE TRADE

To understand how law can shrink trade barriers so as to promote the knowledge economy, a sense of how trade barriers work and how internationalist projects unfolded in the past helps. In the modern era, the significant project that provided a model for future endeavors was the campaign in the first half of the nineteenth century to repeal Britain's Corn Laws (in British English, unlike American, corn includes all grains). This legislation protected farmers, more precisely the landed aristocracy, from imports of grain that would cut into their domestic market share and lower the price that their grains could command. The scheme worked by imposing a tax, called a duty, on foreign grains as they entered the country. Foreign farmers might enjoy natural advantages, such as better soil and climate, better farm machinery, or better farming techniques (seed selection, soil preservation, laborers), that resulted in larger and better crops at a lower cost. The duties offset these advantages, letting British farmers sell lower quality and more costly grains to the British population.

Soon after the Napoleonic Wars, liberal activists, including the founders of *The Economist*, campaigned against the Corn Laws as an unjust tax on the general population for the benefit of the landed aristocracy. They also argued that the Laws served as a subsidy for sloth and backwardness. After thirty years of struggle and in the context of the Irish potato famine, in 1846 the government of the day pushed through repeal. Over the remainder of the century, this abolition of protectionist duties became a template for liberal economic policy, embodied in the United Kingdom by the politician William Gladstone.

Paradoxically, in the late nineteenth and early twentieth century free trade evolved into the battle for empire and the rise of monopoly capital. The story is complicated and controversial, including a vigorous debate among economic historians as to whether economic forces can adequately explain European imperialism. The British, French, German, and Russian empires, the first three overseas and the last contiguous, applied a principle of imperial preference that overrode free trade. World War I ensued, although it would be wrong to say that any single factor, even the battle for empire, caused that catastrophe. The interwar period brought new challenges to the world economy and dealt even more blows to the free trade ideal.

After World War I, governments found new ways of protecting domestic producers, the contemporary counterparts to Britain's landed gentry. The government might ration foreign currency, without which a firm could not buy any foreign-made goods. Or it might impose sanitary and health rules that isolate the specific attributes of foreign products to ban their importation. Environmental and biodiversity projects in the late twentieth century offered further chances to exclude foreign competitors under the guise of pursuing impeccable policy goals.

Seeing these barriers as a threat to economic health and ultimately to peace and security, the western states crafted the General Agreement on Tariffs and Trade, an international agreement that regulates how states limit imports of goods. As Chapter 3 relates, the Uruguay Round Agreements extended and strengthened that instrument. They also created a new international court to apply and enforce these rules.

INTERNATIONAL LAW AND MULTINATIONAL COMPANIES

For much of the nineteenth and twentieth centuries, international liberalism focused on physical goods traded at arm's length. These transactions traditionally involved many firms, including several layers of brokers and distributors separating the producer – in the case of the Corn Laws the farmer – and the consumer – the baker or other food processors who convert grains into comestibles. As the knowledge economy grew, the multinational company emerged as a new means of organizing and controlling business activity, whether manufacturing (think of cars and steel), extracting (think of oil and minerals), or providing services (think of banking, engineering, insurance, law, and telecommunication). Over time, manufacturing, extracting, and service-providing increasingly relied on knowledge advantages, which pushed the firms toward international markets.

The multinational company substitutes for informal relationships that previously had linked businesses internationally, such as correspondent banks or law firms. People use the new form because they believe that it can do a better job of managing projects and risks through a hierarchy run by a headquarters, and that the personal on-the-ground connections that had made independent local firms the preferred business form no longer matter as much. The second part of this calculus implies a belief that law can supplement, although not totally replace, local knowledge.

The central insight is Ronald Coase's, the pioneer in the economic theory of firms. Other Nobel laureates who refined and extended these insights include Douglass North, Elinor Ostrom, and Oliver Williamson.[2] A hierarchically organized firm does better than distributed relationships when the business depends on confidential information, trade secrets, and intellectual property – in other words, commercially valuable knowledge. A centralized managerial hierarchy can discipline people and guard secrets more effectively than independent firms deploying only contract and property law. Of course, this model works only if the central management has good judgment or good luck (let's call it talent). Knowledge-protecting discipline depends on discretion rather than rules, and discretion is not always used wisely. But where a firm can draw on talent to pursue its best interests, centralized management can provide a superior way of administering and dispensing the firm's knowledge.

Firms that extend operations across borders still want to back up their self-help remedies for knowledge protection – the power to discipline and fire people who do not do enough to safeguard the firm's knowledge, whether employees, contractors, suppliers, distributors, or anyone else in the production chain – with legally enforceable remedies. One deterrent to cross-border operations is a fear that, in at least some countries, only local firms can get fair treatment from the authorities and full enforcement of their rights. Replacing

[2] R. H. Coase, *The Nature of the Firm*, 4 Economica 386 (1937); Elinor Ostrom, Governing the Commons: The Evolution of Institutions for Collective Action (1990); Douglass C. North, Institutions, Institutional Change and Economic Performance (1990); Oliver E. Williamson, Markets and Hierarchies: Analysis and Antitrust Implications (1975).

local law and law enforcement with international mechanisms ameliorates that concern, at least among states that buy into the idea of the international rule of law. Even if international remedies still rely on national states for complete implementation, those remedies have bite to the extent that states value the work that international law does.

Thus, as the knowledge economy swelled in the 1990s against the backdrop of the collapse of Soviet-style socialism, multinational companies and their allies looked for new ways to bolster the protection of international business across borders. These allies included not only people with economic ties to global business – lobbyists and consultants, for example – but technocrats, professionals, and academics who believed in the potential of liberal internationalism to spread peace and prosperity and promote human thriving. The search proceeded on three fronts – expanding the multilateral trade regime to cover the other aspects of doing business across borders; extending international protection of foreign investors to more destinations with greater enforcement of rights; and building regional institutions to provide stronger protection than the multilateral ones, limited by the larger number of state parties and the consequent greater veto risk, could deliver. A collateral but important part of the project was protecting people from status-based discrimination and barriers to movement across national borders.

UPGRADING THE INTERNATIONAL LAW OF TRANSACTIONS

At the start of the 1990s, the legal regime for international trade in physical goods was already well-developed but excluded much of the socialist world. As Chapter 3 relates, that decade's reforms brought in the states that socialism had left out, elaborated on the rules applicable to seemingly neutral health, safety, and environmental regulation that may function as a trade barrier, and created a more legalist enforcement mechanism. The authors of the Uruguay Round Agreements implemented this program and extended it to international trade in services (as distinguished from goods) and intellectual property. Internationally traded services largely involve high-skill, expert work such as banking, lawyering, accounting, design, engineering, journalism, and entertainment and thus form a significant part of the knowledge economy.

The way trade liberalization worked for international sales of services is instructive. The method of delivery complicates the regulation of international services. Some services involve a seller crossing a border, as when an accountant travels to another country to conduct an audit. Sometimes the buyer does the traveling, as in tourism and education (before online courses).

A service provider might set up a satellite office in another country while maintaining headquarters supervision, a structure that banks and law firms widely adopt. The rise of better technologies for virtual communication allowed the dematerialization of some services – that is, delivery without any people moving at all. Data services (think of virtual learning, Bloomberg's financial news, Amazon's cloud services, and Microsoft's data storage business), social media, and search engines largely work this way.

An equivalent to customs duties for cross-border services does not exist. Indeed, national tax authorities struggle to capture the normal share of tax revenues from international sales of services, using the taxation of domestic transactions as the baseline. Thus governments that impose income taxes attempt to assess the profits of people that sell goods or services on their territory through a foreign headquarters, and those that rely on value-added taxes (which are more widespread globally than profits taxes) seek to tax sales by foreign merchants to domestic consumers. When transactions are dematerialized, everyone struggles. Perhaps no issue has divided the United States (the greatest exporter of dematerialized services) and Europe (the greatest importer) more than this one.[3]

The authors of the Uruguay Round Agreements chose a menu-based approach to promote international trade in services, rather than a top-down regime. Under the General Agreement on Trade in Services (GATS), states choose to submit specified service sectors (banking, law, engineering, advertising, etc.) and delivery systems (seller moves, buyer moves, local subsidiary, virtual delivery) to international law. They have no absolute obligation to make any submissions, but bargain with each other to find deals that, in theory, make every state better off. Any submission to international discipline entails using the WTO dispute resolution process, which was supposed to mean that the permanent WTO court, called the Appellate Body, had the final say. And states from the South, in particular China and India, mostly got a ten-year phase-in period before the obligations applied.

The Uruguay Round approached intellectual property differently. Instead of inviting states to bargain over their commitments, it imposed a broad, one-size-fits-all regime. The Agreement on Trade-Related Aspects of Intellectual Property Rights identifies minimum standards for the protection of patents, trademarks, and copyrights, using the regimes widely applied in the West as the baseline. All members of the WTO must adopt legislation implementing

[3] Ruth Mason, *The Transformation of International Tax*, 114 Am. J. Int'l L. 353 (2020).

this commitment, although again many states from the South enjoyed a phase-in period. The WTO dispute settlement system, including the Appellate Body, applied.

One wrinkle in the TRIPS Agreement is the absence of express rules about enforcement of intellectual property rights. Some experts read the Agreement as mandating legislative action but not administrative enforcement.[4] Under this reading, states in the South that mostly import intellectual property have no duty to take these rights seriously. Foreign sellers of protected goods, such as software, music, and films, would have no claims against states that failed to investigate or punish illegal copying, and their home states would have no basis for invoking the dispute settlement process.

An alternative reading of the TRIPS Agreement would see the silence on enforcement as much like the absence of mandatory commitments in GATS. Both gaps create space for expectations to grow and for law to fill in with implied duties. Supporters of the Uruguay Round Agreements believed that growth in transnational business based on international law had its own logic. People would see the new economy, increasingly entwined with growth of knowledge and technological prowess, as a good thing and law as a means of making that good thing thrive. Rather than regarding the treaty commitments as incomplete, states, businesses, and the technicians who make the system work (increasingly lawyers) would use the formal obligations as a template that could gradually extend into the blank spaces.

Liberal internationalists, as they reap the rewards of the knowledge economy, believe that they stand for progress and that their project has a kind of manifest destiny. Both GATS and TRIPS reflect that outlook. They anticipate that liberal internationalism will sell itself, that states will submit more sectors of service industries to internationally supervised deregulation, and that states will seek greater and more effective enforcement of intellectual property rights as they take in the benefits of a more robust global economy. Liberal internationalists also leave open the possibility of remaking the treaties, either through another round of multilateral negotiations or by interpretive extension through the dispute settlement process. They could plausibly expect, for example, that the Appellate Body would reject the argument that the silence of TRIPS on enforcement meant an absence of obligation. Surely the WTO dispute settlement system, when confronted by brazen failure by a state's law enforcement officials to respect intellectual property rules, would find in the

[4] Rachel Brewster, *The Surprising Benefits to Developing Countries of Linking International Trade and Intellectual Property*, 12 CHI. J. INT'L L. 1 (2011).

concepts of good faith, reasonableness, and proportionality a jurisprudential basis for requiring real enforcement.[5]

The point generalizes. Liberal internationalists saw the Uruguay Round Agreements as both fulfillment of the movement for liberalization of the international law for trade in goods and as a significant first step in the construction of a deeper and broader body of law governing international business. For example, a project that did not make the final cut in 1994, but for which liberal internationalists have high hopes, would bring competition law – what we in the United States for historical reasons call antitrust law – into the WTO family of international regimes.

Competition law, as noted in Chapter 6, attacks two problems in market economies. Single firms might acquire monopoly power and abuse it. Alternately, separate firms might collude to produce the kinds of abuses that a single monopoly firm can inflict. These simple principles disguise many knotty problems, especially as applied to the knowledge economy.

Regulators, policymakers, and politicians are deeply divided over what counts as "abuse" of monopoly power, and particularly over the relevance of noneconomic abuse such as concentrated power. The knowledge economy raises the stakes in this debate. Many of its most prominent firms exercise significant, if ephemeral, monopolies that do not directly make consumers worse off and do provide them superior value at a low cost. For example, Facebook (now Meta) collects no direct charges from its users, but does appropriate data generated by their posts and collects revenues from advertisers for putting ads on their screens. Its critics contend that it inflicts costs on its users indirectly, such as by spreading misinformation and promoting dangerous behavior in the physical world. Consumers benefit from network effects, namely the worldwide reach of the service due to its many subscribers. Does the company's immense power to shape the information environment constitute an abuse, even if no particular consumer suffers and the scope of its membership enhances the value of the services they consume?

Giving the WTO a role in forming competition policy likely would benefit firms and actors in the knowledge economy. An organization devoted to economic growth and easy-to-measure indicators of consumer welfare has no offsetting interest in distributive politics. It would be unlikely to take on challenging issues such as information compartmentalization and knowledge islands, features of the knowledge economy that undermine democratic

[5] Panel Report, Saudi Arabia: Measures Concerning the Protection of Intellectual Property Rights, WTO Doc. WT/DS567/R ¶ 7.250 (June 16, 2020).

governance. It would likely be skeptical of attempts to block scaling that did not take into consideration offsetting consumer benefits.

INTERNATIONAL INVESTMENT PROTECTION

This chapter has already touched on the use of international law to protect foreign investors and hence international capital mobility. Treaties that require states to protect these investors go back a long way. The 1783 Treaty of Paris, which consummated the revolt against British colonialism by recognizing US independence, obligated the newborn country to restore any property confiscated from British nationals, including US residents who supported the Crown during the Revolution, and to guarantee that the states would not cancel the debts owed British merchants. It did not specify a formal dispute settlement method, although Great Britain likely expected the US government and its courts to see that these commitments were honored. When the Confederation of the United States proved inadequate to the task, the country formed a new state that could do the job. The 1789 Constitution made it clear: the Supremacy Clause (Article VI, paragraph 2 of the Constitution) raises above State law "all treaties made … under the authority of the United States," understanding that the Confederation also was the United States and that the Treaty of Paris was made under its authority. The Constitution's Article III gave its creature, the Supreme Court of the United States, the power to review the decisions of state supreme courts and thus to invalidate judgments from the states that violated the Treaty. One of the Supreme Court's first cases used the Treaty to protect Scottish merchants from the depredations of Virginia's legislature.[6]

During the nineteenth century, the capital-exporting world, initially the rich countries of Europe, crafted an international law governing what host states owed to aliens doing business on their territory. Meanwhile the United States transformed itself from a destination for foreign investment, as in transcontinental railroad building after the Civil War, into an exporter of capital, the world's largest from the onset of World War I. It accordingly gave enthusiastic support to the investor-protection project. During the twentieth century, US Secretary of State Cordell Hull voiced what has become the conventional formula: "under every rule of law and equity, no government is

[6] *Ware* v. *Hylton*, 3 US (3 Dall.) 199 (1796); MICHAEL J. KLARMAN, THE FRAMERS' COUP: THE MAKING OF THE UNITED STATES CONSTITUTION 44–46 (2016).

entitled to expropriate private property, for whatever purpose, without provision for prompt, adequate, and effective payment therefor."[7]

In the wake of decolonization during the 1960s and 1970s, countries in the South pushed back against the West's claims about investor protection. They drew support from many international lawyers in the West who joined them in proclaiming a New International Economic Order (NIEO) based on state sovereignty over domestic resources, an obligation to make reparations for colonialism, and a consequent duty to transfer technology to the host state as the price of investing. The UN General Assembly passed resolutions (always over the opposition of the West), academics proclaimed new rules of customary international law, and a handful of states outside the Soviet-dominated bloc banded together to implement the new order. For example, the 1969 Cartagena Agreement originally included Bolivia, Chile, Colombia, Ecuador, and Peru, with Venezuela joining in 1973. It created an Andean Community – an organization intended to present a united front to foreign investors based on NIEO principles.

The world went a different way. The proliferation of multinational firms based in the West fueled the explosion of BITs in the 1980s. Western firms sought more business opportunities in the South and looked to treaties to strengthen their security. Countries in the South acceded to the treaty commitments as a means of signaling their openness to these propositions. These treaties committed countries that hosted investments to the Hull formula of "prompt, adequate, and effective payment" upon expropriation and imposed additional duties of nondiscrimination (also called national treatment), fair and equitable treatment, and full protection and security. They typically made the World Bank's ICSID Convention the required means of dispute resolution, although other tribunals were sometimes selected. The former socialist giants, Russia and China, signed up for these commitments, although Russia, along with Brazil, India, and South Africa, stayed out of the ICSID Convention. Chile left the Andean Community in 1976, and all its remaining members joined BITs that rejected the Cartagena principles.

For the knowledge economy, the profusion of investment treaties in the 1990s and the proliferation of ICSID arbitrations in this century abetted the expansion of supply chains while protecting proprietary information and the control of the knowledge content of products made or sold in countries with weak domestic legal systems. The treaties' institutional dimension – moving

[7] *Letter of the Secretary of State to the Mexican Ambassador*, Aug. 22, 1938, published in 3 Green Haywood Hackworth, Digest of International Law 658–59 (1942).

treaty interpretation and enforcement to arbitration-based ISDS – increased the security of these operations. International arbitration drew on eminent legal practitioners who have a professional as well as ideological commitment to liberal internationalism. Its growth also meant greater opportunities and revenues for prominent law firms, mostly from the West.

ISDS promoted expansion of the regime. First, the substantive duties – compensation for expropriation, nondiscrimination, fair and equitable treatment, and full protection and security – invite extension by interpreters whose sympathies lay with promoting international investment. The meaning of expropriation, for example, can go beyond direct seizure to acts disguised as regulatory measures. Proponents of investor protection re-envisioned seemingly neutral rules of tax, environmental regulation, and consumer protection as seizures of property.

A case in point that has taken up a large part of my life involves Yukos, once the largest energy company in Russia. After jailing the company's leaders, the government in 2004 imposed a massive tax bill on the company based on one-off theories about how the tax law worked. It also blocked the company from auctioning off its liquid assets to pay the assessment, instead seizing its most valuable oil field. It then sold the field to Rosneft, the state-owned oil company, in a rigged daisy chain of transactions. Bankruptcy followed, with most of the company's remaining assets winding up with Rosneft. Foreign shareholders brought treaty claims for this expropriation of their investment, winning them all. Arbiters awarded over $60 billion to the shareholders (who have yet to collect a penny). All this happened because the Russian government devised a means to tax out of existence a powerful and, in its eyes, dangerous firm, using rules that no reasonable taxpayer could have anticipated.[8]

A dispute between Iranian banks and Bahrain offers another take on how conventional regulation can wind up seen as expropriation. Bank Melli and Bank Saderat, Iranian entities subject to US sanctions, formed Future Bank in Bahrain in 2004. They apparently expected their Bahraini bank to undertake transactions from which they were barred under US law. Bahrain closed Future Bank in 2015, supposedly because of its involvement in corruption and sanctions evasion. It then convicted its senior management of financial crimes. A panel constituted under the Bahrain–Iran BIT described the bank's closure as motivated by a "contrived agenda of political retribution" rather than a legitimate regulatory measure. It thus characterized the bank closure as

[8] Paul B. Stephan, *Taxation and Expropriation: The Destruction of the Yukos Oil Empire*, 35 Houston J. Int'l L. 1 (2013).

an unlawful expropriation. It ordered Bahrain to pay $270 million to the Iranian owners.[9]

What these cases have in common are the submission of ordinary regulatory practice – tax collection and bank integrity regulation – to international review. States claim not that they are entitled to seize a foreign investment as a general sovereign power, but rather that they may engage in ordinary, indeed indispensable regulatory practice and impose appropriate sanctions as a means of enforcement. The international tribunal serves not as a filter to sort out permissible from prohibited regulatory measures, but rather as a trier of fact to determine if the regulations were what they purported to be.

International obligations such as fair and equitable treatment and full protection and security pretty much do the same thing. Both apply to state action or inaction that significantly impairs or destroys an investment. With a sufficiently generous understanding of the causal chain between what a state does or should do and the injury to the investor, the treaty can insure against the legal risk that accompany projects in foreign locations.

The other kind of mission creep that benefits participants in the knowledge economy is the tendency of ISDS to bootstrap the arbitral tribunals' jurisdiction. This can happen in at least two ways. The treaties by their terms limit their benefits to eligible investors – subjects of one of the treaty parties – and specify which benefits apply. Tribunals can take a generous approach to who qualifies as a subject, as well as to theories that multiply benefits.

A generous approach to investor eligibility puts form above substance for the purpose of determining who is an eligible investor. A multinational firm can set up a special-purpose company in a state that has a strong investment-protection treaty with the country destined to host the investment. If one looks at the nationality of the special-purpose entity, and not who owns it, then the entity can claim treaty benefits. This move allows anyone willing to absorb the transaction costs to qualify as an eligible investor.

Philip Morris, for example, used a Singapore subsidiary to run distribution and sales of its tobacco products in Australia. This structure gave a US company access to dispute resolution under the Australia–Singapore BIT, even though Australia had rejected an investment-protection chapter when it negotiated its free trade agreement with the United States. After Philip Morris established its business in Australia, the government imposed a plain-paper packing rule on cigarette sales, arguing that tobacco brands trigger addicts and result in more consumption of a dangerous product. Philip

9 *Bank Melli Iran and Bank Saderat Iran* v. *Kingdom of Bahrain*, Permanent Court of Arbitration Case No. 2017-25, Nov. 9, 2021.

Morris used the Singapore treaty's arbitration process to press a claim that the rule constituted an expropriation of its trademarks. It lost on the merits. But just by asserting jurisdiction over the dispute, the tribunal exposed Australia to the risk of future costly claims.[10]

Another mode of extending treaty coverage is expansion of the rights protected, rather than persons who come under it. A most-favored-nation (MFN) clause, common in BITs, allows eligible investors to claim the protection accorded by other treaties that the host state joins later. The clause thus extends treaty benefits to investors who are not nationals of the state that negotiated for such benefits.

By way of illustration, the Soviet Union, when it still existed, entered into several treaties that allow international arbitration over the amount of compensation due an investor because of an expropriation. These treaties excluded the question of whether particular state acts constituted an expropriation. Its treaty with the United Kingdom did this. Looked at in isolation, the treaty denied UK investors any protection against indirect expropriation. A later treaty with Denmark, however, covered indirect expropriations, and a UK investor argued that the most-favored-nation provision in the UK treaty ensured the same scope of protection as the Danish treaty provided. An arbitral tribunal in one of the Yukos cases agreed.[11]

In each of these stories, international bodies broadened the scope of protection for multinational enterprises beyond that expressly provided in the treaties that established those bodies. The direction of the law reflected the logic of the knowledge economy. It expanded legal rules that lower the cost of doing business, including the costs of regulatory compliance, for multinational firms. Not all those firms had knowledge at the heart of their activities, but as the knowledge economy grew, more did.

SUPRANATIONAL INSTITUTIONS

The previous sections of this chapter show how multilateral international legal institutions such as the WTO and the ICSID Convention advance the agenda of liberal internationalism. The international agreements on which these organizations rest constrain states from limiting the movement of economic goods across borders or harming multinational businesses. They also supply

[10] *Philip Morris Asia Ltd.* v. *Commonwealth of Australia*, PCA Case No. 2012-12, Award on Jurisdiction and Admissibility (Perm. Ct. Int'l Arb., Dec. 17, 2015).

[11] *RosInvest Co. UK Ltd.* v. *Russian Federation*, Case No. Arbitration V 079/2005, Award on Jurisdiction, I.I.C. 315 (Arb. Inst. Stockholm Chamber of Commerce, Oct. 2007).

dispute resolution mechanisms that substitute for national courts as a means of enforcing these commitments.

Multinational institutions, however, have a major shortcoming. As long as international law depends ultimately on state consent, holdout states can undermine an institution's credibility and influence. The principle of state consent implies a unilateral veto. Any project that requires broad participation faces the risk that its least enthusiastic party can torpedo the enterprise.

One way to bypass holdouts is to create regional clubs that draw on common interests, cultures, and histories. Club members can use their commonality both to make deeper commitments than those reached in large multilateral organizations and to delegate greater authority to the club's organs to implement and enforce these commitments. Clubs can organize and implement cooperative projects, whether economic, environmental, or cultural, that are too big and interconnected for individual states but too challenging for diverse multilateral institutions to take up.

The old GATT embraced the concept of clubs, as does the WTO now. It generally imposed a rule of universal concessions through its MFN requirement. Under the GATT, MFN means that any increase in friendliness to imports by a member, such as a lower duty, must apply to all members. Significantly, the Agreement provided several exceptions from this baseline obligation, the most significant of which its Article XXIV codified. That provision allows states to form either a customs union (in which the members have a common customs frontier and no duties for transactions within the union) or a free trade area (in which members impose no duties on transactions within the area but otherwise do not coordinate their customs rules) without having to meet the MFN obligation. The GATT thus embraces local liberalization (free trade) without insisting that states in these arrangements abandon customs duties for the entire world.[12]

Without Article XXIV, the architects of free trade in Europe (originally the governments of Belgium, France, Germany, Italy, Luxembourg, and the Netherlands) would have had to give up their project or abandon the GATT. Instead, they went ahead with building a European economic space alongside the GATT, creating first the Coal and Steel Community in 1952, then the European Economic Community (EEC) in 1957.[13] Denmark, Ireland, and the United Kingdom joined in 1973 and the former dictatorships Greece,

[12] Jagdish Bhagwati, Termites in the Trading System: How Preferential Agreements Undermine Free Trade (2008).

[13] Due mostly to French concerns about governance and power, the founders set up three legally distinct treaties for Coal and Steel, Atomic Energy, and Economics, each governed by a Commission, Council, and Court. Thus the EEC was one of three communities, and the technically correct term for the whole enterprise was the European Communities (EC).

Portugal, and Spain in the 1980s. These twelve states in turn founded the European Union in 1993. The European Union grew to twenty-eight states before losing the United Kingdom in 2020.

The substantive commitments that first the European Communities, then the European Union, imposed grew over the years, but they always demanded greater submission to the club, and thus less national sovereign authority, than did the multilateral GATT, and then the WTO. From the first, the EEC limited the power of a state to keep out goods, services, and firms from the other members. It generally forbade barriers to movement of the members' subjects, whether looking for work or more generous welfare. Early on, the Luxembourg Court (the Community's permanent judicial body, not an ad hoc arbitration mechanism as under the old GATT or today's BITs) required national courts to apply community law, even if that means overriding national legislation or administrative rules. The court can even fine states that fail to comply with its orders.

The European Union not only demands free movement of goods, services, firms, and people, but through its own organs administers several critical policy areas. It takes the lead in making and enforcing the policy and laws governing competition, data privacy and security, consumer health and safety, and the environment. Columbia law professor Anu Bradford sees the organs as generating a "Brussels Effect," leveraging its direct control over access to its large common market so as to impose on the world its choices in these areas.[14]

As a structural matter, displacing national regulation with supranational law enforced by supranational institutions seems exactly the approach that advances the interests of people in the knowledge economy. The EU experience, however, reveals an apparent drawback. Taken as a whole, the bloc has great economic clout, as Bradford rightly claims. At the same time, none of its members serves as the home of cutting-edge knowledge-economy firms, especially those engaged in aggregating and interrogating big data so as to develop artificial intelligence (AI). Rather, China and the United States have the technological lead here. Consequently, the European Union may wield its market power to frustrate the AI superpowers. Both its General Data Protection Regulation (GDPR) and its anti-scaling competition policy suggest to some observers, me included, that striving for technological leadership in this section does not motivate its regulatory policies.[15]

14 Anu Bradford, The Brussels Effect: How the European Union Rules the World (2020).

15 Kai-Fu Lee, AI Superpowers: China, Silicon Valley, and the New World Order (2018); Paul B. Stephan, *Big Data and the Future Law of Armed Conflict in Cyberspace*, in The Future Law of Armed Conflict 61 (Matthew C. Waxman & Thomas W. Oakley eds., 2022).

Supranational clubs like the European Union have another feature, however, that makes it harder for them to sustain regulatory choices that thwart economically fruitful technological change. Its organs, and not the ministries of the individual member states, represent the club internationally on matters of international economic policy. This feature has the benefit of reducing veto points. The EU organs can bind its (now) twenty-seven members without their unanimous consent, just as the post-1789 United States, unlike its predecessor Confederation, doesn't need all its states' approval to act. The European Union as a structure thus makes it easier to reach international bargains that advance the knowledge economy, even if its internal political economy pushes it the other way.

Suppose, for example, that technologists come up with better ways to reassure the people who use the internet about exploitation risks than does the clunky GDPR, which some regard as making privacy protection too costly. Further suppose that Chinese advances, none encumbered by a concern about privacy, threaten vital western interests. The structure of the European Union makes it more likely that Europe and the United States, motivated by Chinese competition, could reach a deal on privacy protection that helps the knowledge economy harvest economic benefits from data, notwithstanding European reluctance to support the activities of foreign firms profiting from data related to its nationals.

Liberal internationalists like the EU model so much that they seek to replicate it elsewhere. The George H. W. Bush administration dreamt of a Free Trade Area of the Americas; the George W. Bush and Obama administrations made progress toward that goal through the 2004 Chile Free Trade Agreement, the 2006 Central American Free Trade Agreement, the 2009 Peru Trade Promotion Agreement, and the 2012 Colombia and Panama Trade Promotion Agreements. Free trade areas lack the thicker governance structures – the organs – of a customs union such as the European Union. They do, however, remove regulatory and tax barriers that crimp the knowledge economy. Many of the US free trade agreements also contain investment protection chapters that replicate and extend the rules and institutions created by the BITs.

Regional liberalization elsewhere remains more aspirational than concrete, but the projects exist. Latin America has its Mercosur (the Global Market of the South), a customs union taking in Argentina, Brazil, Paraguay, Uruguay, and Venezuela. Established in the early 1990s, this structure represented a repudiation of the Andean Community's historic protectionism. During the twenty-first century, national populism in Argentina, Brazil, and especially Venezuela upended the mission, but the pressures created by the knowledge economy may yet reverse these trends. The fifteen-member Economic Community of West African States, originally created as a means of managing the postcolonial transition, in the 1990s sought to repurpose itself along the lines of the European Union. Doing this has proved harder than people thought, but again it suggests a blueprint for bringing liberal internationalism to Africa.

In sum, advancing the goals of the knowledge economy through international legal institutions includes regional projects such as the European Union and the Free Trade Area of the Americas that liberalize markets and support investment. These structures have a secondary advantage of simplifying negotiations in cases where one regional bloc due to parochial interests espouses a regulatory norm that frustrates the knowledge economy. Liberal internationalists want an "ever closer union" around the world.

CYBER POLICY

Online businesses – two-sided platforms such as Airbnb, eBay, and Uber, social media, data management and AI, online delivery of entertainment, and the like – do not define the knowledge economy, but they constitute its public face. They first sprang up in spaces where governments largely weren't. Their connections to the physical world, largely satellite, microwave, and landline networks, as well as their need for finance and payment systems, make them vulnerable to government regulation.[16] In the 1990s, though, the businesses stole a march on the regulators, operating across borders with very few content restrictions. Their principal recreational products were pornography and gambling, largely because states were slow to adapt their enforcement strategies to the new delivery system.

At the time that firms first started to make money in cyberspace, international legal protection from state-imposed obstacles to their business seemed unnecessary. The barriers did not exist. Over the course of this century, states caught up with the firms and started to limit their freedom of action. I consider here what these firms might want from international law and what governments devoted to their interests might do.

Consider first national content regulation and barriers to entering domestic markets. As cyberspace burgeoned, states recognized its influence and began to intervene. European efforts to regulate hate speech got attention early on. China's Great Firewall represents the state of the art of such interventions.

[16] Jack Goldsmith & Tim Wu, Who Controls the Internet? Illusions of a Borderless World (2006).

China complements this surveillance and intervention system with rules that increase the scope of its enforcement. It mandates that foreign firms providing cyber services to people on its territory maintain physical data storage there. The resulting security risk deters most western online businesses from entering its market. A standing threat to bring criminal sanctions against local employees backs up these requirements.

No international regime currently authorizes or limits government control over the content of cyber communications. China and Russia proposed treaties that would endorse content regulation and oblige other states to cooperate with national censorship. Objections from the West blocked them. The GATS allows China (or any other state) to impose limits on foreign cyber businesses such as a physical presence requirement. A GATS party must meet transparency requirements when it regulates, but otherwise can do what it wishes.

Firms in the knowledge economy may regard existing international law as sufficient to deal with these issues. As to content regulation, they might prefer the international status quo. Local rules, whether bans on gambling or on subversive expression, create a market for workarounds. One consequence of the Great Firewall, for example, is a thriving industry producing virtual proxy networks that allow users to circumvent local restrictions. What these firms would oppose are proposals such as those from China and Russia that would raise the cost of circumvention technologies.

Besides creating a market for new products, a diversity of state content regulation may benefit incumbent firms and thus reinforce the tendency toward monopoly in the knowledge economy. Regulations give larger firms with greater resources a competitive edge over startup competitors. Amazon, for example, used locational technologies that it had already developed to accommodate German bans on commerce in Nazi artifacts without abandoning sales elsewhere in the world.

As to barriers to entry, the GATS regime already offers a practical means to address rules such as China's local-presence requirement. The GATS both recognizes a host country's right to impose such rules and offers them an incentive to relax them. Under this treaty, WTO members can offer liberalization in one area in return for reciprocal concessions. China might, for example, suspend its local-presence requirements if the United States and the European Union dropped their national security objections to Chinese products such as Huawei's 5G routers.

The one area where governments early on sought to shape cyberspace was competition policy. The Microsoft litigation, which ran from 1994 to 2002, challenged the way that company used exclusive-dealing contracts and licenses to support its market-dominating products. A federal court of appeals rejected a radical proposal to break up the company and instead curtailed, without banning, its contracts with third parties such as internet-service providers and application designers.[17] In both *Microsoft* and in prominent cases this century, US courts generally have accepted arguments about the benefits of scaling as a justification for an industry concentration.[18]

As noted earlier, the European Union moved later but took a different direction, regarding industry concentration as a problem even where it produced short-term benefits for consumers. The Luxembourg Court, however, has not yet addressed the issue.[19] As with content regulation, no international regime exists for competition policy.[20]

To repeat a core claim of Chapter 6, firms in the knowledge economy gain from scaling. Accordingly, they should prefer the US approach to competition policy to that of the European Union. In a world where the US government saw itself as the ally of big tech (not, to be clear, the present government), it would push the Europeans to accept short-term consumer welfare as a justification for monopoly power. It also would place a heavy burden of proof on regulators claiming that long-term harms outweigh immediate consumer benefits. This pressure could end up codified in an international agreement, more likely bilateral than multilateral.

An emerging issue for cyber businesses is data privacy and protection. In the industry's early days, online data storage and processing benefited from the absence of any rules. Rather than charging users full value for services rendered, many firms instead sought to monetize the data generated by their operations. Some mined the data themselves to improve their marketing and development strategies. Others sold or licensed the data to other firms. The strategy worked because no law clearly gave customers veto rights over the use of the information generated by engagement with these firms. Start-ups entered the sector, but large data-oriented businesses also learned to mine and manage data generated by their transactions. Retailers, first Walmart and then Amazon, learned to target advertising, and banks learned how to do financial risks and opportunities better.

17 *U.S.* v. *Microsoft Corp.*, 253 F.3d 34 (D.C. Cir. 2001); *New York* v. *Microsoft Corp.*, 224 F. Supp. 2d 76 (D.D.C. 2002).

18 *Ohio* v. *American Express Co.*, 138 S. Ct. 2274 (2018); *FTC* v. *Qualcomm Inc.*, 969 F.3d 974 (9th Cir. 2020).

19 Case T-201/04, *Microsoft Corp.* v. *Comm'n*, 2007 E.C.R. II-3601 (General Court).

20 Paul B. Stephan, *Global Governance, Antitrust, and the Limits of International Cooperation*, 38 Cornell Int'l L.J. 173 (2005).

In this century, regulators started to reconsider the premise of this business model. In the United States, California took the first step to limit what cyber firms could do with customer data. The European Union took more ambitious steps, opening a greater divide between it and the United States. The GDPR requires firms subject to EU jurisdiction to obtain customer consent before processing personal data. It addresses both collection and exploitation of personal data, but excludes uses by EU governments in the course of the exercise of their lawful authority. The GDPR also functions as a trade barrier due to its stringent limits on the export of data. China introduced similar legislation in 2021.

Basic economic theory predicts that actors in the knowledge economy will not oppose privacy regulation as such but will resist bans on the monetization of data. An approach to data privacy that draws on property law could satisfy their interests. Firms could adapt to a range of rules assigning initial ownership in data, either to the source or the collector. For monetization to work, however, they would need rules establishing the alienability of data and clarifying the prerequisites for data assignments.

An international regime to standardize rules of ownership, alienability, and assignment of data would not have to prescribe substantive rules. General adoption of a choice-of-law rule governing the ownership, purchase, and sale of data would suffice. That rule would have to reflect the dematerialization of cyber transactions, but this presents only a modest challenge. The law could focus on the nationality of the parties as a substitute for the "location" of the data or its transfer. Thus rules choosing the applicable law based on the nationality of the seller or buyer would work.

Were international practice to settle on clear and stable choice-of-law rules, the need for standardization of substantive rules of property in data and data transactions would diminish. Cyber businesses would resist local regimes that threw up significant obstacles to alienability, perhaps by boycotting those states. As with content regulation, incumbent monopolists might prefer local regimes that made data acquisition costly so as to deter start-ups. They otherwise could adapt to almost any other outcome that reduced legal risk by providing legal clarity.

These conjectures suggest that, in a world where the knowledge economy calls the shots, international agreements standardizing the rules for cross-border sales of data and data products should emerge. Such agreements could supplement local initiatives such as the GDPR and China's comparable legislation. Firms would have to comply with local rules to acquire data but, having established ownership, could do what they want with it.

To summarize, the economic interests of the portion of the knowledge economy focused on online operations support some forms of international law more than others. Firms can adapt to local censorship and privacy regimes but would resist international efforts to embrace and standardize censorship and privacy protection. They would want to adapt existing international trade law, especially the GATS, to encourage liberalization of local-presence rules such as China's. They also would seek to rebalance local competition law with general free trade principles. Accordingly, they would support either a bilateral agreement between the European Union and the United States or a new WTO agreement on competition for the purpose of reducing limits on scaling of knowledge-economy firms.

ANTIDISCRIMINATION AND INTERNATIONAL HUMAN RIGHTS

The battle against tribalism, misogyny, and other habits and customs that divide people for purposes of oppression and domination has deep historical and cultural roots. The barbarities inflicted by German National Socialism, especially the mass murder of Jews during its conquests and later retreats, inspired an international movement to banish genocide and to protect human rights. For the victors, this was complicated. The Soviet Union rejected the idea that human rights included the liberal concept of democracy, and the United Kingdom and United States had hardly purged themselves of systemic racism when the war ended. None of countries at the time supported female empowerment as a matter of right. This last project remained a generation away in much of the West and faced high cultural obstacles in most of the socialist world, egalitarian ideology notwithstanding. Yet the battle had begun.

Over the following decades the struggle continued and grew. The International Convention on the Elimination of All Forms of Racial Discrimination entered into force in 1969, with all of the rich and socialist world (other than North Korea) joining. Women's rights attracted greater support over time and eventually acquired an international instrument, the Convention on the Elimination of All Forms of Discrimination Against Women, which entered into force in 1981. Because its constitution makes treaty ratification difficult and a few cultural conservatives in the Senate objected to the treaty, the United States remains one of the few countries not to have joined it. Federal legislation, however, does regulate sexism even in the absence of any international obligation. The new frontier in this century has become the protection of sexual minorities, a campaign that has made great gains in the West but far less in the South.

These struggles have their own stories and do not often enter into conversations about the world economy. I do not believe that they rest on self-interest, but rather on inspiring moral and compassionate motives. It does not demean them, however, to point out where the struggles converge with the interests of the knowledge economy. My claim is only that the imperatives of the knowledge economy reinforce the struggle against discrimination.

The knowledge economy does not make us better people as it creates wealth. As Chapter 6 shows and Chapter 8 explores in depth, it promotes other kinds of inequality – those based on talent and skill rather than on race, ethnicity, or gender. To the extent that talent and skill are themselves immutable characteristics, or at least hard to change – an empirical question on which the jury manifestly remains out – the knowledge economy contributes to its own kind of invidious discrimination. All that it pursues is stripping away artificial social arrangements that frustrate people, regardless of color, tribe, or gender, from expressing their talent and acquiring the skills suitable to that talent. It runs on competition that rewards talent and skill. What competition does not do is erase disadvantages such as a general lack of ability.

What winners in the knowledge economy want is legal structures that oppose social habits and practices that keep talented people from finding their place in the knowledge economy. There is no reason to think that skin color and gender have anything to do with talents and skills that the knowledge economy values. Perpetuating the subjugation of people of color, women, and sexual minorities offends many values that have nothing to do with material interest, but it also interferes with the harnessing of talent to production. People, firms, and polities that fight subjugation will improve their odds in economic competition and will want the law to help them fight.

Evidence for growing support of these nondiscrimination norms comes mostly from the West, and especially from states where the knowledge economy first emerged. The United States began to tackle racial injustice seriously in the 1960s, and women's rights in the 1970s. The gap between aspiration and accomplishment remains large, but it narrowed over time. President Truman ordered the desegregation of the military in 1948, the Supreme Court proclaimed the essentiality of racial desegregation (while initially not doing much about it) in 1954, and Congress adopted a suite of antidiscrimination laws between 1964 and 1968. The legislators who added a ban on discrimination "on the basis of sex" to the 1964 Civil Rights Act did so hoping to derail the legislation, but the ploy backfired. During the 1970s the Supreme Court increasingly took on sex discrimination, using constitutional and statutory interpretation as tools to do so. Gender discrimination came much later. Only in 2020 did the Supreme Court confirm that the 1964 Act reaches discrimination against homosexuals and transgender people, although a lower court of appeals had reached this outcome in 2017.[21]

Australia, Canada, and the European Union, among leading rich states, followed a similar trajectory, sometimes earlier and sometimes later than the United States. Each has robust domestic institutions to give these commitments bite. In Europe, the Strasbourg Court took the lead, often going further than most of the states governed by the European Convention on Human Rights. Similarly, the Inter-American Court on Human Rights, which has jurisdiction over the majority of members of the Organization of American States, joined the struggle.

Internationally, multilateral treaties applicable to most states exist but have less impressive enforcement mechanisms. The antidiscrimination conventions on both race and women have committees to which people can address their grievances, but the committees can only investigate as well as name and shame, not authorize other sanctions. To date, the United Nations has not advanced any multilateral instrument protecting sexual minorities. In parts of the South, Russia in particular but also China and parts of Africa and the Middle East, opposition to such protection is strong.

IMMIGRATION

Free immigration serves two purposes of firms in the knowledge economy. Mobility of talent makes matches of the right person to the job for knowledge-based production easier. Better matching means higher-quality output. Second, mobility of people lacking high-end skills who can provide basic services at a low cost makes it easier to maintain knowledge workers as they work, and thus lowers the cost of knowledge workers, the essential input of the knowledge economy. Anything that allows an economic actor to increase the quality of its product while lowering the cost of production gives it an edge over its competitors.

There are, of course, other reasons to support freer immigration. First, people tend to migrate to places where they can live better lives and contribute more to society. Not having to deal with rampant corruption or widespread violence, as well as terrible roads and intermittent electricity, represents a life upgrade.

Moreover, many immigrants move not only to improve their lives on the margin, but to escape truly awful circumstances. Gang violence, famine, and

[21] *Bostock* v. *Clayton Co.*, Georgia, 140 S. Ct. 1731 (2020); *Hively* v. *Ivy Tech Community College of Ind.*, 853 F.3d 339 (7th Cir. 2017).

natural disaster drive people from their homes. The people of Haiti, to choose an example of special salience in the United States, in recent years faced a catastrophic earthquake on top of regular hurricane disasters and then a complete breakdown in social order after the assassination of President Moïse, all layered on deeply rooted poverty. Basic human compassion pushes people to find a way to accommodate those who make it to the United States. Those fleeing the humanitarian disaster that is Syria or catastrophic, often climate-change-related conditions in sub-Saharan Africa provoke similar responses from Europeans. Most recently, the Russian invasion of Ukraine drove millions of people west into Poland and the rest of Europe.

As with antidiscrimination commitments, it does not disparage the sincerity of the desire to help people better their life chances to note that it can overlap with the interests of the knowledge economy. Compassion and a desire to create wealth can converge. We can disparage countries that exclude outsiders both because of the meanness of the exclusion and because it undermines that country's ability to compete in an increasingly open international economic system. What benefits the interests of people in the knowledge economy is more immigration, especially of skilled workers but also of people who can provide basic services at a lower cost than their domestic counterparts.

Implementation of these goals in the present world confronts legal obstacles, however. The default in today's world is state control of its borders, with wide variation in the efforts that individual states make to do this. An international regime or club rules can restrict states that frustrate immigrants. Only two broad multilateral treaties currently in force do this, and they have only limited scope.

The 1951 Convention Relating to the Status of Refugees and its 1967 Protocol provide the principal limits on state choices regarding immigration. Members of customs unions or free trade areas sometimes face additional constraints on their power to block immigration from other members. The European Union, for example, generally protects the right of its nationals to migrate within the Union. NAFTA, by contrast, liberalized rules for professionals moving across borders on a temporary (three-year) basis but did nothing for people who lacked exceptional skills but sought to transform their lives. Chapter 16 of the United States–Canada–Mexico Agreement (USCMA), NAFTA's successor agreement, retains this regime.

The 1951 Convention and the 1967 Protocol bestow limited but significant rights, most importantly that of *non-refoulèment*, the right of people at risk not to be returned to persecution. It forbids a state from deporting refugees, defined as people with a well-founded fear of persecution due to their politics or because of membership in a racial, ethnic, religious, or social group targeted for mistreatment in their home country, back to their place of origin. Unless immigrants qualify as refugees, international law (EU law aside) leaves states free to deport them.

Proponents of immigration, from compassion as well as to lower the costs of the knowledge economy, seek to broaden the protected class. They would expand the scope of the categories that define persecution. The Convention and Protocol, for example, do not mention sexual orientation as a category of persecution that entitles its victims to refugee status. One can plausibly argue, however, that sexual minorities belong to a "social group" and, when threatened with violence or legal sanctions for that reason, meet the persecution requirement. An even more ambitious move would regard the desperately poor as a social group and the failure to provide realistic opportunities to improve life chances as a form of persecution. This line of thought would treat anyone fleeing a failed or failing state as belonging to a social group that has a well-founded fear of persecution.

* * *

This chapter reviews the law and institutions that advance the interests of people and firms within the knowledge economy. It describes the emergence and growth of international arrangements that further those interest. The existing legal structures indicate how states might extend them further in accordance with the interests of people in the knowledge economy.

8

Losing and Location in the Knowledge Economy

The View from the Hinterlands and the Chinese Alternative

The knowledge economy makes many people better off and a small minority very wealthy. It also creates new things – drugs, smartphones and their applications, low-cost communication at a distance – that expand the reach and pleasure of all people. It pushes governments to remove impediments to free movement of people as well as to goods, services, and strategic and portfolio investment. Taking down these barriers disrupts and sometimes destroys incumbent firms and displaces their workers. Both knowledge workers and poor people from low-social-capital societies migrate toward sites where the knowledge economy has put down roots. The disrupted and damaged exit the great global cities that drive the knowledge economy and move to hinterlands.

Global cities have local effects. Thriving takes place in specific urban places, not throughout a country. Knowledge clusters attract migrants and drive out incumbents who cannot adapt to the transformations wrought by the knowledge economy. Outside of these knowledge-cluster cities, many workers stay behind when jobs go elsewhere. Either way, the knowledge economy's losers mostly end up in hinterlands, including failed cities. Location thus both molds and reflects attitudes toward the institutions that sustain the knowledge economy, depending on where the winners and the losers concentrate.

LOCALITY

Long before the knowledge economy emerged, economists knew that successful businesses tend to group together, that cutting-edge production "localizes." Looking back at the industrial revolution from the perspective of 1920, Alfred Marshall, one of the founders of the modern economics discipline, attributed the clustering of manufacturing in a handful of cities to three factors – the pooling of a supply of skilled labor that firms could draw on quickly as needs changed, access to infrastructure (such as specialized machinery or construction equipment) that firms could use without shouldering the costs of exclusive ownership, and spillovers in knowledge. Pooling of labor and other inputs gave firms flexibility and sustained higher-quality goods and services at a lower cost. Spillovers allowed knowledge to diffuse more widely without destroying the incentive to create rather than copy.[1]

Updating those findings seventy years later, Paul Krugman refined Marshall's observations and adapted them to the postindustrial knowledge economy. He showed how both Milan's fashion industry and Silicon Valley's tech sector draw on pooled labor and non-labor inputs as well as knowledge spillovers. He noted that leading service industries tend not just to localization, but urbanization. The great global cities such as London, New York, and Tokyo no longer had much manufacturing but sectors such as finance, insurance, and lawyering dominated. As knowledge grew in economic importance, so did locating production (firms) in places with many knowledge workers and people who could look after them.[2]

CITIES

Although Krugman saw cities as a facet of locality, his update of Marshall did not concentrate on them as such. Much of what we know about the economic role of cities, as opposed to localities, is due to urban theorist Jane Jacobs, who, like Marshall, wrote before knowledge had become the dominant factor of production. She was a groundbreaking social theorist and economist in spite of her lack of formal academic credentials.[3] Her central insight is that in the modern world, cities, rather than nation states, provide the focus of economic activity.[4] To understand what happens in a country's economy, an observer must look at what its cities do. Throughout history, she demonstrated, cities prospered when their residents served as a source of insights and adaptations:

1 Alfred Marshall, Principles of Economics 267–77 (8th ed. 1920).

2 Paul Krugman, Geography and Trade (1991).

3 At the stage in her life when she should have been accumulating university degrees, Jacobs faced a high barrier to women in higher education driven by the returning veterans from World War II and a national policy of sacrificing the professional goals of women to the advancement of the men who had served. This obstacle did not stop her from becoming one of the great urban theorists of the later twentieth century. Nobel laureates such as Robert Lucas drew on her work. She is better known today than her younger brother, John Butzner, a successful lawyer who became a much admired judge on the US Court of Appeals for the Fourth Circuit.

4 Jane Jacobs, The Economy of Cities (1969).

> [Cities'] vital functions are to serve as primary developers and primary expanders of economic life, functions that work not in the least like perpetual motion. They require continually repeated inputs of energy in two specific forms: innovations, which at bottom are inputs of human insight, and ample replacement of imports, which at bottom are inputs of the human capacity to make adaptive innovations.[5]

Whether a city could perform these functions well determines whether they, and the countries that claim them, succeed or fail.

Jacobs contrasted the dynamic potential of cities with the hinterlands – what she called "supply regions." These regions might successfully produce goods for the world market, but they lack the dense social and economic networks that facilitate innovation and adaptation to change. She told the story of Uruguay, a country that prospered for several generations as a source of meat, wool, and leather for the rest of the world. After World War II, European measures that limited meat imports along with the emergence of low-cost substitutes for wool and leather devastated Uruguay's livestock-based export economy. Its government's attempts at top-down industrialization misfired, because the country lacked an urban capacity to sustain those projects. Uruguay went from a prosperous democracy to a country plagued by poverty and terrorism.

Jacobs also demonstrated that technological innovations in hinterlands, when they do succeed, can produce massive local costs with ramifications (what economists call externalities) for cities. She looked at the Scottish Highlands in the late eighteenth century and the US rural South in the mid-twentieth century. Both places relied on outdated technology for agriculture, their basic economic activity, and were markedly poorer than other regions of their countries. In the Highlands, technological change came in the form of the Cheviot, a breed of sheep that produced more and better wool than the native variant but also needed more food. The native sheep, which survived on nearly barren land, supported only subsistence production, while the Cheviot generated substantial export revenues. The landowners, themselves impoverished but not as vulnerable as their tenants, adapted to this new technology by imposing enclosures on the land so as to sustain the Cheviot. This exercise of property rights ousted the larger part of the Highland population so that more of the sparse land could be devoted to pasturage. The former tenants migrated to Glasgow and Edinburgh, themselves economically

[5] Jane Jacobs, Cities and the Wealth of Nations 193 (1984).

backward compared to London, Birmingham, Liverpool, Manchester, and Leeds. There they suffered greatly.

In the United States, government interventions during the New Deal and after World War II rapidly increased Southern farmers' access to machinery and other agricultural technologies already widely used outside the region. Output grew and the return to unskilled labor pancaked, driving many former farmworkers to Atlanta and the great cities of the Northeast, Midwest, and West Coast. These cities, already dealing with a sudden growth in labor supply as veterans returned to the workforce, found themselves unable to integrate many of these domestic immigrants into their economies. Racial segregation multiplied the burdens of Black immigrants. Technological improvements thus turned rural backwardness in the South into urban blight elsewhere in the country.

These stories have a common theme – hinterlands upgrade their economic activity through knowledge, if at all, only at the cost of displacing local workers. Jacobs shows that cities must do the heavy lifting in development, either by commanding new technologies (which did not happen in Uruguay) or by finding productive uses for people forced out of hinterlands by knowledge gains (which did not happen in the Highlands during the enclosure period or in the United States during the great migration out of the South).

Jacobs contrasts innovations that push people out of the hinterlands, as in Scotland and the US South, with transformations within cities that pull in people. She cites Italy's North, which drew migrants from its poor South to fill labor gaps in its flourishing economy. As the knowledge economy took off in the West, China's development policy, based principally on luring workers from the countryside to newly dynamic places such as Shenzhen, a wholly invented city, followed the same principle. Concentrating technological changes in urban areas, whether without a government mandate as in Italy or through government planning as in Shenzhen, multiplies the cities' productivity with benign effects on the hinterlands. Unlike innovation in the hinterlands that destroys jobs, urban transformation brings workers to places with great opportunities and physical capital. Here hinterland depopulation means better life chances for more people, not urban poverty, as well as transfer payments (remittances) from the urban workers to sustain those left behind. Either way, increasing the knowledge portion of economic activity broadens the gap between cities and hinterlands.

Jacobs wrote mostly before the rise of the knowledge economy. The trend of the last thirty years, however, involves movement across national borders. Columbia sociologist Saskia Sassen pioneered the study of cities under conditions of increasingly internationalized economies. Writing at the start of the 1990s, she describes the rise of global cities across four dimensions:

> [F]irst, as highly concentrated command posts in the organization of the world economy; second, as key locations for finance and for specialized service firms, which have replaced manufacturing as the leading economic sectors; third, as sites of production, including the production of innovations, in these leading industries; and fourth, as markets for the products and innovations produced.[6]

She shows how these changes in functions both reflect and induce transformative changes in the movement of workers. Knowledge workers flock to these great cities, attracted by the demand for knowledge and skills that the rising economic sectors generate. Low-skill workers from impoverished countries cross national borders to take advantage of the cities' social capital while providing essential services to knowledge workers. The global cities thus exploit global hinterlands as sources of cheap labor.

These migrations, Sassen observes, are intensely urban. She documents the rise of roughly forty global cities, places where the organization and control of economic activity play out. Transnational executives and professionals – all knowledge workers – come to the global cities to do their jobs and largely prosper, while low-income workers, commonly illegal or informal, arrive in even larger numbers. What these immigrants share is a mostly successful search for a more fulfilling and better-paid life. In that sense, both groups benefit from the knowledge economy. What divides them, however, are personal security, legal status, pay, and access to housing, health care, and education.[7]

As Sassen reports, many of these cities use legal regimes that reinforce the social chasm between close neighbors. Chapter 6 notes China's Hukou system. Under Chinese law, people may migrate to the great cities in search of work, but without a local permit (Hukou) they have very few rights. They can live only in quarters provided by an employer, typically crowded and austere barracks. They get only what amenities their employers supply, and family members have no entitlement to the medical care, education, or other forms of social support and integration that a nominally socialist society

6 Saskia Sassen, The Global City: New York, London, Tokyo 3–4 (1991).

7 Saskia Sassen, Territory, Authority, Rights: From Medieval to Global Assemblages 293–95, 315 (updated ed. 2008); Saskia Sassen, Losing Control: Sovereignty in an Age of Globalization 94 (1996).

provides. Because their urban lives are at the pleasure of the employer, job switching is hard. Those who lack a formal job live at the sufferance of the police, who can harass and deport them.

The Chinese approach closely mirrors the *limitchiki* system that the Soviet Union developed to control its urban workers. Everyone in the Soviet Union had to have a domestic passport, and only people with special skill and talents could obtain one for Moscow and the other great Soviet cities. Everyone else could migrate to these places only on the basis of a limited domestic passport that left the worker completely dependent on the employer. An analogy to indentured servitude in Colonial America comes to mind, except that the indentured got full civil rights when their contracts concluded. The *limitchiki* had access only to resources that the employer tendered, rather than to socially provided benefits such as housing, education, and health care that people with unlimited residence permits got as a matter of right. In spite of findings by a constitutional tribunal that this form of oppression violated the country's international obligations, it survived in Russia well into the post-Soviet period.[8]

In the West today, we rarely see such transparent erasure of workers' rights. Informality and indifferent enforcement of immigration law, however, leads to a similar outcome. Sassen shows how Japan, the United Kingdom, and the United States created the status of illegal alien by tolerating undocumented immigrants who work in Tokyo, London, and New York. Relaxed law enforcement serves employers' ends. They exploit the immigrants' vulnerability to deportation and harassment to lower their labor costs and maximize their control.

In the thirty years since Sassen wrote, the great centers of the knowledge economy depend even more on informal immigrants. The number of people willing to face the risks of illegality to build a better life for themselves skyrocketed. In the United States, the Trumpian theater of bigotry, highlighted by separating families at the border and putting children in cages, distracted from the ongoing use of undocumented people in urban service work. Brexit has, if anything, increased London's dependence on informal immigrant labor. The greater share of the knowledge economy in the life of the West has meant even higher demand for low-cost support workers.

[8] Dietrich A. Loëber, *Limitchiki: On the Legal Status of Migrant Workers in Large Soviet Cities*, 11 Soviet Union/Union Soviétique 301 (1984); Paul B. Stephan, *The Fall – Understanding the Collapse of Soviet Communism*, 29 Suffolk U. L. Rev. 17, 24–26 (1995).

HINTERLANDS

Sassen's focus on cities leaves out the urban–hinterland divide to which Jacobs directs our attention. Sassen is a sociologist, not an economist, and not interested in theories that tie urban growth to hinterland desolation. Her portraits of global cities are invaluable. Yet, as recent research by Princeton economists Anne Case and Angus Deaton shows, it is exactly the changes in the hinterland that drive national populism in much of the rich world.

People who come to the great global cities, whether as knowledge workers or low-skill immigrants, mostly do so expecting their lives to get better, even if knowledge workers will harvest a much greater share than others. Notwithstanding the shocking inequality between knowledge workers and low-cost service-worker immigrants, both see the knowledge economy as providing new and better opportunities. In contrast, many people in the hinterland, mostly stay-behinds rather than immigrants, fear that things will get worse. Their deep pessimism, economic and cultural, too often becomes a toxic mix of radical fury and despair. In the South, remittances from urban workers may dull the pain. In the West, however, the sad effects of displacement and disappointment go unmitigated.

The best account of the knowledge economy's human casualties comes from Case and Deaton. They first published their research in 2015, the same year that Deaton won a Nobel Prize for his groundbreaking work on consumption, welfare, and poverty. Their article detected a clear geographical pattern in deaths and morbidities such as addiction and mental illness. They turned their initial research into a bestselling book in 2020.[9]

Case and Deaton study deaths and illness in the United States and the United Kingdom, with emphasis on the former. What first piqued their interest was data indicating a declining life expectancy for White middle-aged men (White used as a shorthand for people who identify as not Black, not Asian, not Native American, and not Hispanic). They find that a sharp uptick in what they call deaths of despair caused a drop in overall life expectancy during the twenty-first century. They track these deaths by locality and link them to a range of socioeconomic factors such as mental health, employment, educational level, and family stability. They show that in the parts of the country most blighted because of the knowledge economy, social failure produces lives in distress that too often end prematurely.

[9] Anne Case & Angus Deaton, Deaths of Despair and the Future of Capitalism (2020); Anne Case & Angus Deaton, *Rising Morbidity and Mortality in Midlife among White Non-Hispanic Americans in the 21st Century*, 112 Proc. Nat'l Acad. Sci. 15,078 (2015).

Case and Deaton build their work around two sets of data, one for causes of death and the other for educational attainment. They define deaths of despair as those resulting from acute liver disease (a good indicator of substance abuse, especially alcoholism), accidental drug overdoses, and suicide. They divide the adult population into those who never attended college, those who attended but did not graduate, and those who possess at least a BA degree. They then track the distribution of these characteristics throughout the country. They also look at other signs of suffering, including chronic pain, obesity, eligibility for disability-based social insurance, mental illness, and broken family life, to trace the connection to mortality.

What their data tells us is surprising and disturbing. The increase in US deaths of despair in this century largely involved Whites aged 25–64 who never attended college. Black people in the same age cohort saw a growth in the rate of death from alcoholism and drug overdoses, but not from suicide. Thus, although deaths of despair grew somewhat during this century for people who identified as Black, most of the growth occurred among Whites, with their annual rate of deaths of despair passing Blacks in 2003 and rising continuously thereafter. The incidence of deaths of despair among people with at least a BA were much lower for both Whites and Blacks in the same age cohort. The death rate over the course of this century for degree holders grew only slightly for Whites and declined a little for Blacks.

Other indicators of unhappy lives – mental illness, chronic pain, social security disability, divorce, and out-of-wedlock children – largely track the never-attended-college variable. These also increased disproportionately for Whites in this century. Turning to income data, Case and Deaton report that, for Whites, the wage gap between those with a BA and those without increased for people the same age as the twenty-first century unfolded, and that employment rates for both men and women who do not have a BA declined steadily during this period.

Case and Deaton take pains to make clear that these data do not undercut our understanding of the disproportionate social and economic burdens borne by Black people in the United States and the United Kingdom. What they show instead is the narrowing of the gap between Whites and Blacks as to certain indicators of misery, but only with respect to those who never attended college. Their work indicates that the twenty-first century has not been especially good for Blacks in the United States and the United Kingdom but nor has it substantially increased their suffering. Whites who never attended college, however, saw a significant drop in well-being, as measured by health data, and a widening income gap between themselves and the better educated. What Case and Deaton uncover are increases in misery, the delta as economists call it, not absolute levels of oppression.

Case and Deaton use county-level data to confirm that these trends play out locally. For recent years, one number, a county's portion of White population that never attended college, gives a good indication of the rate of deaths of despair, percentage of population receiving social security disability benefits, incidence of chronic pain, and diagnoses of mental illness. This correlation did not exist to any significant extent in the twentieth century and grew stronger as the twenty-first century unfolded.

In the United States and the United Kingdom, the places where despair and misery have gone up are socially as well as geographically distant from the great global cities. In the United States, Greater Appalachia and the Deep South lead the way, as also does rural Maine, the West excluding California, upper Michigan, and much of Texas. In the United Kingdom, the contrast is between London and the rest of the country. Case and Deaton describe the localization of misery and death as a product of geographical segregation:

> The worlds of the more and less educated have split apart ... At work, companies are today more likely to be segregated by education, and ... firms are outsourcing many low-skill jobs that used to be done in-house, where people with different levels of education worked together and were part of the same company. The more and less educated are now more segregated in where they live, the successful in places where housing prices are high and to which the less successful do not have access. Greater geographical segregation has widened the gap in the quality of schools attended by the more and less educated.[10]

Substituting "better at navigating the knowledge economy" for "more educated," we get a good snapshot of how the knowledge economy has sorted out winners and losers in the United States and the United Kingdom.

Finally, misery and despair affect entire communities, not just the individual victims. Suicides and deaths from drug abuse and alcoholism affect families and others tied to those who die. These tragedies overwhelm places and regions. Case and Deaton describe them as dying communities – that is, places where individual deaths and misery define the local society.

What we have, then, is both an economic theory about the local effects of the knowledge economy and an abundance of data about the local distribution of misery and despair. The Case and Deaton data bolster and clarify a narrative that first emerged in the United States in the 1970s. It was in that

[10] Anne Case & Angus Deaton, Deaths of Despair, *supra* note 9, at 52–53.

decade that formerly cutting-edge manufacturing industries in the United States, such as cars and consumer electronics, began to move their production offshore or to abandon the market entirely in favor of imports. The owners of the incumbent firms – suppliers of capital – could park their money elsewhere, and the top management could find new outlets for their skills. Workers from the shop floor and other low-skill people who supported production lost their jobs. Government-funded retraining programs did little to help them adapt. Those young and unconnected enough to move within the country to find new work did so. Those who could not took lower-paying, lower-status jobs, retired early, went on disability or welfare, or looked to their families for subsistence. A generation later, deaths of despair exploded.

Over the decades, this story seemed to capture a growing part of American life. The triumph of liberal internationalism in the 1990s accelerated the process of dislocation and displacement. Economists debate the effect of NAFTA, the Uruguay Round Agreements, and admission of China to the WTO on manufacturing jobs in the United States, but a consensus now points in the direction of measurable negative local impacts.[11]

At roughly the same time, a growing number of people from the global South moved to the United States. Some were highly skilled, such as the East and South Asian engineers who populate Silicon Valley. Others lacked formal education or training and took low-wage jobs such as in construction, restaurant work, child care, the bottom stratum of the health-care system, housekeeping, and landscaping.[12] A portion of the people displaced by the immigrants became candidates for the deaths of despair and the other forms of misery that Case and Deaton uncovered. Their misfortune spread throughout their communities.

Meanwhile the beneficiaries of the knowledge economy – not just the plutocrats who made fabulous fortunes, but the well-educated professionals and nimble entrepreneurs who prosper without becoming super-rich, the products of élite schools and plugged-in people who made their livings by manipulating images, words, and, increasingly, code, separated themselves from the displaced as well as the low-human-capital portion of the new immigrants. As Case and Deaton observe, they go to different schools, attend

[11] Daron Acemoglu, David Autor, David Dorn, Gordon H. Hanson & Brendan Price, *Import Competition and the Great US Employment Sag of the 2000s*, 34 J. LAB. ECON. S141 (2016); David Autor, David Dorn, Lawrence F. Katz, Christina Patterson & John Van Reenen, *The Fall of the Labor Share and the Rise of Superstar Firms*, 135 Q. J. ECON. 645 (2020); David H. Autor, David Dorn & Gordon H. Hanson, *Untangling Trade and Technology: Evidence from Local Labour Markets*, 125 ECON. J. 621 (2015).

[12] Giovanni Peri, *Immigrants, Productivity, and Labor Markets*, 30 J. ECON. PERSP. 3 (2016).

different churches, join different clubs, exercise at gyms rather than in public parks, and largely work apart. The move to remote work during COVID-19 widened this separation. The beneficiaries of the knowledge economy neither see nor understand the despair embedded in the communities from which they live apart. The segregation is both cultural and geographical.

THE POLITICS OF LOCALITY

In a democratically elected representative government, geographical segregation matters where the voting rules require discrete localized victories, rather than a single overall referendum. In both the United States and the United Kingdom, the national leader is not chosen by a nationwide ballot, but rather on the basis of who wins the most electoral districts. In the United Kingdom, all parliamentary seats are local, and Parliament selects the Prime Minister based on party blocs. In the United States, the voting system for the President doubles down on locality. It allocates electoral votes state-by-state, with the weight of each state determined by its representation in both houses of Congress. The Constitution by design does not distribute Senators on the basis of population but by state, which skews electoral vote share toward the less populous states. Because the national government in both countries allocates power, both executive and legislative (granted that in the United Kingdom the two are largely the same) on the basis of locality, local conflicts have national political ramifications.

Geographical segregation does not only give real-world effect to expressions of local and regional divergence. It also undermines democratic politics by making the traditional method of smoothing out political differences – in-kind bartering known as logrolling – more difficult. The lack of ongoing contacts and a shared culture make it harder for the representatives of the two sides to find the range of mutually acceptable compromise. Mutual distrust bordering on paranoia makes any concession seem like unconditional surrender.

In both countries, the fundamental political conflicts track onto the division between global cities and the hinterlands. The regions most economically connected to the European Union, either because of trade ties (Northern Ireland) or the EU subsidies called cohesion funds (parts of Scotland and Wales), voted to remain, as did voters in London and its vicinity. The London votes, which by numbers outweighed the rest of the "remain" bloc, reflect the local gains of the knowledge economy. The "leave" votes, the majority overall, came largely from the hinterlands.

The other significant election in 2016 was, of course, for the US President. Trump's shocking win cried out for explanation. For many, the primary candidate for a post hoc account of his support was White resentment combined with lack of education. An analysis by *The Economist* shortly after the vote showed otherwise. A county-by-county study of the increase (delta) in Republican votes between 2012 and 2016 revealed that a variable aggregating the percentage of White and no-college-degree residents did track larger Trump gains, but that poor-health metrics had a stronger correlation. Taking their cue from Case and Deaton's 2015 article, *The Economist*'s analysts constructed a county-based index combining life expectancy and the prevalence of obesity, diabetes, heavy drinking, and lack of exercise. Even after controlling for other demographic and economic factors, including race, the poor-health metric outperformed all other attempts to explain Trump's votes. By looking at counties rather than larger units, the data captured community effects: places where death and poor health prevailed increased their share of Republican presidential votes compared to 2012. This data doesn't prove that these Trump voters were former Obama voters, but the inference seems very plausible and complicates the White-resentment story.[13]

Case and Deaton's book reports a complementary finding. Looking at Trump's percentage of the vote, rather than his gains over Romney in the previous election, on a county-by-county basis, they find that the incidence of people in physical pain, based on self-reporting, correlates with the Trump share. They also observe that in the United States, in contrast to many other countries with comparable data, increases in pain over the twenty-first century peak in middle age rather than later in life. The increase comes mostly from Whites without BA degrees. Trump voters in 2016, especially those who had voted for Obama four years previously, disproportionately lived in parts of the United States that lost ground due to the rise of the knowledge economy and suffered accordingly.[14]

Elsewhere in the rich world, similar patterns emerge, if perhaps not as starkly as in the United States and the United Kingdom. In France, support for the Front National, a revisionist political party that opposes the European Union and immigration, polls best outside of Paris, especially in the struggling northeast, and does poorly around Paris and Toulouse, the homes of its high-tech firms. Germany's AfD, its most prominent populist party, does best on the territory of the former East Germany, which remains a depressed hinterland

[13] Illness as Indicator, *The Economist*, Nov. 19, 2016, www.economist.com/united-states/2016/11/19/illness-as-indicator.

[14] Anne Case & Angus Deaton, Deaths of Despair , *supra* note 9, at 86–89; David Autor, David Dorn, Gordon Hanson, & Kaveh Majlesi, *Importing Political Polarization? The Electoral Consequences of Rising Trade Exposure*, 110 Am. Econ. Rev. 3139 (2020).

since the 1990 reunification. Hungary and Poland, the countries in the European Union where national populism has formed governments, lack great global cities and do not participate as much in the knowledge economy.[15]

Tracking the geography of populism in the global South is complicated. In China, the rise of the knowledge economy did not disrupt industrial incumbents because none existed. The Great Leap Forward and the Cultural Revolution already had ravaged what manufacturing industries it had. Rather, the economic reforms drew people from countryside to cities, not because technological innovation in the countryside drove farmers out but because the new jobs in the cities offered better life opportunities, notwithstanding the rigors of the Hukou system. In Russia, by contrast, the economy depends much more heavily on harvesting natural resources, which takes place far from cities. Many of its workers in the knowledge economy serve the state, supporting redistribution rather than creation of wealth. In both countries, populism largely means hostility to western élites, not to the national regime.

KINDS OF ECONOMIC INEQUALITY

As the divide between winners and losers in the knowledge economy widens, people debate where in the socioeconomic spectrum this gap is located. In the United States, a common trope identifies plutocrats as the wielders of pernicious power. These are a small class of super-rich, whose enormous wealth translates into lopsided political influences and the ability to corrupt public discourse. The problem becomes the 1 percent, people who engage in obscene displays of privilege and influence. In US history, the Gilded Age offers a precedent. It inspired acute social critics such as Vernon Louis Parrington and Thorstein Veblen, whose insights remain relevant today. So contemporary center-left politicians such as Joseph Biden, Bernie Sanders, and Elizabeth Warren and economists such as Thomas Piketty propose tax levies and regulatory interventions that target the super-rich and the supposed sources of their extraordinary fortunes, such as concentrated high-tech firms.[16]

[15] Political Cleavages and Social Inequalities: A Study of Fifty Democracies, 1948–2020 (Amory Gethin, Clara Martínez-Toledano & Thomas Piketty, eds. 2021); Pippa Norris & Ronald Inglehart, Cultural Backlash: Trump, Brexit, and Authoritarian Populism 17–18 (2019).

[16] Thomas Piketty, Capital in the Twenty-First Century (2013).

At least in the United States, this conception of economic inequality has little appeal for the dislocated and despairing as well as all others attracted to national populist politics. They instead go after a class that British sociologist Michael Dunlop Young first described in the 1950s in his ground-breaking study *The Rise of the Meritocracy*. Young saw the underside of a society where talent and skill become the basis of social rank and political power. He feared that a technocracy based on merit suffers from the hubris of the winners as well as the lack of common ground between the ruling class and those ruled.

Young's critique had some traction during the counterculture of the 1960s, but the ascendancy of Thatcher and Reagan seemed to render him irrelevant. In the last few years, however, Young's ideas have enjoyed a renaissance. Philosopher Michael Sandel, as well as public-policy thinkers such as Frederick DeBoer and Richard Reeves, draw on his core concern about the failings of merit-defined social differentiation.[17] They describe an upper middle class, defined by education, intelligence, and talent rather than inherited wealth and privilege, that dominates the economy, politics, and culture. In the United States, first degrees from competitive colleges and universities (schools that reject more than a handful of applicants, a minority within the US system) provide the best marker for membership in this class. Roughly 20 percent of the adult population belong to this group, a more broadly based, dispersed, and formidable ruling class than the so-called 1 percent.

Meritocrats can also be defined as those that rise in the knowledge economy. They are mostly knowledge workers who prosper as that system gains throughout the world. Their success makes it more likely that their consumption preferences dictate both material and, increasingly, knowledge products such as news and entertainment. Organizations that make knowledge workers – besides employers, mostly educational institutions, although uniquely in the West the US military also plays an important role – both cater to and help to form those preferences.

Driven by the politics of resentment, national populism in the rich West focuses on meritocrats, not plutocrats, as its main enemy. Its opposition to the status quo extends beyond politics to the construction of knowledge itself. This

[17] Michael Young, The Rise of the Meritocracy (1958); Christopher Lasch, The Revolt of the Elites and the Betrayal of Democracy (1997); Richard V. Reeves, Dream Hoarders: How the American Upper Middle Class Is Leaving Everyone Else in the Dust, Why That Is a Problem, and What to Do About It (2018); Michael J. Sandel, The Tyranny of Merit: What's Become of the Common Good? (2020); Frederick deBoer, The Cult of the Smart: How Our Broken Education System Perpetuates Social Injustice (2020).

means not only embracing the category of "fake news" and weaponizing constructs such as "mainstream media," but also attacking people whose job it is to make knowledge authoritative. Among such people are lawyers.

Many in the knowledge élites see this growing skepticism as a scam run by plutocrats to save themselves from the righteous anger of the masses. An arresting example is the 2017 book *Democracy in Chains* by Duke historian Nancy MacLean.[18] It tells a story of covert influence by the billionaire Koch brothers to brainwash Americans and pervert politics. In MacLean's telling, the Kochs implemented a strategy developed by publicists such as Lewis F. Powell, Jr. (before he joined the US Supreme Court) and academics such as Nobel laureate economist James Buchanan. This campaign supposedly pulled off an intellectual takeover of US politics to the benefit of the extreme right. Her scholarship purports to demonstrate that national populism in the United States rests on a deception perpetrated by the richest of the rich, an insidious conspiracy rather than a deeply rooted political and cultural trend. As it came about through false consciousness, a righteous light will clear away the fog.

Before saying more, I should declare an interest. Powell was my mentor for twenty years, from the time I worked for him as a law clerk until his death. I knew Buchanan and used his public-choice scholarship in my own work for much of my career. As best I can tell, Powell's effort to revitalize public support for US free enterprise had no impact at the time he chaired the commission that MacLean paints so darkly; indeed, during his lifetime he saw the effort as a flop. I also did not recognize anything of Buchanan's career or thought in MacLean's portrait. Many reviewers from a wide range of political and ideological points of view found glaring errors of characterization and omission in the book. Yet the story it tells comforted many who wanted it to be true, and it was nominated for a National Book Award.

The reasons for the left-behind's hostility to the meritocrats are more complex and harder to exploit than MacLean's just-so story would have it. The left-behind are not merely unequal in an absolute sense, but dislocated in a temporal sense. Work, friends, family, and civic institutions erode as good jobs disappear. It happened quickly, making adjustment hard. Suddenly upended, these people confront a burgeoning regulatory industry at the local level, often with encouragement and funding from the national government. Employers increasingly insisted on educational certifications that, strictly speaking, jobs don't require, such as having a BA degree. One study estimates

[18] Nancy MacLean, Democracy in Chains: The Deep History of the Radical Right's Stealth Plan for America (2017).

that 7.4 million qualified jobseekers lost the chance to hold good jobs in the US economy because of unnecessary BA requirements.[19] In addition, access to artisanal trades such as hair braiding or locksmithing, jobs that people could learn informally at no risk to the general public, increasingly required a state license based on expensive training and passing an exam. The avenues for the dislocated to get back on their feet shut down.[20]

None of these barriers to economic recovery for the left-behind reflects the power of monopoly capital or the whims of plutocrats. Rather, they suggest the overmighty ambition and self-satisfaction of low-level meritocrats, holding sway over people because they can. No wonder that the dislocated and despairing hate them, and not the billionaires.[21]

NATIONAL POPULISM'S LEGAL AGENDA

It may be true that tribalism, however it manifests itself, becomes more evident during hard times, but this should not obscure that hard times drive the dynamic. Whatever the prospects of anti-racist projects around the world, the economic forces that shape life opportunities will remain critical. Both will depend on law and legal institutions. I look here at what those who fell behind in the knowledge economy, especially those who turn to national populism, demand from law. We can see that the knowledge economy produces losers as well as winners and segregates them both geographically and culturally. Chapter 7 shows what the winners want from the legal system. But what about the losers?

For many of the left-behind, asking what law can do for them kind of misses the point. Their general disillusionment leads to a conviction that legal systems – both domestic and international – are largely corrupt, rigged to sustain those who prosper in today's world while holding down those who don't. Opportunistic politicians some products of the finest law schools play on this attitude, inviting their supporters to think of law as just another means of wielding power, not as

[19] Opportunity@Work, Rise with the STARS: Building a Stronger Labor Market for STARS, Communities, and Employers, Jan. 14, 2022, https://opportunityatwork.org/wp-content/uploads/2022/01/Rise-with-the-STARs.pdf

[20] Morris M. Kleiner & Alan B. Krueger, *Analyzing the Extent and Influence of Occupational Licensing on the Labor Market*, 31 J. LABOR ECON. S173 (2013).

[21] U.S. DEPT. TREASURY OFFICE OF ECONOMIC POLICY, COUNCIL OF ECONOMIC ADVISERS & U.S. DEPT. LABOR, OCCUPATIONAL LICENSING: A FRAMEWORK FOR POLICYMAKERS (2015) (outlining problem); Sandeep Vaheesan & Frank Pasquale, *The Politics of Professionalism: Reappraising Occupational Licensure and Competition Policy*, 14 ANN. REV. SOC. SCI. 309 (2018) (invoking Koch-conspiracy theory while making the case for licensing).

something independently justified. Those of us in the United States who went through the Trump moment recall the juxtaposition of extreme claims about legal discretion ("Article II means I can do whatever I want") with quick-trigger resort to preposterous legal claims, such as the First Amendment-based suits against Facebook and Twitter for deplatforming Trump.

Where anti-liberal revisionists came to power, their legal moves concentrated on rolling back the projects of the past few decades. They wanted law to make radical changes, but in the direction of a mostly imaginary past. They often sought to bolster the executive, largely by the removal of legal restraints. Political leaders act without waiting for legislative approval, as Trump did with his Muslim ban and Johnson with Brexit. In both these instances the courts pushed back.[22] From an illiberal perspective, the judicial defeats indicated only work that remains to be done on the courts. Once free to act, the revisionist leader can dismantle commitments that empower the knowledge economy and bring about a restoration when the country can be great "again."

Another part of the illiberal agenda is to unmake international law and institutions. This move assumes that these regimes were the product of the economic forces that deranged the hinterlands and that their destruction will make it easier to push back against those forces. Revisionist states, aggrieved by the existing international order, seek to discredit the international legal status quo generally and to dismantle the regimes that express it.

One way of attacking international law is through formal legal channels that comply with its established procedural rules while trampling its substantive norms and principles. Brexit provides a good example. The United Kingdom worked entirely within the framework of the EU treaty, taking the exit rules as it found them and complying with them during the exit negotiations. It undermined international law not through violating it, but rather by demonstrating a will to take advantage of an international organization's vulnerabilities.

Most of what Part III of this book describes are moves like Brexit, law-based unwindings of international law. Revisionist states identify the weak links in international institutions, typically escape clauses meant to preserve the rudiments of national sovereignty in emergencies, and exploit them. A persistent pattern of resort to such measures brings the entire international law enterprise into disrepute. It shows how much international law depends on political will driven by state interest, not simply on a desire to comply with the rules.

Another way a revisionist state can undermine international law is by re-envisioning what it says. It can destabilize an international regime by

[22] *Trump* v. *Hawaii*, 138 S. Ct. 2392 (2018); *R ex rel Miller* v. *Prime Minister*, [2019] U.K.S.C. 41; *R ex rel Miller* v. *Secretary of State for Exiting the European Union*, [2017] U.K.S.C. 5.

announcing new standards and acting consistently with them. Both the acting and the explaining disrupt international law by exposing its contingency even in the absence of express escape clauses.

An example of one such move, the subject of Chapter 12, weaponizes the fundamental premise of international law that it exists because states create it. For most of the twentieth century international lawyers assumed that international law could not impose obligations on a state that had the effect of negating what makes a state a state. According to this position, international law cannot strip a state of the core attributes of its sovereignty.[23] In the twenty-first century, a growing number of states declared, often through their courts, that they would not recognize any international obligation that contradicted their constitutional order. The new claim reserves to a state the power to discover upon reflection, and in light of its evolving domestic jurisprudence, that it cannot honor an international obligation that seemed valid at the time that it acceded to it.

An alternate strategy that plays out much the same way is for a revisionist state to adopt a surprising interpretation of what it understands its international legal obligations to be. A much studied example from the past decade involves Russia's annexation of Crimea. Aside from its general obligations under the UN Charter not to use force or threats to interfere with another state's territorial integrity, Russia had made several treaties with Ukraine during the 1990s that committed it to respect Ukraine's borders and territorial integrity. Yet in March 2014 it used proxies in Crimea to hive off that territory from Ukraine and to absorb it as its own. It did not directly employ its military in these events, although its agents in Crimea threatened violence and its military did act elsewhere in Ukraine. Seemingly the operation constituted a flagrant violation of international law as well as a serious threat to international peace and security.[24]

Not so, said Russia. It had several explanations of why its actions complied with international law. Crimea had simply exercised its right of national self-determination consistent with the UN Charter. Ukraine had no right to object because it had no duly constituted government at the time of Crimea's secession.

The most interesting argument, however, was that the annexation was necessary to deter Ukraine from violating a fundamental norm in international relations that overrides any international legal obligation. Ukraine wanted to join NATO, a move that would unbalance the military, economic, and

23 Alfred von Verdross, *Forbidden Treaties in International Law*, 31 Am. J. Int'l L. 571 (1937).

24 Oona A. Hathaway & Scott J. Shapiro, The Internationalists: How a Radical Plan to Outlaw War Remade the World 390–94 (2017).

political relations between the West, led by the United States, and Russia, the present embodiment of an ancient orthodox civilization that the West had bullied and harmed for over a millennium. Gobbling up Crimea forestalled a greater danger to the international system, a NATO-armed Ukraine posing an intolerable threat to Russia from the territory of the former Soviet Union.[25]

Russia persuaded almost no one about the rightness of its position, but that wasn't its purpose. What it achieved was the spread of doubt and insecurity among those states that had relied on the international rule of law. Like the people in the hinterlands of the rich world, Russia regards existing international legal structures as threats, not as opening a path to its peace and prosperity. It may lack the power to destroy these structures, but it can undermine them. Its use of force in violation of an international norm that supposedly defines the existing international order, coupled with a willingness to back up its actions with novel arguments that mock liberal internationalist premises, threatens more damage to the order than would an exclusively military attack.

As I write this, the world's attention has returned to the Ukrainian story. Russia has resumed the war against Ukraine begun in 2014, extending across much of the country's east and producing terrible casualties while absorbing greater military costs than it anticipated. Russia points to NATO expansion as its fundamental grievance, repeating the arguments heard at the time of Crimea's annexation. The invasion indicated an inability of the United States and Europe to project credible deterrence as well as Russia's joy in displaying its contempt for international law as the West sees it. Its consequences remain to be seen.

THE CHINESE ALTERNATIVE: ADVANCED CAPITALISM IN ONE COUNTRY

Because of scaling, the knowledge economy prospers when markets increase in size. This does not mean, however, that this method of production requires global markets. Protected economies still can take advantage of knowledge and make knowledge products. For one country's economy to outcompete others, it must only do better than its rivals.

A century ago, socialists proclaimed that workers had no homeland and that their movement was inherently international. Under this banner Lenin accepted Imperial Germany's help to overthrow the provisional government

[25] Paul B. Stephan, *Wars of Conquest in the Twenty-First Century and the Lessons of History: Crimea, Panama, and John Bassett Moore*, 62 VA. J. INT'L L. 63 (2021).

that had replaced the Tsar. The Bolsheviks fought through a civil war and against foreign intervention to establish what they called the Russian Soviet Federal Socialist Republic, soon reincorporated as the Union of Soviet Socialist Republics. After a few failed indigenous attempts to establish Soviet-style socialism in places like Hungary, Bavaria, and Gilan (a province in northern Persia), the Soviet Union found itself the world's only socialist state. Many of the other Bolshevik leaders fretted, but Stalin had an answer. Socialism in one country was a viable path toward worldwide socialism, and indeed the logic of the dialectic demanded it. Armed with this formula, Stalin murdered his domestic adversaries and, at terrible cost, prevailed over foreign enemies. At the end of World War II, the remaking of Central and Eastern Europe as a family of Soviet dependencies and the triumph of a Soviet-backed regime in China seemingly vindicated his claim that socialism in one country was a winning strategy.

Today we find ourselves considering the possibility of advanced capitalism in one country, namely China. The variant of national populism that prevails in China fosters suspicion of foreigners, but apparently not of domestic élites. China adheres to a form of autocracy that concentrates political and administrative power in the Party and the People's Liberation Army (PLA) while tolerating a wide range of private economic activity, subject to administrative prerogative. Checks on the use of this administrative prerogative come from within the party, the PLA, and the state structure they control, not from an independent judiciary, the press, or civil society. Prosperity remains the goal of the autocrats and they seek to exploit the knowledge economy as much as they can, consistent with retaining ultimate control over economic life. But the new formula speaks of common prosperity, implying a kind of populist revolt against the excesses of the people that drove its economic rise.

Substituting administrative fiat for legal security and imposing border controls over information flows prevent a country, and therefore its people, from maximizing the benefits of the knowledge economy. If China alone took this path while the rest of the world sought the best ways to extract value from economic processes tied to knowledge, it might lose ground, much as the Soviet Union did in the 1970s and 1980s. But if the rest of the world descends into trade wars, information protectionism, and enhanced administrative discretion, the picture changes. All that China needs to do to become the global economic hegemon is to keep its own house in order while divisions within the United States, Europe, and the remainder of the rich world fester.

Safeguards against administrative capriciousness generally induce greater investments in knowledge, but China might be able to forgo this advantage and still overtake the West. The size of China's economy, given its large population and territory, may enable it to realize much of the gains from scaling knowledge-based innovation, even if it can't fully scale internationally. All that matters is that competitor states also face barriers to international scaling. As long as China's stock of human capital grows, which depends on the size of educated, skilled, and talented population, it has a chance of overtaking and surpassing the others.[26] All it has to do is keep its competitors from taking advantage of their people's human capital and slow down the replenishment of their stocks.

I do not consider China an inevitable global hegemon. As Chapter 13 discusses, it faces distinct challenges as it implements a strategy of advanced capitalism in one country. Marrying autocratic politics with market economics sometimes works over the short- to mid-term, as in Chiang Kai-shek's Taiwan, Lee Kuan Yew's Singapore, Suharto's Indonesia, and Park Chung-hee's Korea. But these were all relatively small economies at the time of their take-off. It's not clear if such marriages can handle the tensions and complexity of large expanding economies facing continuous creative destruction.

Leaving autocrats to police their own administrative prerogatives in the face of growing wealth presents a serious risk of wasteful competition over rents from regulation, including corruption. An autocracy can and probably will morph into a kleptocracy, a system inhospitable to the knowledge economy. A takeaway from Soviet economic history, for example, emphasizes the rise of corruption in the face of initial economic success. The postwar Soviet Union, most decidedly not a market economy, enjoyed high growth rates during the 1950s and early 1960s. These were large enough to lead Paul Samuelson to assert that the Soviet Union would overtake the United States in GDP within thirty years. Yet by the 1970s and 1980s, competition over private gains from rigging central planning largely wrecked the economy. China may yet face a similar fate, if abuse of administrative discretion has the same fundamental effect as rigging central planning.

Still, liberals the world over must worry that the Chinese approach might prove the best adaptation to the knowledge economy. The Xi regime prizes knowledge workers and allows its firms to harvest the gains from innovation and inventions, subject to not-completely-defined boundaries based on the imperatives of regime preservation and economic oversight. Its relentless development of surveillance technologies, explored in detail in the next chapter, tamps down the risk of political and social division that plagues the

[26] Paul M. Romer, *Endogenous Technological Change*, 98 J. Pol. Econ. S71, S94–96 (1990).

West. China may have its own deaths of despair, but they seem to be quieter and lack a ripple effect. It may yet achieve the common prosperity that it touts but does not define.

* * *

Nationalist populism arises from the world's hinterlands to oppose the knowledge economy and its various cultural products, including international law in the service of liberal internationalism. A reassuring take, if cold-hearted, regards this movement as a last-ditch struggle by people already overtaken by forces beyond their control and waiting to be ground down further. Between COVID-19 and deaths of despair, this perspective holds, these people are doomed; the only question is how much damage they can do before their inevitable disappearance as a political force.

An alternate view regards displacement as a permanent and widespread feature of the knowledge economy. Societies that do not find a way to reconcile the losers and winners in this mode of production face enduring, not ephemeral, conflict. The struggle between these groups may doom liberal democracy as practiced in the rich world. China, an authoritarian regime with a world-class surveillance state, might rise up as the incumbent rich states fall back.

PART III

Battlegrounds

Part I of this book covered the gradual erosion of the liberal-internationalist accomplishments of the 1990s during this century, punctuated by the tumult and distress of the last five years. Part II explored how the ascendant knowledge economy contributed to these problems. The knowledge economy represents humanity's best hope for peace and prosperity but also poses the greatest threat to successful navigation of the ensuing crises.

This part looks at the emerging crises in depth. Throughout, it focuses on two things: the battles spawned by the knowledge economy and liberal-internationalist institutions and practices as battlefields. Attacks on international law illuminate a broader struggle over mastery of the world economy. The legal battlefields point to the stakes in play.

Across the board, the most important states, rich incumbents and revisionists from the South alike, take increasingly bold steps to unravel the bonds of international law. The undoing of legal commitments reflects doubt and disorder across fields and subjects, from international security to human rights to trade and investment to law generally as a tool for cooperation. As challenges mount, all linked to the transformations that the knowledge economy has wrought, the nations of the world grow increasingly reluctant to trust each other in the face of potentially profound threats that demand collective responses.

9

International Security, Cyber Disruption, and Human Rights

This chapter looks at areas that make up the heart of what specialists call public international law – war and peace as well as the interests of humanity in the face of state power. It shows how the cyber world, a visible manifestation of the knowledge economy's effect on the twenty-first century, has become an ever more dangerous place. Cyber insecurity in turn endangers peace and human rights. The general instability brought on by this century's cascade of crises underscores the dangers.

I focus on six looming threats to global well-being, to each of which the knowledge economy has at least indirectly contributed. Russia has gone to war against Ukraine; China might conquer and annex Taiwan; Iran may soon become a nuclear power; climate change might ruin us all; cyberspace is already a bad place but threatening to become much worse; and the international institutions that hold states to their human rights obligations are unraveling. The West's dependence on the Chinese economy as well as its growing disarray make deterrence of any adversary difficult; technological advances make it easier for a country such as Iran to acquire nuclear weapons; the knowledge economy might find solutions to climate change, but for it now it contributes to carbon dioxide emissions more than it ameliorates them; innovations in data processing and surveillance make cyber disruption and predation harder to deter or defeat; and national populism makes international human rights institutions easy targets. We have much to dread.

PEACE AND SECURITY

A thread that ran through the twentieth century was the hope of replacing the great-state balance of power with collective security. Many leaders and thinkers thought that the world needed something better than the old regime to protect peace and stability. From the 1907 Hague Peace Conference through Versailles in 1919 to the 1921–22 Washington Naval Conference to 1928 Kellogg–Briand Pact to the 1945 UN Charter, internationalists aspired to build a global institution that would mediate and even arbitrate international conflicts. Both world wars represented disastrous failures of the balance-of-power system. The end of communism meant that survival of humanity no longer would rest on the nuclear balance of terror. Serious people thought that the world could find new ways to meet future dangers without the risk of balances upending.

In the new world order of collective security, war would not necessarily end. Instead, putting an international organization in the way of war would, people hoped, make armed conflict less likely. Granted, neither Versailles nor the United Nations pulled it off, but people could still believe that humanity over time would come to accept that it had no better alternative. Beginning with the first Gulf War and the Security Council's engagement with the operation, it became possible to think that that day had come.

As we saw in Part I, that belief proved unsustainable. Focusing specifically on the United Nations as the last great hope for collective security, we can trace the failures. Libya's unraveling in the wake of the Arab Spring gave the UN Security Council its last chance to wield any influence over an armed conflict. China's and Russia's claim, feigned or not, that the United States went beyond its authorization there led them to block all further efforts by the Security Council to take jurisdiction over matters involving state violence.

Since then, grave threats to international peace and security – the supposed domain of the Security Council – emerged, but it failed to respond. The Syrian civil war entailed more intensive and extensive armed force than Libya's. Outsiders, including a western coalition, Iran, Russia, and Turkey, joined in the hostilities. The Security Council remains confined to the spectators' seats. The General Assembly pushed back against Russia's annexation of Crimea, but the Security Council did nothing. The ouster of the western coalition from Afghanistan may or may not advance stability and reduce violence, but again the Security Council had nothing to do with these events. Wars in the Horn of Africa, Armenia, and Ukraine proceed without any Security Council intervention. Even its role in the efforts to keep Iran from acquiring nuclear weapons, which I discuss later, is as a depository of an international agreement, not its enforcer.

The gravity of future threats seems especially real because of the changes wrought by the knowledge economy to international interests and politics. Russia's collapse and its later efforts to claw back its regional, if no longer global, influence distracted people in the West, especially the United States and Europe, from the steady rise of China as a technological, not merely economic power. Only with the Xi regime, openly revisionist, nationalist, and ambitious, has the prospect of real conflict fought outside the bounds of international institutions concentrated minds in the West. What seemed in the 1990s US hegemony behind a façade of multipolar governance has become, due largely to the workings of the knowledge economy, a dangerous world of diverse great powers.

A large and well-funded industry, of which I am not part, exists to foresee future security threats. I do not pretend to predict where the next war will break out. Three ongoing national security situations, however, seem sufficiently evident and potentially dangerous to merit speculation about how collective security might play out. The first is Russia's invasion of Ukraine, the second Taiwan's possible reunification with the mainland, and the third the prospect of Iran's acquisition of nuclear weapons.

The Ukrainian situation represents a reprise of the 2014 crisis that cost that country Crimea. Russia justified its action then as an appropriate response to what it regarded as a second episode of intolerable western interference in Ukrainian politics.[1] Sensing growing dysfunction in the United States and Europe, the Kremlin leadership has judged the moment ripe to undo the persistence of NATO and the balance of power in Europe. Whether inspired or folly, the move does away with the sense of security that Europe had enjoyed that the calamities of the twentieth century would not haunt the twenty-first.

The liquidation of Hong Kong's one-country-two-systems status and the generally risk-taking tone of the Xi regime drives fears about China's intentions. Taiwan's economic significance, highlighted by its globally dominant semiconductor industry, amplifies the dangers of its seizure. Unfortunately, international law provides little guidance for this crisis.

The deal between the United States and China memorialized in the 1972 Shanghai Communiqué accepts that both regard Taiwan as part of China and leaves it to history to decide which government ultimately will wield power over the single country. Deliberately ambiguous, the Communiqué did not spell out what limits might exist on efforts by either state to give history a hand. China maintained that "no other country has the right to interfere" in the resolution of what is a Chinese "internal affair," while the United States endorsed "a peaceful settlement of the Taiwan question by the Chinese themselves." Deliberately left out was any commitment by China

1 Paul B. Stephan, *Wars of Conquest in the Twenty-First Century and the Lessons of History – Crimea, Panama, and John Bassett Moore*, 62 VA. J. INT'L L. 63 (2021).

to an exclusively peaceful approach, or by the United States as to its course of action if an unpeaceful approach transpired.

Four months earlier, the UN General Assembly had transferred all powers attributable to China's membership, including its seat on the Security Council and accompanying veto power, to the mainland government. Thus a background assumption of the Shanghai Communiqué is the effective incapacity of the Security Council to take any action should armed force become part of the reunification picture. It thus cannot judge whether any steps China takes comply with international law.

In the absence of collective security, the old principle of balance of power applies. The current state of technology preserves the risk of mutually assured destruction and thus makes the use of nuclear weapons unlikely. The more interesting question is whether China and the West, particularly the United States, have attained such a state of economic interdependence that escalating economic sanctions and counter-sanctions is also unthinkable. Both sides watch with fascination and dread the outcome of the sanctions war between Russia and the West.

I have no idea how the Taiwan issue will unfold. My point is that, if no disaster transpires, it will not be thanks to the United Nations. Peace and prosperity, if it prevails, will do so because of the capacity of the two sides to threaten to inflict severe pain on each other. As we learned from the twentieth century's world wars, as well as Russia's Ukrainian adventure, these threats sometimes fail disastrously as disincentives. Yet to address this looming challenge, perhaps the gravest threat to the contemporary world order, we have no better alternatives.

Another alarming challenge, more immediate than the Taiwan issue if not the Ukrainian one, is Iran's program to acquire nuclear weapons. The regime denies that such a program exists, but few seem willing to accept its reassurances. Untrained in the field as I am and not having any inside information (including classified intelligence), I cannot say with any confidence how close Iran is to matching, say, North Korea in its nuclear arsenal. What follows is speculation only.

For thirty years, only the great powers had nuclear weapons, with the United States and the Soviet Union controlling who could join the club. Even Israel, the one unofficial and undeclared nuclear power to cross the threshold during this period, did so, it would appear, with the complicity of the United States, although we do not know the details of what the Johnson administration did. India and Pakistan broke the pattern in the 1970s but did not immediately set off a wave of defections by other states from the non-proliferation regime. Several regional powers, in particular Iran, Iraq, Libya, and North Korea, started to explore the nuclear path but also joined the UN nonproliferation treaty.

When the world changed at the beginning of the 1990s, only North Korea saw the advantage of becoming a declared nuclear power. I assume, without knowing, that technological progress in nuclear bombmaking had progressed to the point where a once rare and terribly expensive set of skills and capacities had become within the reach of one of the world's poorest countries. The Kim regime's strategic calculus was daring but not crazy. It believed that the United States would not go to war to stop it, and China would not use its existential economic power to thwart the nuclear program. It first reached an accommodation with the United States during the Clinton administration but, like Iran today, continued research and testing so that it could switch over to nuclear weapons when the opportunity arose. That happened as the United States launched its invasion of Iraq. North Korea denounced the Nuclear Nonproliferation Treaty in 2003 and conducted its first bomb test in 2006.

During this period, Libya also had a nuclear weapons program. Whether it collaborated with North Korea is a matter of suspicion and conjecture. Its reaction to Operation Enduring Freedom was the opposite of North Korea's. Gaddafi ended his program and submitted to full international inspection and supervision. His regime negotiated out of its status as an international outlaw and a supporter of international terrorism. It paid massive settlements to the victims of the latter.[2] In return, when the Arab Spring erupted a few years later, the United States led efforts to overthrow him and showed no regret over his murder.

Considering how North Korea sustained itself after passing the nuclear weapons threshold, and comparing what happened to Gaddafi after his regime abandoned its program, I have trouble imagining why Iran's rulers would not want nuclear weapons. They seem a means of keeping even an absolutely crazy regime safe from destruction. At the same time, from a global perspective a nuclear-armed Iran is a clearly bad thing, if only because the risk to international stability increases, perhaps exponentially, as the number of potential users goes up.

I am prepared to believe, although I certainly do not know, that Iran already has passed key engineering hurdles and could move quickly from developing to having nuclear weapons. The technology seems relatively easy to achieve, compared to where it stood in the 1940s. If these guesses are reasonable, then the question becomes what measures might have a decent chance of widening

[2] Jonathan Schwartz, *Dealing with a "Rogue State": The Libya Precedent*, 101 AM. J. INT'L L. 553 (2007).

the gap between Iran's current capacity and the consummation of the project. How much time has become the only issue, but more time is still better than less.

The Security Council took jurisdiction over this problem in 2015 through the Joint Comprehensive Plan of Action (JCPOA). It endorsed this international agreement, which Iran, Germany, and the five permanent members of the Security Council joined. The agreement trades sanctions relief for Iran in return for Iranian compliance with a regulatory regime designed to delay it from converting its current nuclear program into weapons attainment. The JCPOA, as implemented by a Security Council resolution, obligates the parties to suspend particular economic penalties targeted at Iran. The deal's enforcement mechanism, unusual for Security Council programs, includes a snapback procedure. Any of the six states can complain to the Security Council that Iran has breached its commitment. Unless the Security Council decides otherwise, after a period for investigation and negotiation the sanctions go back into effect.

When the Trump administration came to power in 2017, backing out of international commitments became part of its brand. Accordingly, in May 2018 the United States repudiated the JCPOA and resumed all its sanctions against Iran. It waited until August 2020, however, to invoke the snapback procedure, which would have rendered reinstatement of its sanctions consistent with the JCPOA. The other parties took the position that, having left the agreement, the United States surrendered its power to use snapback. In February 2021, the new Biden administration withdrew the US attempt to invoke snapback, but did not end the sanctions.

Beginning in May 2019, Iran tested the other parties by engaging in incremental breaches of JCPOA. It defended these as lawful countermeasures against illegal US sanctions. None of the five remaining parties pushed back. As I write this, Iran has proposed to return to compliance with the JCPOA. It is not unreasonable, however, to suppose that during this period it managed to shorten the time needed before it can become a nuclear power.

The shorter the interval, the less important JCPOA is. Restoration of the collective sanctions authorized by earlier Security Council resolutions would matter only until the breakout. Once Iran tests a nuclear bomb or otherwise demonstrates convincingly that it has become a nuclear power, new sanctions would follow in any event. Iran presumably would take this possibility into account before taking this path. Evidence that Iran will accept remaining outside the nuclear club remains scant.

As with the Ukraine and Taiwan situations, a nuclear-armed Iran presents us with a grave problem, a potential spiraling out of control of a deep-rooted regional conflict that puts millions of lives at risk, with nothing more than the old balance of power to keep a lid on things. The JCPOA has not yet failed – that won't happen until Iran gets nuclear warheads – but it offers little evidence that collective security works as a means of dealing with real threats to peace and security.

CLIMATE CHANGE AS A NATIONAL SECURITY THREAT

When the COVID-19 crisis winds down, states may find time to worry about the environment. Current scientific thinking indicates that increasing carbon dioxide in the atmosphere will produce severe climate changes with large if unpredictable effects on the planet. Forced migration and battles over scarcer resources such as water and habitable land seem likely, with follow-on national security effects. Some states may disappear under the water, and others might find themselves at war.

Reduced to its simplest terms, a solution will require reduced emissions into the atmosphere and, in all likelihood, increased extraction of carbon dioxide from the atmosphere. Because climate change does not care where carbon dioxide originates, it offers up a classic collective action problem. Both emission reduction and carbon dioxide extraction involve great costs borne by particular states, while the benefit of reduced levels is a public good, neither rivalrous nor excludible. Anyone's emissions harm the global ecosystem, and anyone's emission reductions or extractions benefit the entire ecosystem, not individual states. The problem cannot be solved, then, without some mechanism that deters defection by states that seek to avoid their appropriate share of the costs.

Setting that appropriate share of global costs presents significant challenges. First, we must determine an acceptable carbon dioxide level in the atmosphere, which may or may not exceed the current level. Second, we must come up with reasonable guesses about how emission-reduction and carbon-extraction technologies will work, when for the most part effective technologies do not yet exist, aside from standing down the world economy. A short cut might involve imposing quotas for every state as to how much carbon dioxide they may release over a set period, understanding that negative numbers might be used. We then would need reliable technology to monitor and measure local emissions and extractions, which we also do not have at present.

To complicate the problem further, states have legitimate arguments about distribution of the costs. Human-generated carbon dioxide emissions did not appear simultaneously and evenly around the world. Rather, the carbon-emitting technologies associated with industrialization largely emerged in today's rich West. If we look at the problem as a matter of redistributive justice with the burden on carbon emitters to rectify their past wrongs, we should assign the costs largely on the basis of emission history. Those who wielded industrial economic power in the past should pay for the cleanup, whatever their current wealth, power, or technological capacities.

If we look at the problem instead as reducing future risk, we should assign the costs differently. Thinking of these costs as a kind of tax, we might use principles used to design tax systems, such as ability to pay. Income taxes exemplify this principle. We might, for example, link costs to a state's GDP, a reasonable marker for its economic capacity.

Once we devise a generally acceptable distribution of this burden, we might then create a market to let cost-bearers pay other states to carry out their assigned tasks, thus implementing a least-cost-avoider principle. We have already seen the development of a carbon-credit concept. Our experience to date, however, suggests that existing auditing methods do not inspire much confidence that these credits help. At least some sellers of carbon credits likely overstate how their actions reduce emissions.

So, in addition to achieving breakthroughs in technologies that substitute low-emission energy for high-emission sources and extract carbon dioxide from the air, we need to come up with reliable ways to measure at a reasonable cost the carbon impact of particular projects. Due to geographically distributed supply chains, this task can be even harder than measuring nationwide emissions or extractions. A technology that substitutes for a high-emitting technology doesn't do us much good if deploying the low-emission technology involves lots of carbon emissions. Imagine, for example, solar panels that generate no-emission energy, but the manufacture of which produces lots of carbon dioxide.

Once we have met all these challenges, we still would have to design an enforcement mechanism that holds states to their carbon dioxide obligations. What we do in many areas – allow reciprocal relation through calibrated and proportional lifting of other states' obligations – would not work here, just as we don't punish torturers by doing our own torture. Given the size of the costs envisioned, we need either a technological revolution to shrink those costs or sanctions that generate costs at least commensurate with those of compliance.

What the international community has done so far is make strategically incomplete agreements that rely only on social pressure and socialization to drive cooperation. The 2015 Paris Agreement – the most recent comprehensive international agreement on climate change – leaves it to states to self-assess their compliance burden. It assumes synergy between compliance and ambition and does not make it legally obligatory to do any more work than memorializing intentions. The 2021 Glasgow Agreement extends this process but does not transform it.

The Paris and Glasgow Agreements leave so much open, both because states remain unwilling to bear the cost of significant carbon reduction and because so much of reduction depends on technological breakthroughs that have not yet happened. We do not know how to create an economy that maintains the world's current standard of living while reducing our dependence on activity that emits carbon dioxide; we do not know how to survive while radically reducing well-being; we have not yet discovered how to extract carbon dioxide from the atmosphere at the needed scale; and we have not designed good auditing systems to determine how much particular activities contribute to emission reduction or extraction.

The new products of the knowledge economy that have popped up seem to make things worse. The blockchain mechanism, on which cryptocurrencies and NFTs depend, places an enormous load on energy resources. At its current level, bitcoin production produces as much carbon dioxide annually as New Zealand, with the amount increasing rapidly and dramatically.[3] China, a state that has many reasons not to like the financial secrecy and flexibility that bitcoin facilitates, adopted a blanket ban on its mining and trading in September 2021. But because mining and trading can take place anywhere and have the same environmental effect wherever they occur, only a global system can cap this new source of emissions.

Despite this failing, I cannot imagine managing climate change on any other basis than technological innovation. The industrial manufacturing economy may bear the blame for excessive carbon dioxide emissions, but the knowledge economy offers the only path toward maintaining current levels of prosperity and human flourishing while sustaining the planet ecologically. A solution requires new means of reduced-emission production, carbon dioxide extraction, and atmospheric monitoring. It also will have to provide the developers of these technologies the right incentives to achieve these feats.

Whether the world is up to this task remains the big question. The discoveries necessary to meet the challenge will not occur everywhere at the same time. It is unlikely that they will take the form of easy-to-transfer knowledge, such as pasteurization, Lister's sanitary measures, or the mosquito-fighting measures that abated Yellow Fever in the Americas. Certain people and places

3 Shangrong Jiang, Yuze Li, Quanying Lu, Yongmiao Hong, Dabo Guan, Xu Xiong & Shouyang Wang, *Policy Assessments for the Carbon Emissions Flows and Sustainability of Bitcoin Blockchain Production in China*, Nature Comm. No. 1938, April 6, 2021.

will gain temporary monopolies over the discoveries and want a return for selling their knowledge. Envy, frustration, and anger will result. Political struggle, as people rise up against the individuals and firms that grow fat on the climate-saving technologies, and conflicts among states, as the masters of the discoveries also seek a return – of power and influence if not monetary – seem likely. Struggles within states may heighten conflicts among states. Preemptive acts to thwart these returns, or a failure to make credible promises that they won't be thwarted, might discourage the inventers.

Finding a way out of the climate-change nightmare will require that much of the world make peace with a large chunk of the knowledge economy. Otherwise the destabilization of the international order brought about by the transformation in the way we produce things and the products we make will seem child's play compared to our future. A disordered world with more dangerous and better armed states will await us. Yet looking at the recent past, the prospects for such a peace seem slight.

FEAR, LOATHING, AND THE WORLD WIDE WEB

This book at many points touches on the utopian hopes raised by the enormous increase in virtual connectivity inspired by the knowledge economy. Advanced thinkers thought that the evolution of the Web, the Cloud, social media, and ubiquitous personal computers, smartphones, and internet cafes would transform social and political arrangements by empowering ordinary people at the expense of the state. As we have seen, something closer to the opposite happened. Once state authorities recognized the challenges to their power, they adapted. The West's big data, social media, and search engine companies found it more profitable to sell their services to those seeking to influence great numbers of people than to offer products freeing them from such influence. In the meantime, China and Russia developed technologies to control access to their cyberspace so as to manage outside influence. The technologies that first held out promise of a new dawn of freedom and prosperity, and now seems closer to the opposite, are the poisoned fruits of the knowledge economy.

The future may bring even greater threats. I focus on two here, the possibility of deepfakes and the death of privacy. Put simply, as matters currently stand, there is more money to be made from cyberattacks than from cyber defense. Here this means that coming up with technologies to fool audiences through fake images and sounds is likely to be better rewarded than the development of fake-detection technology, and that penetrating security to amass valuable data is likely to generate a higher return than designing ways to impede penetrations.

Misinformation pollutes cyberspace everywhere. Malicious actors can exploit the algorithms that social media use to maximize looks, introducing dangerous lies that propagate far more quickly than criticism and correction. In a post-truth world, the line between malicious actors and passionate partisans might fade into nothing. Deepfakes extend the problem by making criticism and correction even harder.

We have plenty of experience with doctored broadcasts used in political and cultural combat. Think of the Protocol of the Elders of Zion, a 1903 invention of the Tsarist secret police that inspired credulous antisemites for more than a century and still has fans today. As the analog environment became a digital world, executing these fakes became easier, their impact wider, and the chance of quickly exposing them smaller.

At present, most of the fakes in cyberspace are cheap fakes that play on established memes to reinforce the convictions of targeted audiences. Misinformation has not needed technological enhancement to flourish. Think of the doctored videos that circulated on the internet depicting presidential candidate Biden or House Speaker Pelosi losing command of their faculties. It may have been fairly easy to show they are fakes, but the intended audience didn't seem to care.

What lies just over the horizon are tools that generate high-verisimilitude audio and visual products. As it becomes easier to make sophisticated deepfakes, malicious actors will use them more frequently to greater effect. Bad people will be drawn to high-impact products targeted at time-sensitive events. In democracies, these will occur more frequently as election days or similarly salient deadlines approach. Recall the forged document published by Dan Rather on CBS just before the 2004 US presidential election designed to bolster the claim that George W. Bush was a draft dodger. Back then the use of an anachronistic font established the fakery relatively quickly. In the near future, even more serious and persuasive interventions will occur and survive scrutiny longer. The increase in lives lived online, all due to the achievements of the knowledge economy, multiplies these risks.[4]

For malicious actors, a representation that lasts long enough to embed itself in public memory and frustrates definitive detection as a fake represents the ultimate goal. But even less enduring fakes may move the needle for enough time to achieve the object of the fraud. They also have a secondary effect by undermining confidence in representations generally. Enough sufficiently

[4] U.S. Department of Homeland Security, Increasing Threats of Deepfake Identities (Sept. 14, 2021), www.dhs.gov/sites/default/files/publications/increasing_threats_of_deepfake_identities_0.pdf.

well-done deepfakes may convince broad audiences that they cannot trust any news from any sources, creating the liar's dividend.[5] In this future, a great deal of social capital will disappear.

The problem with deepfakes is that the malicious actors can capture almost all the gains from their actions, while the benefits of thwarting deepfakes tend to be general and dispersed. People on offense know what result they want to achieve. People on defense face a multitude of adversaries, some of whom they may not even imagine. To the extent a deepfake draws down social capital, an entire society bears the cost, which means no one person has a sufficient stake to justify an adequate investment in cyber detection.

Where private incentives do not lead to optimal outcomes, the traditional response is to bring in the state to redress the balance. In the case of politically disruptive deepfakes, however, special problems arise. A strand of liberal democratic thought, mainstream if not necessarily a consensus, holds that state intervention in public political contests presents distinct problems due to the peculiar and malign interest of states to protect themselves from challenges. The US approach to its First Amendment expresses this attitude, although not to everyone's satisfaction.

The state might, hypothetically, criminalize or otherwise punish the authors and publishers of deepfakes. Present US law is decidedly to the contrary. Under current Supreme Court doctrine, publishers enjoy exceptional protection from accountability for sending out harmful publications touching on public affairs, and online publishers seem to enjoy even greater immunity, depending on which interpretation of Section 230 of the Communications Decency Act prevails. As to authors, even if we can get past communication privileges currently provided by law, the technical challenge of attribution would remain.

Alternatively, the government might invest heavily in detection technology for broad public use. If DARPA can invent the internet, the argument goes, surely it can save us from its vulnerabilities. This is true up to a point but overlooks the gap between invention and application. Unless we ask the government not only to invent the technology but to run it, the skewed incentives between those on offense and the defenders will remain. And taking a centralized, command-and-control approach to deepfake detection has its own shortcomings.

I am not a technologist and make no claim about the seriousness of the deepfake risk or the costs of countermeasures. My point, rather, is that from a

[5] Robert Chesney & Danielle Keats Citron, *Deep Fakes: A Looming Challenge for Privacy, Democracy, and National Security*, 107 CALIF L. REV. 1753 (2019).

position of technological ignorance, the deepfake threat seems significant, the potential harm to society in general and liberal democracies in particular seems great, and the incentives as currently aligned do not give us much comfort. Perhaps a genius will save us and reveal my fears to be groundless. But until the genius comes along, everyone should worry about this particular product of the knowledge economy.

Assaults on privacy are structurally similar to misinformation and have even greater stakes. Predators – states tracking down troublemakers, public and private entities using private information to build big data as the foundation for artificial intelligence, spies and gangsters seeking to raid and disable valuable databases – have a systematic advantage over defenders. They get to keep the benefits of their raids. Defenders must organize private data gatekeepers who often do not have sufficient reasons to invest in security adequate to repel these attackers. They typically do not bear all the costs of the data compromise and do not want to assume the wasteful cost of protecting against attacks that never happen. Governments with the skills to defend data security also act as predators. All attack foreign cyber targets for national security reasons, and some also use these skills to suppress domestic threats. They therefore also lack the right incentives to provide the optimal level of security.

Not all predators act out of greed. Some breach protected data to advance a political agenda or shift the distribution of power, seeking fame and virtue in the process. Snowden, Manning, and Assange, their fans claim, meant to benefit the world by revealing the cruelties and abuses of US national security and foreign policy. The publishers of the Panama and Pandora papers see themselves as exposing corruption and holding the privileged and powerful to account. Certainly people see state espionage differently depending on the identities of perpetrator and target. I do not rule out that in some cases predation may produce benefits that exceed its costs. My point is only to unpack those costs and relate them to a world that increasingly has moved online.

Online communication and data processing and storage lose value if users cannot trust the technology. Not all data accumulation and analysis undermines trust, but compromising private and protected information does. Chapter 5 talks about ransomware attacks as a symptom of the failings of cyberspace. The problem generalizes. Anything stored online is vulnerable to theft and destruction, from financial transactions to medical records to pipeline management to air traffic control.

A particular problem with the predatory possibilities of the cyberworld is the potential for insulating state power from outside accountability. Throughout history, autocracies have spied on their subjects to detect threats and plots that might unseat the autocrat. Even liberal democracies have been known to engage in this behavior, if not to the same degree. Existing and developing technologies make that task much easier.

As noted elsewhere in this book, China provides a model of how this works. First, its Great Firewall strains out messages and opinions that the authorities do not want heard. Having lived with feeble Soviet attempts at the same thing during the 1970s and 1980s, I find current Chinese capability amazing and see no reason why it can't get even better. Second, China's insistence that foreign providers of networked services – social media, search engines, and news outlets – have a physical presence within the country makes it easier to penetrate and surveil what happens on those networks. Third, the subordination to the state of nominally private and increasingly popular domestic network-services providers such as Tencent gives the authorities unrestrained access to online life just as many more of their subjects move into that space. Big data combined with ever better artificial intelligence enhances the prediction and negation of threats to entrenched power. The subjugation of Hong Kong provides a powerful example of how a state can wield this power and to what ends.[6]

China represents the epitome of autocratic self-preservation, but similarly minded states aspire to catch up. Russia has scoured social media to identify and punish dissenters to its Ukrainian war. Rumblings in the press suggest Saudi Arabia has similar aspirations. As the technology becomes cheaper and more pervasive, the odds grow shorter that more states hostile to democratic accountability will follow.

These capacities need not remain confined to the South. As national populism captures more territory, and as more states in the West give in to attacks on liberal democracy, the temptation to resort to surveillance and repression will grow. The Polish government acknowledged that it had acquired Pegasus spyware, an enhanced surveillance technology, although it denied using this capability against domestic political opponents. The Greek government owned up to spying on its opposition. We may yet come to a point where the confidence of the 1990s about the invincibility of liberal democracy will exactly reverse itself. People may accept as the natural order a world where rulers choose their subjects, rather than the opposite.

The point remains the same. Liberal democracy may draw on the knowledge economy to make more people happy and prosperous, but it does not necessarily have the means to protect against those of its accomplishments that threaten its very existence. The game may not yet be lost, but the challenge is great.

6 Dimitar D. Gueorguiev, Retrofitting Leninism: Participation without Democracy in China (2021).

THE TURN AGAINST HUMAN RIGHTS

The West, first in the wake of World War II and then more intensely and legalistically during the waning of the Cold War, advanced human rights as a category of entitlements that bound all states universally as a matter of international law. This project dovetailed with the knowledge economy, I show in Chapter 6, by advancing what I call liberal equality. More generally, liberal democracy, which the West puts at the center of its conception of human rights, aspires to check state power. This checking may protect knowledge workers and the firms that organize their work from what they see as wasteful state interference.

The West's conception of human rights largely excludes those entitlements that might advance economic equality.[7] The ascent of the knowledge economy does not fully explain why that understanding of human rights necessarily went in this direction. But the advance of knowledge-infused means of production certainly did not lead to greater efforts to promote economic equality. As I explain in Chapter 6, economic equality threatens knowledge workers and the firms in which they work with a redistribution of the returns from their talents, a prospect that few truly embrace.

One of the casualties of national populism is universalism. As Chapter 5 observes, there are at least as many flavors of nationalism as there are nations. A common core, however, is resistance to the idea that universal values and practices exist and play a significant part in the shaping of people, their societies, and their politics. The assumption that human rights are universal runs up against a belief in essential national histories and qualities. Revisionist political forces, including regimes in power in the South and, increasingly, the West, depict the version of human rights that grew up in the 1970s as an insidious attempt to cancel national culture and its achievements and promise.

If revisionists come to power in more places, we can anticipate further degradation of the human rights commitments made in earlier times. Probably this will start with backing away from the human rights courts that either were created or greatly expanded their authority in the 1990s, namely the ICC and the Strasbourg Court. Independent international courts are an affront to nationalist regimes that deny the right of outsiders to judge what they do. Unlike civil society or the name-and-shame measures of other states, the courts also wield a measure of direct power, including ordering arrests (in the case of the ICC) and imposing fines (in the case of Strasbourg).

7 Samuel Moyn, Not Enough: Human Rights in an Unequal World (2019).

Of the two, the ICC is newest, least established, and accordingly most vulnerable. As Chapter 3 notes, no country that has a serious capacity to project military force outside its borders joined the Rome Statute. France and the United Kingdom, which did, may possess nuclear weapons but have woefully underfunded militaries that act only as part of larger coalitions or in low-impact interventions in their former colonies. The Court has spent billions of dollars with only a handful of convictions, all African, to its credit. This imbalance led Burundi, Gambia, and South Africa to moot withdrawal. South Africa remains only because its constitutional court forbade the government from pulling out. The Philippines, recently subject to an ICC investigation, has vowed to do whatever it takes to thwart the Court.

As for the Strasbourg Court, a growing number of countries subject to its jurisdiction have turned to defiance of its edicts. Chapter 12 explores these cases in detail. Even though the Council of Europe, the international body to which the Court is attached, predates the ancestor of the European Union by several years, the United Kingdom has floated the idea of abandoning that court in the backwash of Brexit. As Chapter 4 mentions, the Hungarian and Polish governments have already made clear that Strasbourg means nothing to them. Were the National Front or a similar party to capture France, a French renunciation of the Council accompanying a withdrawal from the European Union seems likely. Macron's survival in the 2022 presidential election postponed that prospect but did not erase it.

A turn away from human rights based on international law, in both Europe and the rest of the world, follows naturally from a more general movement away from liberal democratic governance. States might back away from the international courts, however, even if they hew to political systems that rely on checks and balances, the rule of law, and democratic accountability to limit what government can do. States could come to the conclusion that the concept of fundamental rights is culturally specific enough, and that their own institutions are sufficiently independent and robust, to make international oversight unnecessary if not undesirable.

Still, ending outside oversight of human rights might complement the erosion of liberal political institutions more broadly. A revolt against the knowledge economy might take on both. The rise of China as a global power might accelerate the process, if only because that would undercut the belief that liberal democracy represents the best way of coping with an uncertain and challenging world.

* * *

Prospects of war, nuclear proliferation, climate catastrophe, the degradation of cyberspace, unstoppable surveillance, better armed authoritarian states, and a retreat from human rights shape our future. The knowledge economy, where we might seek workarounds to limit these threats, so far has been part of the problem. Neither peace nor prosperity seems in the offing.

10

Immigration

In Europe after 1989, one of the earliest visible signs of the world's transformation was the changing mix in peoples you could hear and see on the streets. In Paris in the 1990s, I increasingly heard Polish and Russian around town, on the street, at tourist sites, and in restaurants. By the end of the century, busloads of Chinese tourists appeared in the Louvre and the Champs-Elysées. Central and Eastern Europeans too poor to stay or dine in Venice would take the train from Treviso for day trips, packing their meals and glorying in the grandeur without spending anything. Human mobility became manifest.

Tourism is all well and good and a critical source of revenue for some places, but the movement of workers in search of jobs has a more enduring impact on life around the world. In my niche industry – legal education – our customers (law students) increasingly came from the global South and did not necessarily return home upon receiving their degree. We symmetrically hired more foreign-trained academics to staff our faculties. The global law firm comprising thousands of lawyers in offices around the world emerged as a new template for legal practice.

What happened in education and law took place in many industries that relied on talent and skill to deliver specialized services and make technologically sophisticated products. Knowledge workers became cosmopolitans, living away from their homeland for months on end or picking up stakes altogether to live in a new place, usually a great global city. Expat communities swelled in places like London, Melbourne, Moscow, New York, Paris, Prague, and Sydney, cities where I lived and worked from 1991 to 2002.

My first morning at work in Vienna in 1998, I met the cleaning staff, all ladies dressed in traditional country clothing from the Turkish countryside and speaking no English and not much German. This was another face of worker mobility, one involving menial work and none of the skills that the knowledge economy prized. Yet their work was essential for the office to function. The women from Turkey did their jobs well and, I suspected, better and at a lower price than Austrians from the countryside whom the university might otherwise hire to clean the offices.

ANTI-IMMIGRANT POPULISM

This happy face of immigration – me as a knowledge worker from the United States and the women from Turkey – had a dark underside. A year later, the *Freiheitliche Partei Österreichs* (FPÖ), a national populist party opposed to Islamic immigrants, came second in the parliamentary elections and entered government in coalition with Austria's Christian Democrats, the *Österreichische Volkspartei* (ÖVP). The European Union immediately punished Austria for allowing the FPÖ to share power, maintaining that its policies had no place in a modern European order. Mostly the sanctions involved barring the government from participating in various meetings of EU functionaries and thus EU governance.

The momentary success of the FPÖ, which lost power three years later, did not lead to a mass expulsion of people like the university's cleaners. It did, however, send a warning signal. A significant number of votes were to be had by opposing the kind of personal mobility that the European Union embodied. The euro had just been adopted, prefiguring a transformation in daily life. Many people weren't happy with this rupture in history and embraced politicians who promised to resist the busybodies in Brussels. Turning on immigrants who did the jobs that, educated people thought, no one else wanted was part of the resistance.

In this century, the most visible and impassioned battlefield between the interests of the knowledge economy and the agenda of national populists is immigration. The knowledge economy thrives on free mobility of knowledge workers. Vesting legal protection in these people when they migrate further encourages them to move to places that best take advantage of their skills. The knowledge economy also likes free immigration of other workers, but not necessarily the bestowal of legal rights on them. Low-skill workers make life easier for knowledge workers, thus lowering the cost of knowledge-worker labor. Not giving them full legal protection allows their employers to capture a greater share of the economic surplus created when low-skill immigrants work in high-social-capital societies. As long as the cost to these immigrants of incomplete legal protection does not exceed their portion of the gain from moving to a better place, economic logic predicts that immigration will still unfold.

For those in the hinterlands who became the victims of the knowledge economy, both kinds of immigrants fuel their fury, but for different reasons. Foreign knowledge workers disrupt their sense of entitlement. Not only are the left-behind not getting a share of the prosperity produced by the economic transformation, but people who do not look like them, talk like them, or share any substantial cultural contacts with them do benefit. Success enjoyed by people with whom they have nothing in common inspires greater anger and resentment than that of people with whom they may have some ties, however superficial.

Low-skill immigrants attract even greater anger and resentment because they compete directly with the knowledge economy's victims. Simply by their numbers they drive down the price of low-skill jobs. People who had worked on assembly lines could move into construction or yard work without too much loss of dignity or pay, were the labor supply sufficiently tight. Low-skill immigrants make that less likely. To be sure, economists disagree about the extent of substitution of immigrant labor for incumbent and the income effects. But that some effect exists for some people seems clear enough.[1]

The informality of the immigrants' status reinforces the anger. People who arrive clandestinely, as do undocumented immigrants throughout the West, or without regular visas, as do those who claim refugee status under international law, can be accused of not playing by the rules and, in some cases, as lawbreakers. People who assert refugee status but do not wait for an official determination before moving into a society and taking on work fall into this category. The incumbent left-behinds rage that these people get a free pass from the law while they suffer.

Of course, many of the dispossessed may dislike immigrants simply because they have different-colored skin and come from another culture. Racism remains a force just about everywhere. Economic resentment and selective concerns about legality may mask something far uglier. It does not require much historical imagination to compare hostility to immigrants in contemporary western societies to the antisemitism that motivated Russian anger at the status quo in the years before the Revolution (remember the pogroms) or, even more obviously, that inspired Germans in the 1930s.

However toxic the brew, it remains true that resentment of low-skill, informal immigrants prevails in much of the West and provides great opportunities

[1] *Compare* David Card, *Immigrant Inflows, Native Outflows, and the Local Labor Market Impacts of Higher Immigration*, 19 J. LAB. ECON. 22 (2001), with George J. Borjas, *The Labor Demand Curve Is Downward Sloping: Reexamining the Impact of Immigration on the Labor Market*, 118 Q. J. ECON. 1335 (2003).

to politicians willing to exploit it. We can debate whether addressing the causes of economic resentment and legalizing the status of all immigrants would abate these opportunities. These measures are unlikely over the short run. If the source of resentment is not plutocrats but the knowledge economy and those who thrive in it, liberalizing immigration becomes even more challenging.

The alternative and more likely outcome is a worldwide battle against cross-border migration even as environmental, economic, and military forces make more of the world unsafe. In a contest between compassion and decency, on the one hand, and hard political and economic interest, on the other, interest has a way of coming out ahead. Consider what the battle over expansion of asylum might look like and what it might cost.

IMMIGRATION AND INTERNATIONAL LAW

I focus on the legalities first. In Europe, the rule of free movement of people rests primarily on the Schengen Agreement, an international treaty that includes all EU and European Free Trade Association members except Bulgaria, Croatia, Cyprus, Ireland, and Romania. Movement among Schengen countries is largely free of border controls, no matter what nationality the traveler might have.

Were the European Union to retrench or reorganize in the wake of a withdrawal by, say, France, the unraveling of Schengen would likely follow in short order. Indeed, even if the European Union were to survive to the end of the 2020s, it seems likely that the member states will more frequently and for longer periods invoke the emergency exception that allows restoration of border controls. Either way, significant impairment of the present borderless regime for much of Europe seems likely.

Restriction of movement within the Schengen area matters because not all European countries face equal exposure to immigrants from the Middle East, Africa, and now Ukraine. For most of this century, those claiming refugee status and others who hope only for a better life enter through Italy or Greece by crossing the Mediterranean or transiting through Turkey. More recently, Poland has come under pressure from immigrants passing through Belarus as well as a new wave coming out of Ukraine. These destination states adamantly reject their frontline status and will take in more informal immigrants only if interior European states agree to share the burden. Germany under Merkel did this, but the ensuing backlash makes future cooperation from interior states less likely.

These pressures will also invite rich destination states – the United States even more than the Europeans – to reconsider who counts as a refugee under international law and how to implement the obligation to protect those who qualify for this status. Just as a matter of technical lawyering, three issues arise: (1) Who counts as a refugee facing a well-founded fear of persecution? (2) When do a state's duties to refugees attach? (3) Do refugees already in a state that does not threaten to persecute them have the right to go somewhere that they think affords them better opportunities?

Chapter 8 describes the basics of refugee status under international law. A state may not deport a person who meets the definition of a refugee to a country where a risk of persecution exists, although it may move refugees to another country where their lives would not be threatened. Refugees are people who fear persecution due to their characteristics, such as political commitments, religion, or ethnic identity. The broadest, or at least the most indefinite, of characteristics that trigger refugee status is "social status." Lawyers seeking to expand who counts as a refugee argue that people facing a risk of persecution due to their identity as a woman or a sexual minority meet this test. For example, Grover Rees, at the time general counsel for the Immigration and Naturalization Service during the George H. W. Bush administration and a long-time conservative Republican activist, ruled that Chinese women affected by that country's one-child policy qualify as refugees under international law.

A generous approach might regard subjection to the chaos of a failed state as persecution and treat anyone lacking the resources to protect against such an evil as having the "social status" from which persecution flows. The law could treat "poor and weak" as a social status. This strategy would allow people fleeing from famine or disorder to count as refugees, even if their risk were general rather than based on traditional characteristics such as politics or minority status, and even though the threat of persecution stemmed from government powerlessness rather than active measures. In a world of greater conflict and environmental catastrophe, driven by climate change as well as a decline in international order, such an approach could accommodate the human casualties of these disruptions.

If hostility to immigration grows, however, we are more likely to see governments looking for ways to shrink the protected class. They might insist that "social status" be understood in reference to the more specific categories mentioned in the treaties – "reasons of race, religion, nationality ... and political opinion" – and focus more on the kinds of active persecution that originally motivated the treaty, such as that of Jews by the Germans. The world does not lack today for persecution of well-defined groups, such as the Uighurs in China, the Rohingya in Myanmar, and the Yazidi in the Middle East and South Asia. A growing number of governments would restrict *non-refoulement* to members of these kinds of groups as well as traditional categories such as political refugees. People terrorized by gangs and civil war in El Salvador or Guatemala, for example, would not qualify, because a failure to protect from nonstate violence would not count as persecution. Many will see this as retrogressive, as indeed it would be. But progress and humanity in matters of high policy cannot be taken for granted.

A more technical question is the evidentiary standard used to establish a "well-founded fear of persecution." The Supreme Court interpreted this requirement as mandating only proof of a reasonable fear, not of the objective likelihood of persecution. It distinguished refugee status, defined by international law and implemented in relevant legislation, from people entitled not to be deported under US law even if another country would take them. The latter must show that it is "more likely than not" that they will be persecuted if repatriated. Asylum-seekers, the Court held, face a lower burden of proof because what they get, as a matter of international obligation, is less than what the United States bestows on people objectively facing persecution.[2]

In a more rigorous and less generous world, states might move toward equating "fear" with objective probability. To qualify for asylum, refugees would have to present objective evidence to persuade the authorities that they face a clear and present danger that the country in which they live singles out people with their particular characteristics for persecution. Fear based on chaos and state failure would not suffice.

BARRIERS TO ENTRY

A collateral issue is when the *non-refoulement* obligation attaches. This question arises when the naval forces of a state intercept people claiming asylum before they reach that state's shores. Friends of asylum argue that as soon as a state exercises control over people found on the high seas, it acquires the duty under international law to process the asylum claim and must host those people on its territory while doing so. So Harold Koh, a Yale law professor representing Haitians fleeing chaos in their homeland, argued to the Supreme Court in 1993. Only Harry Blackmun, Koh's former boss, bought the argument. The remaining justices found no support in the treaties or international practice.[3] Afterwards, however, several international human rights bodies, including the Inter-American Commission on Human Rights, the UN High

[2] *I.N.S.* v. *Cardoza-Francesca*, 480 U.S. 421 (1987).

[3] *Sale* v. *Haitian Centers Council, Inc.* 509 U.S. 155 (1993).

Commissioner for Refugees, the Strasbourg Court, and an Australian court embraced Koh's view.[4]

For states that face seaborne immigrants hoping to claim asylum status, the issue matters. It probably affects Europe even more than the United States and is a focus of Australian politics. If opposition to immigrants continues to mount around the rich world, we might expect greater use of naval resources to keep asylum seekers offshore. Australia might supply the model. Its government stores intercepted immigrants in offshore facilities either under its jurisdiction or, more frequently lately, on island microstates that host asylum seekers in return for Australian remittances.

These strategies seem cruel, especially as the craft on which asylum seekers travel often are unseaworthy and sometimes pose a deadly risk. Well-publicized tragedies have followed the turning back of immigrant-loaded ships in the Mediterranean and the English Channel, and Caribbean deaths are not unknown. But in a crueler world, states may regard these casualties as worth the price of appeasing domestic resentments.

For immigrants coming by land, the issue becomes what measures a state can take to prevent them from entering. From one point of view, rights under international law attach no later than when a person claiming asylum touches the territory of a state. From that moment, the argument goes, a state must give asylum seekers a personal hearing to determine whether they qualify for *non-refoulement*. This is true even if a mass of people storm a border and touch the territory as a mob. Presence alone matters, regardless of how a person attained the presence.

Some states reject that argument and assert an inherent right to protect their borders from lawlessness. They argue that they may expel people who arrived as part of a mob without first providing each person an individualized and necessarily time-consuming procedure to establish eligibility for refugee status. A border means nothing, they claim, if a state cannot use at least limited force to protect it.

The Grand Chamber of the Strasbourg Court, interpreting the asylum right as incorporated into the European Convention on Human Rights, gave a qualified endorsement to a state's power to expel asylum seekers who arrive as part of a mob. It ruled that, as long as a state (here Spain) has in place a mechanism to provide the requisite individualized hearing, it can insist that people seeking entry comply with reasonable time-and-place rules about where to present themselves for processing. A state therefore can evict people

4 *Hirsi Jamaa* v. *Italy*, App. No. 27765/09, (2012) 55 Eur. Hum. Rts. Rep. 21; *Plaintiff M70/2011* v. *Minister for Immigration and Citizenship*, 244 CLR 144 (2011) (Austl.).

who flout those rules without giving them a hearing first. It rejected the assertion of the UN High Commissioner that Spain did not have reasonable rules in place at the time of the incident.[5]

A later decision by a panel of that Court somewhat walked back that ruling. It ruled that a group that arrived illicitly in a country enjoyed at least a right to a safe expulsion. When Croatia returned a large Afghan family to Serbia without alerting authorities on the other side that they were coming, it bore legal responsibility for the death of one of the children in an accident that Serbian police, if alerted, could have prevented.[6]

In the United States, territoriality does a lot of work, but the government still uses mass expulsions. A 2021 Haitian episode provoked high-profile resignations from the Biden administration, including Harold Koh from the State Department. It involved people who had found their way into the United States en masse and whom US authorities put on airplanes without tendering them individual hearings to determine asylum eligibility. If history provides any guidance, lawsuits will follow and US courts yet may speak on the issue.

We don't know whether the European doctrine of safe expulsion will migrate to other countries. The current direction of European politics, however, points toward greater discretion to expel informal immigrants, not less. If the Strasbourg Court pushes too hard the other way, it may have to give ground or, even worse, see states flout its edicts.

The Australian strategy and the mass expulsion controversy implicate another legal issue built into the treaties governing refugees. People seeking entry into the rich world almost never arrive directly from the site of their persecution. Instead, they collect in transit states such as Mexico (for the United States), Belarus, Libya, Tunisia, and Turkey (for Europe), and Indonesia and Malaysia (for Australia). Almost without exception, no one trying to come to these rich states claims that these transit states intend to persecute them. Rather, their grievance is that they are unwelcome in the transit state, housed in awful camps, and have terrible life prospects for themselves and their children.

The Luxembourg Court added a pro-asylum gloss to this question in a decision resting on EU law rather than the Refugee Convention itself. Hungary adopted a law permitting categorical rejection of asylum applications whenever the applicant came from a country where the applicant did not face persecution or a risk of serious harm. The corresponding EU legislation, meant to control implementation of the Convention, permits denial of asylum

5 *N.D. and N.T.* v. *Spain*, Apps. No. 8675/15 and 8697/15 Eur. Ct. H.R. (2020).

6 *M.H. and Others* v. *Croatia*, Apps. No. 15,670/18 and 43,115/18 Eur. Ct. H.R. (2021).

to people coming from a "safe" country. The Luxembourg Court added a gloss to the "safe" requirement. It ruled that a country could be considered safe only if the applicant had some connection to it so as to make it reasonable to go there. Hungary, it held, did not take this gloss into account and therefore violated the legislation, if not the Convention itself.[7]

Arguably the international law *non-refoulement* obligation applies only to people who have arrived on a state's territory and can prove their entitlement to asylum. The Luxembourg Court did not rule that a state that closes its borders to people fleeing persecution who find themselves in a transit state violates its obligation under international law, however uncharitable and uncooperative such acts may be. Paying the transit state to take the asylum seekers off their hands, as the European Union does with Turkey, Australia with the microstates, and the United States could do with Mexico and Central American states, complies with the letter of international law, if not, perhaps, the spirit.

What we might see more of in the future, then, is immigrant dumping. As political upheaval and climate crises drive more people from their homelands, more people will arrive at the gates of the rich world. Rather than taking them in, rich countries will pay poor ones to store them. Decent people will claim that international law demands more than storage, that basic human rights include a fair opportunity to flourish and includes a right to housing, health care, and education. But as people pile up in camps for ever longer stays, these pleas are increasingly likely to fall on deaf ears.

THE FUTURE OF BORDER CONTROL

What might states do about border control in the near future? Recall that, regional structures such as the European Union and international refugee law aside, states retain a wide range of discretion about whom to allow into their countries, especially as to people seeking access to domestic labor markets. What might they do with this discretion as national populism wields greater influence?

For large continental states such as the United States and the BRICS, the issue would turn on resources as much as political will. As surveillance technologies proliferate and improve, the cost of tracking the legal status of residents likely will go down. Experience gained monitoring the vaccination status of people during the pandemic might end up pointing to inexpensive

7 Cases C-924/19 PPU and C-925/14 PPU, Országos Idegenrendészeti Föigazgatóság Dél-alföldi Regionális Igazgatóság, 2020 E.C.R. I-367 (2020).

means of confirming who is and is not documented and entitled to remain in the places where they dwell.

Over the last twenty years or so, the United States has dithered about deploying technologies that would oblige businesses to show they do not use undocumented aliens. Business groups vigorously resist, as they understandably prefer the wage savings attributable to the legal insecurity of these workers. As pressure mounts about border controls, however, the fruits of the knowledge economy might come into play. Just as people have had to show proof of vaccination to dine out in certain cities or attend live entertainment, cell phone apps and similar devices might enable employers, landlords, and merchants to determine quickly the legal status of people with whom they deal. The deployment of tamper-resistant forms of identification tied to official records would seem well within reach, even though we have not yet taken this step for vaccinations.

In this world, states could substitute verification technologies for expensive and largely ineffectual border compliance measures such as fencing. States that wanted to attack supply effects on low-wage labor by cutting back the informal economy would have a tool to do that. With credible means of tracking down new arrivals, they might even begin the process of identifying undocumented people who enjoy valuable ties where they currently reside with an eye to regularizing their legal status. With good detection technologies, an amnesty for legacy undocumented workers need not become an incentive for new arrivals.

I can imagine a completely different approach to immigration. As Chapter 6 shows, countries like the United States, the United Kingdom, France, Italy, and Australia have done well, among other reasons, because for much of their history they took in large numbers of people from troubled parts of the world. They have blended these immigrants with their incumbent populations in ways that enriched all sides both materially and culturally. No country has done this better and at greater scale than the United States. It is this quality that distinguishes the United States from China and Japan, the countries with the second and third largest economies, and holds out hope of future adaptation, resilience, and even progress, relative to these economic competitors.

BLEAK FUTURES

As long as the politics of resentment continue to shape the rich world, however, advocates of immigration need more than evidence that it makes a net contribution to national well-being. The net is the problem: discrete and significant segments of society do not see those benefits. Unless we can address that problem, we face the prospect of lower labor mobility around the world. These barriers might even extend beyond workers who directly compete with those left behind by the knowledge economy. Blocking immigration of knowledge workers would hurt the modern world economy exactly where it has done best.

A dystopian future might consign immigrants fleeing chaos and deprivation to dead-end camps just as the rich world starves itself of the talent needed to innovate and prevail. Differences in how national economies perform will turn more on each state's ability to grow human capital within its own borders, a race that the West could well lose to China. The costs of our present conflicts may scale. International law will not help us here.

* * *

Even more than fancy new toys and online life, the face of the knowledge economy has been the cross-border movement of people. The new economy gives many more people around the planet the chance to travel across borders to learn new skills, make new connections, and find new work. Some leave their homes for years and others migrate more or less for their entire working lives.

In much of the world, states react to these movements in ways that make it harder for people displaced and demoralized by the knowledge economy to adapt to the new work environment. They have many beefs with the new status quo but concentrate on immigration as a proxy for the others. The left-behind hate it that low-skill immigrants service the new economy's winners while blocking their path to finding dignifying work, often doing so informally and in a sense illegally. The left-behind come to see these immigrants as not only harmful but a symptom of élite corruption.

The attacks on immigration that result will put not only prosperity, but ultimately peace, at risk. As natural forces and civil war drive more people from their homelands, no-hope camps will grow and fester near the now closed borders of rich countries. They will breed violence and terrorism. Great-power rivals will seek to weaponize these forces, or at a minimum refuse to cooperate to defuse threats. Misery and danger will threaten all, not just the wretched of the earth.

This book's final part considers whether we can expect to return to a world where people have a reasonable chance of finding their best lives regardless of national borders. The best answer is that tremendous, perhaps insurmountable obstacles lie ahead. A more venturesome response is that we should not give up hope, but that much patience is needed. Of only one thing I am sure: we do not have a magic bullet that will fix the immigration crisis any time soon.

11

Trade and Investment

Trade and investment may seem prosaic topics, of interest to specialist technocrats but not to the general public. For national populists, however, blandness is part of the problem. They see technicalities as masking the ravages of corrupt élites. International flows of goods, services, and capital, both strategic and portfolio, provide the life's blood of the world economic system that empowers the knowledge economy. As populists see it, stopping the free movement of economic activity across borders is the only way to save good people and their national societies from the oppression of liberal internationalism. That this target comes clothed with a veneer of law-based international respectability makes it more dangerous, not less.

Students of twentieth-century history see trade and investment as critical not only for prosperity but for peace. World War I had many causes and ultimately may have been so irrational as to defy any interest-based account. Yet the construction of empires as bulwarks against free trade and investment certainly laid some of the groundwork for the cataclysm. The nationalist reactions to the Great Depression of most economically significant states, including throwing up trade barriers, helped pave the way to an even more dreadful conflagration. The measures taken in the wake of World War II, principally through the GATT and, from 1965 on, the Bank's ICSID facility for investment disputes, rested on a hope that they would place speed bumps on the road to war.

Undoing these arrangements thus means more than repudiating the ideological overreach of the 1990s. Not only would the world lose a great engine of economic growth, but it would weaken the incentives that induce smart, creative people to contribute to the knowledge economy. Perhaps capitalism in one country based on Chinese hegemony will suffice as a substitute. But, as Chapter 8 points out, and I reconsider in Chapter 13, Chinese hegemony still has a lot going against it. As we wind down the institutions that promote free trade and investment, we may face as an unintended consequence a more dangerous, as well as a grimmer, future.

Chapters 2 and 3 describe what the Washington Consensus meant for international trade and investment. The liberal internationalism that Washington prescribed took hold first and most deeply in economic fields, as these provided the most direct opportunities for the knowledge economy. Both multilateral organizations such as the WTO and ICSID and regional ones such as the European Union and NAFTA offered international legal support for free trade in goods and services and the movement of enterprises and capital across borders.

Brexit and the election of Trump as President represented noisy attempts by two of the leading architects of liberal internationalism to walk away from these structures. The United Kingdom diminished the European Union by leaving it; folks in Brussels live in fear that Brexit will not diminish the United Kingdom. Trump redid NAFTA as well as the US–Korea Free Trade Agreement. The damage that the United States did to the WTO, however, seems the bigger story.

THE RETURN OF PROTECTION AND UNDERMINING THE WTO

Under US trade law, the president may restrict imports of particular goods through higher duties or other barriers, such as a quota or ban, if imports present a threat to the country's national security. Section 232, the provision bestowing this authority, was a central part of the Kennedy administration's principal legislative initiative, the Trade Expansion Act of 1962. President Ford invoked it in 1975 to impose licensing fees on oil imports, a measure that won the Supreme Court's blessing after an importer's legal challenge. The Court took a generous view of the President's discretion to determine what constitutes a national security threat as well as what measures will suffice to abate it. The case illustrates the reluctance of the US judiciary to constrain a president's intervention in international trade, no matter how amorphous the national security claim, on the basis of an open-ended legislative delegation.[1]

No President took greater advantage of this authority than did Trump. His administration launched eight investigations by the Department of Commerce, six of which resulted in positive findings of a national security threat and five of which he accepted. His response was transactional rather than interventionist. He used the positive findings to launch negotiations with

1 *FEA* v. *Algonquin SNG, Inc.*, 426 U.S. 548 (1976).

other countries. These sought to induce exporting states to reduce what they sold into the US market, rather than putting the burden on the United States to maintain a trade barrier.

In the case of steel and aluminum, Trump imposed special duties, with exceptions for countries in preexisting trade agreements with the United States. When negotiations failed, as they did with Turkey, the administration increased duties above the baseline in the original notice. Importers litigated whether the second-stage increases fit within the statute's time limits, but the one federal court with appellate jurisdiction over these duties upheld them.[2]

Since coming to office, the Biden administration has left these measures in place and launched new Section 232 investigations of other imports. It did negotiate a special deal with the European Union, adhering to Trump's transactional model, that substitutes export-state-imposed controls for US import barriers. According to press reports, it seeks to do the same for Japan. It remains committed to the same basic strategy that Trump used of unilateral trade measures resting on dubious national security claims.

Questions of domestic legal authority aside, the Section 232 measures call into question the US relationship with the WTO. Under WTO rules, a state "binds" itself to a schedule of duties (a tariff) from which it can move downwards but not exceed. The Uruguay Round Agreements also provide for exceptions to this rule. They permit a state to impose temporary trade barriers called "safeguards" to address sudden surges of imports to the detriment of its domestic producers. Safeguards must comply with other WTO rules, in particular that requiring equal application of the measure to all members (most-favored-nation treatment). This law allows other states to retaliate with proportional increases in their duties on the goods exported by the safeguard imposer. States can also impose extra duties, called antidumping duties and countervailing duties, that negate benefits that the exporter derives from specified anticompetitive practices or proscribed state subsidies. Elaborate rules apply to the imposition of both these kinds of fairness-based penalties.

The United States relies on none of these exceptions for its new measures. It instead rests these duties on the most problematic of WTO exceptions, that applying to the protection of national security. This particular exception is problematic not because it allows states to take their national security into account. Such rules are pervasive in trade and investment agreements and in any event seem unavoidable in a world where states must attend to their

[2] *Transpacific Steel LLC* v. *United States*, 4 F.4th 1306 (Fed. Cir. 2021).

security. Rather, the provision sets up a conundrum because it seems to allow a state to decide for itself what it can do under the national security umbrella.

Article XXI(b) of GATT allows a state to disregard its obligations under the GATT system when:

> taking any action *which it considers* necessary for the protection of its essential security interests ... (ii) relating to the traffic in arms, ammunition and implements of war and to such traffic in other goods and materials as is carried on directly or indirectly for the purpose of supplying a military establishment; (iii) taken in time of war or other emergency in international relations.

The question that jumps out is the scope of the "it considers" modifier. What room does this language leave for adjudication of disputes by the WTO?

At least three plausible interpretations present themselves. First, the WTO, acting through its dispute-resolution organs, might address only the question whether a state does "consider" the otherwise unlawful measure necessary for its national security interests. Second, the WTO might decide that, as an objective matter, the measure is connected in some way to military procurement or is taken in the context of an emergency in international relations. Third, the WTO might judge whether a state's claim as to what measures it considers necessary is made in good faith, enabling the WTO to make an independent assessment of the measure's necessity in response to either procurement needs or an international crisis.

These three approaches represent points along a continuum running from easy invocation, meaning effortless shrugging off of WTO obligations, all the way to rigorous scrutiny of a state's motivations and the real basis of its concerns, meaning third-party oversight dominating a wide range of trade disputes. A prior issue, however, is whether the "it considers" language permits any third-party review at all.

A state might plausibly argue that when it invokes its essential security interests, all WTO supervisory jurisdiction disappears. Efforts by the WTO to argue otherwise must then be considered illegitimate. In technical language, the "it considers" language denies the WTO the capacity definitively and authoritatively to determine its jurisdiction – what in Europe is known as *kompetenz kompetenz*.

If this argument has any bite, the WTO has a problem. Without third-party enforcement, the WTO rules don't function as law so much as desiderata. Rule compliance as such drops out of the system. Instead, more general and hard-to-pin-down qualities such as a state's tendency toward cooperation or disruption do all the work. Robust resort to a national security exception, when this choice easily and perhaps automatically ousts formal dispute settlement, seems to nullify the WTO as a rules-based system that constrains states in the pursuit of a greater good.

For the first twenty years of the WTO, no one sought to test the dispute-settlement system by invoking Article XXI(b). Commentators suggested that the logic of mutually assured destruction applies. The risk of creating an easy way out from formal dispute settlement, and thus undermining the WTO agreements as a legal system, deterred states from opening up the national security Pandora's box.

Mutually assured destruction or not, other WTO states went down this path before the Trump administration did. Russia imposed trade sanctions on Ukraine to discourage it from upgrading its economic ties with the European Union. Saudi Arabia led a coalition to boycott Qatar for its supposed support of revisionist populist movements inspired by the Arab Spring. In both cases, the target of the sanctions sought a ruling from the WTO that the measures violated the Uruguay Round Agreements. Russia and Saudi Arabia both invoked Article XXI as a defense.

In the Russian case, an arbitral panel formed by the WTO ruled that it had jurisdiction to decide whether the elements of a national security defense exist – whether the measures advance a national security interest arising out of a crisis in international relations – and thus rejected self-judging by the respondent state. It explained that an implied

> obligation of good faith . . . applies not only to the Member's definition of the essential security interests said to arise from the particular emergency in international relations, but also, and most importantly, to their connection with the measures at issue. Thus, . . . this obligation is crystallized in demanding that the measures at issue meet a minimum requirement of plausibility in relation to the proffered essential security interests.[3]

Having asserted its right to review the factual basis of Russia's national security claim, it then declared that it found Russia's account satisfactory.

A later panel went further. It rejected Saudi Arabia's argument that a measure was necessary to meet a conceded national security interest. As part of its boycott of Qatar, the Saudi government refused to take action against a private broadcaster operating in its territory whose programming included copyrighted programs belonging to a Qatari firm. Qatar argued that this failure to respect its intellectual property violated its rights under the TRIPS agreement. Enforcing copyright law against a pirate acting within its own

3 Russia – Measures Concerning Traffic in Transit, WT/DS512/R ¶ 7.138 (April 5, 2019).

territory, the panel concluded, would not require the Saudi authorities to interact with Qatari nationals in any way that might create a risk of subversion. Thus, although the government's inaction arose out of an "emergency in international relations" under Article XXI(b)(iii), it was not necessary within the terms of that article, even though Saudi Arabia asserted otherwise. Notwithstanding the "which it considers" language, this call, the panel asserted, was for it to make, not the Saudi government.[4]

Turkey, joined with a number of other WTO members, has a case pending against the United States based on the Section 232 measures. The WTO convened an arbitration panel to address the dispute, but it has delayed because of the pandemic. We cannot expect to hear from the WTO for some time. Because the United States does not recognize the WTO's jurisdiction in the matter, it is unlikely to take part in the proceedings.

The US case tests the meaning of Article XXI to a much greater extent than the Russian or Saudi disputes. Russia was not merely worried about Ukraine, but, at the time it imposed its sanctions and since, effectively at war in Ukraine's Donbas region. Similarly, the members of the Saudi-led coalition faced what they viewed as serious and violent domestic opposition to which, they believed, Qatar gave aid and comfort. In both situations, people died and more casualties were expected. The US measures, by contrast, invoke no specific threat from any adversary, but rather a general sense that existing trade patterns weaken the country.

Shoe-horning the US argument into the language of Article XXI is a reach. If anything less than unrestrained self-judging applies, the claim fails. Indeed, a bloody-minded observer could interpret the US position as a deliberate provocation, meant to expose the disconnect between the formal rules that the WTO applies and the actual balance of interests that sustains the multilateral trade regime. Can the WTO ignore such a challenge?

Complicating the question is the US decision to cancel the Appellate Body, the ultimate arbiter of all disputes addressed to the WTO by its members. As Chapter 3 describes, the Uruguay Round Agreements created this permanent court as part of the WTO's new organizational form. The Appellate Body reviews the decisions of ad hoc arbitral panels so as to impose consistency and lend authority to WTO dispute resolution. A dissatisfied party can appeal its decisions to the entire membership, but only a consensus vote that includes the state that prevailed before the Appellate Body can overturn a decision.

[4] Saudi Arabia – Measures Concerning the Protection of Intellectual Property Rights, WT/DS567/R (June 16, 2020).

The Appellate Body is supposed to have up to seven members who serve staggered four-year terms and sit in panels of three. Going back to the Obama administration, the United States blocked the replacement of any member of that tribunal. For that administration, this was a warning signal indicating dissatisfaction with how the Appellate Body had performed and intended to provoke reform; for the Trump administration, it was a means to another end – the undoing of international supervision of trade law. The Appellate Body lost a quorum to convene in 2019, and has had no members since the end of 2020. The Biden administration, as of this writing, has not reversed its predecessors' course.

Once the Appellate Body lost its quorum, China and the European Union established an alternative appellate body to function as long as the regular one remains out of commission. This mechanism cannot affect the United States or the other states that did not joined that agreement. For the indefinite future, then, we have lost a multilateral dispute settlement process for trade issues just at a time when the government of the world's largest economy wields a legal theory allowing it to disregard any WTO obligation it chooses.

A plausible interpretation of the WTO rules gives no legal effect to a panel's decision when a dissatisfied state has a right of appeal, even though that right is empty because a working appellate mechanism doesn't exit. As a result, current panel decisions, including those interpreting Article XXI, rest in legal limbo. On the one hand, every state that has invoked the national security exception to call off its WTO obligations can fairly argue that the WTO has yet to authoritatively decide against it. On the other hand, the WTO has lost the capacity to authoritatively decide any dispute, including the extent of national security self-judging.

At the end of the day, one cannot tell whether unilateral actions by leading states and consequent tit-for-tat retaliation will undo the international legal order for trade, or whether knocking the WTO out of commission as a dispute settlement body will do the trick. The point is that the WTO today has greatly diminished credibility as an arbiter of trade disputes. If we do successfully navigate the present challenges to the international trading system, it won't be because the WTO will lead us through the storm.

RESHORING SUPPLY CHAINS

Other forces push against reintegration of the world economy. The COVID-19 shock disrupted international supply chains and the shipping that makes them work. In the wake of these events, politicians and pundits call for onshoring supply chains, arguing that the gains from specialization in production do not offset the cost of supply insecurity. The creation of supply chains reflects the decisions of private firms based on their judgment as to where the greater profit lies. Onshoring thus will require massive government intervention, implicating and devaluing WTO rules.

The onshoring argument recapitulates the defense of the British Corn Laws in the first half of the nineteenth century that Chapter 7 recounts. An indefinite national security risk justifies a definite cost in the form of higher prices and lower quality of essential goods. In 1846, Great Britain had enough confidence in its naval hegemony to accept the risk of interruption in the food needed to feed its population and therefore repealed those laws. Today, the question is whether future conflicts, made possible by the dissipation of the power of rich states, make long-term stoppage of supplies sufficiently likely to require a sacrifice of the value gained by this mode of production.

Two tropes, old but hardy, dominate discussion of this kind of issue. On the one hand, the Munich metaphor, referring to British Prime Minister Chamberlain's capitulation to Hitler in 1938 that greased the path to World War II, suggests that threats may be larger than they seem and that stalwart resistance deters greater catastrophes down the road. On the other hand, Smoot–Hawley, a reference to the eponymous 1930 statute that erected a tariff wall around the US economy in reaction to the 1929 financial crisis, stands for the claim that defensive measures, specifically new trade barriers, provoked by a local crisis can invite retaliation with a pinwheel effect that metastasizes the crisis. Smoot–Hawley contributed to the worldwide Great Depression and made things worse in the United States, not just for the rest of the world.

Both tropes are clichés that invite the suspension of critical thinking. This does not mean that they always fail to get at something important. The Smoot–Hawley metaphor, for example, captures a big piece of the story behind the terrible performance of the economies of the former Soviet states in the years immediately after the breakup of the Soviet Union. Soviet central planning was hostile to vertical integration and thus made most enterprises dependent on other firms as both suppliers and customers. When the Soviet Union ceased to exist, many of these connections suddenly faced customs frontiers as well as insecurity-driven hoarding by traditional counterparties. Sales and purchases froze, with larger enterprises taking years to recover and the general population suffering a sharp and steady immiseration. The residue of this failure reinforced convictions across the post-Soviet area, excepting perhaps the three Baltic republics that fell into the arms of the European

Union, that liberal economics as well as liberal democratic institutions were a con, not a path to prosperity.[5]

Onshoring supply chains similarly would disrupt established commercial ties. In isolation, the breakups would test individual firms' resilience and perhaps feed the optimistic narrative of creative destruction. Undertaken en masse, an unwinding of the supply chain economy could lead to systematic uncertainty and the freezing of an important slice of economic life, much as happened on the territory of the former Soviet Union. The Smoot–Hawley horror story could come back to haunt us.

Yet we seem headed in exactly this direction. The increase in international insecurity, driven by the recent system shocks and then the joint trauma of rising national populism and the COVID-19 pandemic, leaves states more vulnerable than ever to self-harm justified by self-sufficiency. Bipartisan support for such measures exist in the United States, and any further unraveling of the European Union likely would create new barriers to distributed production. The consequences may be great.

WITHDRAWING PROTECTION FOR INTERNATIONAL INVESTMENT

As Chapter 7 shows, cross-border capital flows drive the knowledge economy every bit as much as the movement of goods and services. Supply chains work because financial capital and know-how can migrate to places that create the most value for the investment required. Barriers to investment sunder existing relations and block the search for new arrangements that could make use of comparative advantage in the production process. More generally, strategic investments typically transfer commercially valuable knowledge to places where they can generate profits.

The legal mechanisms that protect cross-border investment are diverse. The investor can invoke whatever protections the host state's legal system provides through its property and contract law as well as what constraints it imposes on state administrative discretion. In most rich states, these protections satisfy most investors. But in states with weak legal systems, especially those that opened up to foreigners only in recent years, the domestic remedies may not inspire confidence. In these instances, an international mechanism might help.[6]

5 Paul B. Stephan III, *Privatization after* Perestroyka: *The Impact of State Structure*, 14 WHITTIER L. REV. 403 (1993).

6 Paul B. Stephan, *International Investment Law and Municipal Law: Substitutes or Complements?* 9 CAPITAL M'KTS L.J. 354 (2014).

International investment law, unlike trade law, focuses more on the back end of transactions. The WTO rules aspire to limit what states can do to keep imported goods and services out. Most of the international law of investment, by contrast, deals with regrets that arise when things don't turn out as hoped. The host state relies on changes in circumstances to justify costly intervention or argues that the investor brought misfortune on itself. The investor claims to have suffered from a bait-and-switch, that the host state did something to upset its legitimate expectations at the time of investment.

As described in Chapter 3, the substantive content of this law evolved in the nineteenth and twentieth century against a backdrop of conflicting views on the part of formerly colonial and formerly colonized states. The late twentieth century, as part of the turn toward liberal internationalism, saw a significant change in the enforcement mechanism on which international investment law rested. Increasingly states entered into BITs that not only spelled out the investor's legal entitlements, but moved disputes from state-to-state negotiation to investor–state dispute settlement (ISDS) based on compulsory arbitration.

Empowering private investors to sue host states proved good news for the international lawyers who process the claims and sit on the arbitral tribunals that adjudicate them. I must acknowledge that, for much of this century, these cases have given me lots of interesting and reasonably well-paid work, mostly acting as an expert witness on questions of foreign law rather than as a litigator. Whether creation of this private right of action benefits either host states by allowing them to claim a larger share of the returns from projects, or investors by allowing them to intimidate and exploit host states, is deeply controversial.

Economists and lawyers have looked at investment flows and concluded that treaties either increase investment somewhat or have no effect, depending on the methodology used in the study. Investment flows, however, is not what needs measuring, if the goal is assessing the impact of the treaties. Investments may come or go depending on technological changes or economic circumstances that affect the value of projects independent of the extent of legal protection. The real issue is not whether the presence or absence of a treaty determines if an investment occurs, but rather whether treaty rights affect the terms for which an investor will bargain in the process of risking its assets in a venture.

No one has figured out a way to measure directly the variable that matters, namely the effect of legal security on the host country's return from projects. In economic theory, these investments suffer from the problem of holdup. Once the investor sinks money in the project in advance of any revenues, the host state can demand a renegotiation giving it a greater portion of the returns as the price of leaving the investor unmolested. Knowing that host states will have a good reason to do this, investors will demand more rights up-front. Legal enforcement provides one means to render credible the host country's promise to behave, thus lowering investor resistance.[7] Ideally, we would like to know if host countries can obtain more concessions, such as tax revenues, local sourcing of inputs, hiring of local skilled workers, or a larger ownership share, if they make legally enforceable commitments to secure the investor from downstream holdup.

Critics of investment protection treaties argue that the ISDS regime empowers well-funded investors, often large multinational corporations, to thwart beneficial regulatory responses to newly arising problems. These exploiters, the story goes, take advantage of naïve governments either by bullying them into settlements or by getting huge awards that can deter needed general welfare regulation, especially environmental and labor protection. Panels that tolerate abusive practices to create jurisdiction while embracing legal theories that extend the scope of investor protection beyond what existed at the time of the treaties' formation exacerbate the problem. In some instances, emerging-market states create two levels of dispute resolution that divide investors into different classes. Small businesspeople must rely on the local courts, often lethargic when not corrupt, while plutocrats can structure their investments as international ones through offshore shell companies and thus get access to world-class legal protection.[8]

This critique gets a lot of support in the academy and from at least a handful of politicians. Senator Elizabeth Warren, a once and future presidential candidate in the United States, embraces an across-the-board critique of investor–state arbitration. She describes the process as "corporate courts that give multi-national companies special treatment while stiffing American workers." In 2011, Australia's government under Labour Prime Minister Julia Gillard took up the anti-arbitration banner. She argued that it was fundamentally unfair to provide a foreign investor any greater legal rights than domestic businesspeople enjoy.

National populists also have no love for arbitration-based ISDS. They distrust the cosmopolitan lawyers and technocrats who run arbitration. Populist leaders in the West prefer to have injured investors seek out their help to remedy wrongs, rather than having an autonomous international mechanism get the credit for whatever succor the investors get. Revisionist states in the South increasingly reject the system as neocolonial.

[7] Robert E. Scott & Paul B. Stephan, The Limits of Leviathan: Contract Theory and the Enforcement of International Law 65–68 (2006).

[8] Delphine Nougayrède, *Outsourcing Law in Post-Soviet Russia*, 6 J. Eurasian L. 383 (2013).

In the face of these attacks, the evidence of the concrete impact of treaty-based arbitration is surprisingly scant. Neither the United States nor Australia has lost a treaty-based investment dispute. Nor do the sums won from other states through international arbitration seem so vast.

A database maintained by the UN Commission on Trade and Development (UNCTAD) covers 1,104 investor–state treaty disputes filed between 1987 and 2020. According to this data, as of 2021, 975 of these filed cases produced an outcome, with the remainder still pending. In nearly a quarter of the cases (241), the investor got some recovery, with awards varying from $30,000 to $40 billion. In the remaining three-quarters, investors got nothing. In the cases that count as wins, investors received settlements totaling $17 billion and have outstanding, and often unsatisfied, judgments of $87 billion. We have no comprehensive data on judgment satisfaction, but resistance, lengthy delays, and outright defiance seem the norm. Defaults on settlement agreements also happen. Formal enforcement through judicial measures almost never works, because states enjoy something close to judgment-proof status because of widely accepted doctrines of sovereign immunity.[9]

Of the apparently unpaid judgments, $66 billion are owed by Russia ($51 billion) and Venezuela ($15 billion), two countries that manifestly regret earlier treaty commitments and vigorously resist all efforts to collect on the awards. If we kick Russia and Venezuela out of the pool, over a thirty-year period investors have got total settlements of $17 billion and still unsatisfied claims of $21 billion. These numbers seem large, but they average to about $1.4 billion a year.

Nor are the claimants usually the multinational giants that the critics decry. They are far more often small, privately held firms. None of the largest international oil and gas giants – British Petroleum, Chevron, Exxon, Royal Dutch Shell – shows up in the UNCTAD database as a successful claimant. A casual review of all the successful cases suggests that firms too small and specialized to self-insure or to pressure host governments in other ways are the ones that avail themselves of formal treaty protection.

Still, the tide that spawned the proliferation of BITs at the end of the twentieth century now recedes. Australia is not alone in rejecting these treaties. Bolivia, Ecuador, India, Indonesia, and South Africa started programs to terminate all of their treaties, and Bolivia, Ecuador, and Venezuela denounced the ICSID Convention, although Ecuador rejoined in 2021 after a change in government. India, which like every member of the BRICS group

9 Emmanuel Gaillard & Ilija Mitrev Penushliski, *State Compliance with Investment Awards*, 35 ICSID Rev. 540 (2020).

save China never joined ICSID, has denounced or begun renegotiation of its BITs. In particular, it wants to require investors to litigate in local courts before resorting to international arbitration.

Given the widespread political opposition to the current investor-protection regime, its subsidence, if not outright abolition, seems likely. As it does little real work, perhaps only the international lawyers and specialists (like me) that make money from it will regret this. Yet, in context, the fading away of investment protection further undermines liberal cosmopolitanism and the interests of the knowledge economy.

The real problem with the decline of treaty-based investor protection is the many opportunities it gives revisionist states to express their contempt for international law. The Kirchner regime in Argentina led the way in defying international investors unwilling to go along with its sharp left turn in the early years of this century. In recent years, Russia showed even greater resolve and ingenuity in attacking the international system. As Chapter 12 describes in detail, it amended its constitution and the jurisdiction of its constitutional court to procure seemingly authoritative judicial rulings asserting the invalidity of its obligation to honor the rulings of international courts and tribunals regarding foreign investments. It becomes increasingly easy to see even the most concrete international legal commitments as hollow.

CAPITAL, CALVO, AND CLEAVAGES: EUROPE V. UNITED STATES V. CHINA

The fading away of international legal protection of cross-border investment represents only one threat to the knowledge economy. The more concrete challenge involves apparently legal measures by which knowledge have-nots attack centers of the knowledge economy. Targeted taxes became the weapon of choice for Europe as it faced US ascendancy in online capitalism. These instruments represent a wonderfully ironic reprise of the historic Calvo Doctrine wielded by exactly the states against which Calvo had directed his theory.

Carlos Calvo, an eminent Argentinian diplomat and scholar of the second half of the nineteenth century, opposed the growing dominance of European capital and power in Latin America. His eponymous doctrine asserts that foreigners may claim no greater rights to legal protection in their business affairs than what the subjects of a state enjoyed. If Latin American debtors defaulted, as they were wont to do, their European creditors could seek only such relief as local law provided, even though no local subjects operated at the scale of the Europeans and local law thus skewed toward debtors.

At the time, Europeans replied not so much with reasoned arguments as with gunboats. The United States sought to mediate under the cover of its Monroe Doctrine. Ultimately, a 1907 treaty sponsored by the Hague Peace Conference outlawed military intervention as a means of asserting creditors' rights. Withholding of future credit became the principal sanction for defaulting states in the Western Hemisphere.

In the twenty-first century, unlike the nineteenth, European states see themselves as the victims of exploitation, with the digital giants as the principal agents of a new kind of empire. US knowledge firms such as Alphabet, Amazon, and Facebook (Meta) harvest advertising revenues and data from their European operations but largely avoid income taxes and some value-added taxes. Rather than restructure their general tax bases to capture these revenues, an increasing number of European states adopted special levies on gains from digital operations and defined their application so as to apply only to the US companies. Others have such legislation in the pipeline. Standing on the Calvo doctrine, they defend these taxes as permissibly neutral general levies, even though their practical effect is to burden only US businesses.[10]

The United States threatens retaliation, although so far no one has mentioned gunboats. A global agreement negotiated in 2021 under OECD auspices might persuade the Europeans to substitute a minimum corporate tax for the digital taxes already on the books or in the works. The Biden administration promotes this solution. Peace might break out, but probably won't.

First, enough states might fail to comply with the agreement or reject it outright to convince the rest that a multilateral solution will be unavailing. Second, European states might design minimum taxes that target unpopular US firms, especially the knowledge giants, while leaving local enterprises unscathed. Third, European states might decide that a minimum tax does not do enough to capture their share of tax revenues from US firms and reinstate digital taxes. This prospect seems especially likely if the European Union comes undone as more large states follow the United Kingdom in exiting. Under any of these scenarios, the digital taxes would invite an unpleasant US response. Fourth, a future national populist administration in the United States could see European taxation of US firms as a ground for retaliation, whatever the justice of the European position or its conformity with the OECD treaty.

The larger point is that as long as cutting-edge knowledge economy firms arise in the United States rather than Europe, European states will have a

[10] Ruth Mason, *The Transformation of International Tax*, 114 Am. J. Int'l L. 353 (2020).

reason to resent and harass them. Chapter 7 shows how data privacy regulations serve as a means to express this resentment. Taxes do so even more directly and concretely. The more that European governments come to think both that the future lies with big data and that they have not found a way to catch up, the more likely that these conflicts will come to represent not mere competing economic interests, but determined struggles over the future.[11]

Something of the same anxiety drives recent US measures against Chinese technology companies. After years of regarding the growth of that sector as a benign development likely to check the political leadership's authoritarian tendencies, the United States reversed course during the Trump administration. The executive used several statutes to block access of Chinese knowledge companies to the US market. These included the International Economic Emergency Powers Act (IEEPA), a statute enacted during the Carter administration to organize various powers that presidents had used to impose economic sanctions on adversary states, Section 1237 of the National Defense Authorization Act of 1999, a provision designed to bar the Chinese defense industry from infiltrating the US economy, and the Foreign Investment Risk Review Modernization Act of 2018 (FIRRMA), the latest codification of the interdepartmental structure that reviews foreign investments in the United States for national security risks. Several affected firms obtained preliminary injunctions barring enforcement of these measures against them. In some instances, they argued that they fell outside the statutory descriptions of regulated companies.[12]

The Biden administration accepted these legal defeats but issued new executive orders expanding the reach of rules barring specified Chinese companies from US capital markets.[13] A bipartisan consensus supports doing this and otherwise thwarting China's technology projects. Meanwhile, the United States shows no signs of weaning itself from a bond market largely funded by Chinese trade surpluses. Indeed, the Biden administration's

[11] Anne van Aaken & Jürgen Kurtz, *Beyond Rational Choice: International Trade Law and the Behavioral Political Economy of Protectionism*, 22 J. INT'L ECON. L. 601 (2019).

[12] *Luokung Technology Corp.* v. *Department of Defense*, 538 F. Supp. 3d 174 (D.D.C. 2021); *Xiaomi Corp.* v. *Department of Defense*, 2021 WL 950144 (D.D.C. March 12, 2021); *TikTok Inc.* v. *Trump*, 507 F. Supp. 3d. 92 (D.D.C. 2020).

[13] Executive Order No. 14,032 – Amending Executive Order 13959 Addressing the Threat From Securities Investments That Finance Communist Chinese Military Companies, 86 FED. REG. 30, 145 (June 3, 2021); Notice: Continuation of the National Emergency with Respect to the Threat from Securities Investments That Finance Certain Companies of the People's Republic of China, 86 FED. REG. 62,711 (Nov. 9, 2021).

showcase infrastructure plans, both enacted and proposed, could deepen US dependence on Chinese finance.

A prolonged struggle over control of the knowledge economy seems to await us. The United States, long comfortable as the world technological leader and generally relaxed about the centrality of the private sector for this mode of production, now wants governmental controls to ward off a perceived Chinese threat. China, both ascendant and insecure, seeks to dominate the knowledge economy and to translate the fruits of that domination into political influence and national security. Unwinding the two economies is likely to spawn large and expensive disruptions to the harm of both nations. Alternate courses have not yet materialized. A sanctions war provoked by the Russia–Ukraine war already threatens the world economy. One prompted by the seizure of Taiwan would blow up everything

* * *

The obstacles to the free trade and investment that so greatly benefit the knowledge economy grow ever larger. The international organizations and structures set up to suppress these obstacles, the WTO, regional structures such as the European Union and NAFTA, and the BITs, face bleak prospects. Meanwhile, different hopes for and fears about the future divide Europe, the United States, and China from each other. Serious unwinding of current economic interdependence threatens – a process that is not likely to go well for anyone.

A worldwide economic crisis as powerful as the Great Depression is not inevitable. Perhaps invoking the Smoot–Hawley meme is alarmist and lazy. The current drift in international economic relations, however, points in that direction, and the absence of international organizations and legal structures to slow down this trend is worrisome. Measures to restart the world economy after COVID-19 provide more opportunities for mischief. Populists and revisionists on both left and right may hate global capitalism in its current incarnation enough to risk all for its destruction. They, and the rest of us, may come to regret their getting what they want.

12

The Treason of the Clerks

Judicial Revolts against International Law[1]

Piecemeal resistance to international legal obligations at some point becomes across-the-board revolt. International organs like the WTO panels and the Strasbourg Court still put up resistance, the former most recently by rejecting state arguments about the scope of trade law's national security exception and the latter by imposing new duties on states expelling immigrants. As we become accustomed to states ignoring what international tribunals tell them, a realization dawns: international authority no longer works because deference no longer exists.

A worrisome trend, first emerging in 2008 and accelerating thereafter, involves the highest courts of important states expressly rejecting international law in general and the orders of international courts and tribunals in particular. These acts of rebellion involve a wide range of policy areas, from criminal justice and human rights to the separation of powers and the reining in of overbearing executives. In some instances, the domestic courts back up local authority in a manner that seems suspect, even craven, but in others the courts resist powerful domestic political actors to defend broad constitutional principles as they understand them. More significant than the choices made by domestic judiciaries is the widening gap between international and domestic courts across many issues. Battles over the rule of law become struggles over whose rule of law, with the international realm increasingly coming up short.

The contradictions between international rule of law and domestic sovereignty reach their peak when a country's highest judicial body, not merely its government, rejects the demands of international courts and tribunals. The specific rulings of legalized international organs, which exercise authority based on a state's consent to their jurisdiction, distill international law to its

[1] Julien Benda, La Trahison des Clercs (1927).

essence. If international law means anything, it means honoring a commitment, freely undertaken, to comply with such acts. A state's highest legal organs, however, bear ultimate responsibility for its compliance with the rule of law. If disloyal servants of the state assume international obligations that they have no right to impose on their subjects, doesn't a court have a legal duty to free the state from an invalid commitment?

Obviously, both arguments about the rule of law cannot be true. International and domestic law each has its own domain, and courts with the authority to do so must distinguish their limits. Yet domains overlap, courts do not always agree as to which supersedes the other, and conflicts arise. The greater the conflicts and the less often they reach resolution, the emptier the rule of law becomes.[2]

This chapter traces the battles between the courts. It begins with two challenges to the UN legal system, one by the Luxembourg Court and the other by the Supreme Court of the United States. Both saw UN measures as threatening fundamental values embodied in the legal systems that they supervised and protected. Reflecting different cultures and styles of legal argument, the courts differed dramatically on their strategies for deflecting the question of which legal system enjoyed a preferred hierarchical position. They both, however, took the path of resistance. Later decisions by top national courts joined in, although in different circumstances and on different grounds. The latest round of litigation, coming from countries where various flavors of populism reign, express categorical rejection of liberal internationalism and the institutions that minister it.

PUTTING HUMAN RIGHTS ABOVE INTERNATIONAL LAW

In response to the 9/11 attacks on the United States, the UN Security Council established a counterterrorism committee to organize worldwide economic sanctions against those who give material support to terrorist operations. Good liberals generally prefer economic measures to the use of force as a means of countering threats. Collective sanctions, if effectively administered, do a better job of focusing the pain and preventing evasion than do single-state measures. Recognizing terrorism as a unique threat to the international order, the Security Council's Resolution 1373 set up a body, the 1373 Committee, to identify targets. It ordered every UN member to freeze the assets and block all financial transactions of people and entities listed by the Committee.

[2] Paul B. Stephan, *Competing Sovereignty and Laws' Domains*, 45 PEPPERDINE LAW REV. 239 (2018).

In due course, the 1373 Committee identified Yassin Abdullah Kadi, a Saudi national who, after 9/11, resided mostly in Switzerland and Turkey, and the Al Barakaat International Foundation, a Swedish entity set up by Kadi, as funders of al-Qaeda. The evidence supporting the case against them came mostly from the United States and some was classified. The European Union met its obligation to implement decisions of the 1373 Committee by adopting a Regulation (an EU legislative act that takes effect directly in the legal system of its members). Kadi then sued in the EU courts (as well as in Switzerland, the United Kingdom, and the United States) to overturn the regulation and free his frozen assets.

The Luxembourg Court had no difficulty determining that the process by which the 1373 Committee listed people did not comply with fundamental principles of even minimum procedural fairness. The Committee did not give suspected supporters of terrorism advance notice of their potential listing. Once listed, people could ask the Committee to reconsider but had no right to such reconsideration or to see the evidence against them. If fairness was a condition of the validity of the designation, then Kadi had every right to complain.

The problem is that the Security Council, not the European Union, was the author of this unfairness. Under one conception of international law that rests ultimately on the language of the UN Charter, a state may not argue with the Security Council once the latter has acted. Although the European Union itself is not a state and thus not a party to the Charter, its lawyers assume that it bears the same obligations as its members with regard to the United Nations, including the fundamental obligation to comply with the legally binding determinations of the Security Council.

Not so, said the Luxembourg Court. Even though the European Union, at the time of the *Kadi* decision, lacked a written charter of fundamental rights, its legal order contained certain unwritten but fundamental principles. These include a commitment to procedural fairness, which the Section 1373 Committee had denied Kadi. Implementing the Committee's decision through national freezing orders would extend that unfairness and could not be tolerated in Europe.[3]

The question of legal hierarchy remained, but the Court never addressed it. It might have argued that, although the duty to comply with Security Council resolutions applies to member states, it lacks the authority to enforce that obligation. Only the Security Council, it might have said, had the capacity to

3 Joined Cases C-402/05 P and C-415/05 P, *Kadi and Al Barakaat Foundation* v. *Council*, 2008 E.C.R. I-6411.

compel compliance with its rulings. The Court might instead have claimed that it has the right to select which Security Council resolutions to enforce, based on its judgment as to whether the resolution in question advances or hinders the overarching principles of the European Union. Instead, the Court seemed to indicate that its duty ran only to European law, and it thus had nothing to say about the relationship of EU law to the UN Charter. Yet its order necessarily forced the member states to defy the Security Council.

Several European academics leapt into the breach to reconcile *Kadi* with international law. The most comprehensive was that of André Nollkaemper, an international lawyer currently serving as Dean of the law faculty of Amsterdam University. He argued that the international rule of law does not require a rigid adherence to legal hierarchies and may require (rather than just allow) departures from a hierarchical rule that leads to violation of a core element of the rule of law. He regarded the principle of fundamental fairness as such an element. In *Kadi*, he concluded, the Court rightly backed away from a strict rule giving priority to compliance with the Security Council. Adhering to that rule in the circumstances of the case would have inflicted a serious violation of rights (here rights in property rather than in personal integrity) based on an exercise of power that flouted procedural fairness.[4]

At one level, the *Kadi* case had a happy ending. Whatever ties Kadi had to al-Qaeda and Osama bin Laden, if indeed any existed at all, were not deep or enduring. The Security Council removed him from its list in 2012, and the United States ended his designation as a material supporter of terrorism in 2014. Yet the case, however benign its intentions and generous its outcome, put the worm in the apple. An important rule of international law, here the duty to comply with Security Council resolutions, could be cast aside when other considerations required. Here the other consideration was promoting the rule of law in Europe, something easy to like. But different ideas might seem as compelling to other audiences.

FINDING A PLACE FOR SOVEREIGNTY

The same year that the Luxembourg Court decided *Kadi*, the Supreme Court put an end to a legal campaign that unfolded over a decade and provoked it to intervene in four earlier cases. The United States belongs to a treaty, the Vienna Convention on Consular Relations, that governs the rights and privileges of consuls of foreign states (not to be confused with ambassadors). Among

[4] André Nollkaemper, National Courts and the International Rule of Law (2011).

their other powers, consuls may assist subjects of their state who run afoul of the host state's laws. To implement that power, police authorities must notify the relevant consul after they have arrested a foreign national, leaving it to the consul to decide how to assist the person arrested.

The right to provide consular assistance matters to individuals as much as to the consuls themselves. Triggering assistance requires only a phone call or some other contact, and the Convention imposes no deadlines. Yet the Convention gave the United States two big problems. First, most arrests involve local police, often small departments whose officers do not always get much legal training. Especially in the 1990s, many had no idea that they needed to reach out to a consul when arresting foreign nationals. Second, parts of the United States still have capital punishment, something not true in Europe or Latin America (except, in a few Latin American states, for truly exceptional crimes such as treason). Foreign nationals, many of whom live in the United States, could commit a capital offense and not get access to a consul until late in the process. Foreign states do not like to see their subjects put to death in the United States and seized on the Vienna Convention as a means for blocking executions.

The United States had accepted the Vienna Convention's Additional Protocol. This separate treaty conveys consent to the jurisdiction of the International Court of Justice (ICJ) over disputes arising out of the Convention. This mattered because the ICJ, the United Nations' judicial body, may issue a judgment only against a state that has agreed to let it hear a case, and only if another state or a component of the United Nations (rather than an individual, firm, or nonstate organization) brings the claim. Using the Optional Protocol, first Paraguay, then Germany, and finally Mexico brought cases in the ICJ to stop the United States from putting their nationals to death.

The first two times this happened, the complaining state did not initiate proceedings at the ICJ until execution was imminent. Both times the ICJ ordered the United States not to take any action pending its consideration of the case. The Supreme Court threw out suits to implement these orders that would have enjoined Virginia and Arizona against going ahead with scheduled executions.[5] The respective governors denied clemency, effectively ending the disputes. Mexico did better, bringing a case at a moment when fifty-four of its nationals with Vienna Convention claims found themselves in death row in nine US states, but none faced imminent execution. The ICJ conducted hearings and in 2004 issued its *Avena and Other Mexican*

[5] *Breard* v. *Greene*, 523 U.S. 371 (1998); *Federal Republic of Ger.* v. *United States*, 526 U.S. 111 (1999).

Nationals judgment. It determined that the failure of US authorities to notify consular officials of the arrest of the condemned men violated the Vienna Convention and that United States could not allow the states to carry out the sentences until it has rectified this violation.[6]

The United States never denied its responsibility for violations of the right to consular notice. Beginning with the first case and extending through *Avena*, it argued instead that, under its legal system, victims of a Vienna Convention violation had the duty to raise the issue with the relevant court as soon as they had reason to know of its existence. A decision to bypass this opportunity, under the law of most US states as well as the federal constitutional law of criminal procedure, amounts to a waiver and, absent good reason such as ineffective assistance of counsel, bars later consideration of the claim. In all of the cases, the United States argued, the criminal defendants had competent counsel who knew or should have known about the Vienna Convention and failed to raise the consular notification issue until after the state criminal proceedings had run their course and the condemned had exhausted all direct appeals of the sentence.

The ICJ rejected the waiver argument in a single sentence. It appeared dumbfounded that such a rule could exist. It could not understand how the choices made by legal counsel could have any bearing on the rights of a criminal defendant.[7]

When the case returned to the United States, procedural complications ensued. President George W. Bush ordered Texas, which had the lion's share of the victims including those closest to execution, to provide the hearing ordered by the ICJ. In the same memorandum, Bush directed US withdrawal from the Optional Protocol, thereby ending ICJ jurisdiction over new cases against the United States concerning consular notification.

Texas's top court responded that it could not comply with Bush's order in a case where the victim had failed to raise the issue in a timely fashion. In *Medellín* v. *Texas*, the Supreme Court held that Bush lacked the authority to interfere with state criminal proceedings in the absence of a legislative or constitutional mandate. It further ruled that the ICJ had got the Vienna Convention wrong by failing to take the waiver argument into account. Nor

6 Case Concerning Avena and Other Mexican Nationals (Mex. v. U.S.), 2004 I.C.J. Rep. 12 (March 31).

7 Paul B. Stephan, *International Law as a Wedge between Legal Systems*, in The Common Law and the Civil Law Today: Convergence and Divergence 1 (Marko Novakovic ed., 2019); Paul B. Stephan, *The Political Economy of Judicial Production of International Law*, in The Political Economy of International Law: A European Perspective 202 (Alberta Fabbricotti ed., 2016).

would it give force to the ICJ judgment, even though the UN Charter obligated the United States to comply. Nothing in the UN Charter or the Optional Protocol to the Vienna Convention, the Court argued, gave the federal judiciary the power to enforce ICJ judgments that ran contrary to US law. Here US law included the Vienna Convention, and the ICJ judgment violated the Convention by rejecting the possibility of waiver that the Court found in the Convention.[8]

Medellín, much more than *Kadi*, dismayed many international lawyers and academics. First, the decision allowed an execution to proceed, a far more consequential outcome than letting a suspected supporter of terrorism get his money back. Second, the Supreme Court repudiated not the decision of a committee set up by the Security Council, but a judgment of the ICJ, a body sometimes depicted as the supreme judicial authority on international law. Pushing back against UN bureaucrats, even if backed by the Security Council, was one thing, but contempt for the ICJ by the top court of the world's supposed leading proponent of liberal internationalism amounted to a disaster for international law.

RIGHTS AND RESENTMENT

Before long, other national courts followed *Medellín* in flouting the orders of the ICJ. Prominent is the example of the Italian Constitutional Court, which annulled a law adopted to bring Italy into compliance with an ICJ judgment. On the one hand, the Italian decision indirectly vindicated a kind of human rights claim, a right of access to the courts to prosecute a civil claim for reparations by a victim of a war crime. On the other hand, the judiciary to which the victim asserted a right of access, the Italian civil courts, are famous throughout Europe for their dilatory practice and ineffectual protection of legal interests. The Constitutional Court thus elevated a hollow right under Italian law over a concrete order from an authoritative international court.

The dispute involved unfinished business from World War II. Luigi Ferrini, an Italian soldier whom the Wehrmacht had made a prisoner of war and then transported to Germany to work as a slave laborer, sought reparations for what he claimed had been a grave war crime. Germany over the second half of the twentieth century doled out various payments to victims of National Socialism, but concluded in 2000 that it would not extend this program to persons who had the status of prisoners of war and did not fit within narrow

[8] *Medellín* v. *Texas*, 552 U.S. 491 (2008).

exceptions. Ferrini then sued Germany in an Italian court. Germany asserted state immunity from suit and refused to participate in the proceedings. With no one on the other side, Ferrini managed to procure a reasonably prompt money judgment against the Federal Republic.[9] He then tried to enforce it by attaching Germany's Italian real estate holdings. At that point Germany invoked the ICJ's jurisdiction to assert its right to immunity under international law.

In *Jurisdictional Immunities of the State*, the ICJ ruled that Germany enjoyed immunity from the jurisdiction of Italy's domestic courts and that the attachment order therefore violated international law. Customary international law did not recognize an exception to the default rule of state immunity in cases where someone sought reparations for a grave war crime. It noted that the Strasbourg Court and most states that had considered the issue had reached the same conclusion, and saw no reason for the creation of a new exception to the general rule of state immunity.[10]

Respectful of the ICJ, and perhaps mindful of the provision in the Italian Constitution that places international law higher in the country's legal hierarchy than domestic legislation, the Italian legislature promptly adopted a law foreclosing further judicial consideration of the dispute. Ferrini then turned to the Italian *Corte Costituzionale* (Constitutional Court). It obliged him with a ruling that the new law violated the Italian Constitution and thus was invalid. The hierarchal priority of international law, the *Corte* argued, did not extend to fundamental human rights, one of which was access to civil justice. Accordingly, it would not permit Germany to invoke state immunity to avoid a judicial reckoning with its history of violating the rights of Italians.[11]

Many observers found the *Corte*'s position hard to defend. Granted, the bar to state immunity allowed a human rights claim to go ahead, but at the expense of the international legal structure on which those rights rest. State immunity from the jurisdiction of the courts of other states reflects core principles of international law, not least the concept of sovereign equality enshrined in the UN Charter. Only in a world where protection of human rights, however defined, trumps all other legal rules, however systemic and fundamental, does the *Corte*'s judgment make sense. Yet Italy held its ground.

9 *Ferrini* v. *Federal Republic of Germany*, Decision No. 5044/2004, 87 Rivista di diritto internazionale 539, 128 Int'l L. Rep. 658 (Corte di Cassazione 2004).

10 Jurisdictional Immunities of the State (Germ. v. It.), 2012 I.C.J. Rep. 99 (Feb. 3).

11 Italian Constitutional Court, Judgment No. 238 of October 22, 2014, unofficial translation by Alessio Gracis at https://itdpp.files.wordpress.com/2014/11/judgment-238-eng-alessio-gracisnr.pdf.

REINING IN THE EUROPEAN UNION

The *Corte Costituzionale* may have given vent to a deeper, darker impulse – resentment of German domineering within the European Union. Italy did fight alongside Germany in World War II, but at least it switched sides before the end. For the remaining seventeen months of the war, it suffered gravely at German hands, a memory that remains fresh and on which the *Ferrini* suit drew. That Italy only a few years after the war found itself in a supranational structure built around German capacities, both benign (a rebuilt economy) and not (the lingering risk that Germany would return to its old ways as a predatory aggressor, a course it had followed long before National Socialism came on the scene), rankled.

A vision of European peace and security based on a Germany embedded in and entangled with the rest of Western Europe drove the founders of the European Communities. As German economic power grew, the afterglow of peace faded somewhat, while resentment of German fiscal values, emphasizing sobriety and a revulsion toward improvidence, irritated others. In 1990, France insisted on surrender of the Deutschmark as the price of German reunification, but Germany adjusted. It obtained a decisive voice in the governance of the euro, the currency that would supplant the Deutschmark, through the ECB. The *Corte* reached its judgment just as Italy fell under a kind of receivership administered by the ECB. It couldn't free the country from the new German-inspired financial shackles, but Italy's voters embraced several outsider parties that all rejected the political status quo and some of which broached the possibility of jettisoning the European Union.

The *Corte*'s decision thus came at a time when, for Italy, membership in the European Union translated into submission to German domination. One can see the *Corte*'s revolt against the ICJ as a gesture against the contemporary oppressor. One of the great ironies of the moment, though, was Germany's opposite perception of the European Union. For it, its membership did not mean getting to leverage its preference for financial austerity so that it applied to the entire club, but instead a grave threat to its financial probity. As the *Corte* refused to bend to the ICJ, so the *Bundesverfassungsgericht* (Federal Constitutional Court) stared down the European Union.

For parties to the Treaty of Lisbon, the relation of the individual state to the Union is equivalent to the relation of the Union to the United Nations. In both instances, an international treaty assigns places in the legal hierarchy. A member of the European Union must comply with the demand of EU law, just as (in theory) the European Union should honor Security Council resolutions. *Kadi* opened the door to overturning that hierarchy in the face of different policy preferences. Over the last several years, Germany did the same for the European Union and its principal judicial body, the Luxembourg Court.

As part of its efforts to rescue the PIGS from the consequences of their financial incontinence, the ECB instituted a Public Sector Asset Purchase Program (PSPP), not unlike the quantitative easing program the US Federal Reserve developed to buttress the US economy during its share of the Great Recession. In effect, the ECB substituted its own credit for that of distressed state debtors so as to restore investor confidence in new infusions of finance. Germany believed that the ECB lacked the authority to undertake these transactions. Putting its own assets at risk endangered its viability and crossed a line that the Germans believed had been drawn at the time of its creation.

The ECB set up the PSPP in 2015, and German stakeholders immediately brought suit in the *Bundesverfassungsgericht* to bar the Bundesbank from participating. The claimants argued in essence that the ECB lacked the authority under EU law to do what it did, and further that even if EU law permitted these transactions, Germany could not support them because of the very strong constitutional protection against financial improvidence. Seeking to resolve the EU law first, the *Bundesverfassungsgericht* asked the Luxembourg Court to determine whether the ECB had the authority to undertake the PSPP.

In its *Weiss* decision, the Luxembourg Court determined that EU law gave the ECB the power to run the PSPP.[12] The case went back to the *Bundesverfassungsgericht*, which ruled that the Luxembourg Court had violated the Lisbon Treaty by reaching an objectively unreasonable outcome. Germany, the *Bundesverfassungsgericht* declared, could give no cognizance to Luxembourg's interpretation of European law or otherwise take part in the PSPP.

For decades, the *Bundesverfassungsgericht* had kept Brussels and Luxembourg on notice. The *Solange* cases, commencing in 1974, had always upheld German implementation of EU law in the face of a constitutional challenge. Each time, however, the Court had warned that it retained the capacity, and indeed the duty, to stand in the way of any demand from EU organs that transgressed the fundamental rights protected by the German Constitution. In the *PSPP* case, it finally pulled that trigger.[13]

[12] Case C-493/17, Weiss and others, 2018 E.C.R. I-1000.

[13] Peter Hipold, *So Long Solange? The PSPP Judgment of the German Constitutional Court and the Conflict between the German and the European "Popular Spirit,"* 23 Camb. Yb. Eur. Leg. Stud. 159 (2021).

Other national courts had resisted the primacy of EU law and the priority of Luxembourg Court decisions, but none seems as consequential as the *Bundesverfassungsgericht*'s. Back in 2016, Denmark's Supreme Court refused to obey an order from the Luxembourg Court to apply an EU prohibition against age discrimination in employment. The Luxembourg Court had developed its rule teleologically, rather than textually, and that rule directly contradicted Danish legislation.[14] The Supreme Court made clear its unwillingness to bow to Luxembourg, but Denmark's accession to the European Union involved some unique bargains that may limit the general relevance of its take on European law.

With all due respect to the Danish, the *Bundesverfassungsgericht* stands in an entirely different place in the European legal firmament. Not only is it the most prestigious constitutional court in Europe, but it provides a legal anchor to the European Union's most important state. Moreover, Germany built legal order into its core ideology of ordoliberalism. Its élites see that ideology as the foundation of its break with its Nazi past. On top of that, the matter in dispute – the authority of European institutions to manage the ongoing debt crisis – is critical to the viability of the European Union.

German academics as well as many European lawyers find the *PSPP* outcome dismaying. It creates a direct conflict between the hierarchical aspirations of the two most important courts in the EU system and indicates no space for deals that might reduce the tensions. Moreover, the conflict unfolds against a background of other inter-court combat with greater political salience, if not necessarily more long-term significance.

The most interesting battle is that between Luxembourg and the Polish Constitutional Court. As Chapter 5 notes, Poland's government, organized by the Law and Justice Party, incorporated court reform into its populist agenda. Its strategy including restaffing the Constitutional Court with people in sympathy with its program and enacting new laws to constrain the regular courts, mostly populated by incumbent judges lacking ties to Peace and Justice. Supporters see these measures as a necessary part of going in a new direction free of judicial obstruction; opponents see a naked attack on judicial independence and the rule of law. Judges and litigants offended by the reforms obtained rulings from the Luxembourg Court that the reforms constituted backsliding from the liberal order required of members of the European Union and thus were invalid.[15] The Polish Constitutional Court responded

[14] Case C-C441/14, *Dansk Industri (DI)* v. *Estate of Rasmussen*, 2016 E.C.R. I-278; Case No. 15/2014 *Dansk Industri (DI) acting for Ajos A/S* v. *Estate of* A, Dec. 6, 2016.

[15] Case C-204/21 R, *Comm'n* v. *Poland*, 2021 E.C.R. I-593.

with a determination that Poland, consistent with its own constitutional order, could not comply with the provisions of European law on which the Luxembourg Court relied.[16] As of this writing, the standoff persists.

Romania soon followed. The issue, as in Poland, involved a constitutional court that critics saw as hostile to a liberal conception of the rule of law. Civil society organizations sued in the Luxembourg Court attacking rulings of the *Curtae Constituţională*, Romania's Constitutional Court. That body had dismissed several anticorruption cases on procedural grounds. The Luxembourg Court held that European law requires Romanian courts to ignore rulings if they provide impunity to corrupt officials.[17] The *Curtae* responded immediately with a press release directing the judiciary to disregard the Luxembourg ruling unless and until the country amended its constitution to permit such action.[18]

Looking at the arc of Luxembourg's jurisprudence from *Kadi* to the Polish and Romanian cases, the myth of Icarus comes to mind. His father Daedalus invented for him wings made from feathers and wax, which enabled Icarus to reach heights previously beyond the grasp of humanity. Ignoring his father's warnings, he flew ever higher, the sun melted the wax, and he fatally plunged into the sea. Friends of the European Union might regard the metaphor as melodramatic. As the leading courts of ever more member states rise up against Luxembourg, however, I marvel at Luxembourg's earlier confidence as it instructed the rest of the world (acting through the Security Council) as to what it had gotten wrong about fairness.

WALKING AWAY FROM THE WEST

As revolts by national courts against international authority go, none matches that of Russia's Constitutional Court (KSRF). At its founding in 1991, it embodied the new regime's liberal promise amid great hopes from the West. US Supreme Court Justice Antonin Scalia, with my help, arranged for its members to get formal robes (they previously wore business attire) as a means of expressing the exceptional and inspirational nature of disinterested justice.

16 Judgment in the Name of the Republic of Poland No. K 3/21 of Oct. 7, 2021, Assessment of the Conformity to the Polish Constitution of Selected Provisions of the Treaty on European Union.

17 Joined Cases C-357/19, C-379/19, C-547/19, C-811/19 and C-840/19, *Asociaţia "Forumul Judecătorilor din România" v. Inspecţia Judiciară, Consiliul Superior al Magistraturii*, Înalta Curte de Casaţie şi Justiţie, 2021 E.C.R. 1034.

18 Comunicat de presa, Dec. 23, 2021, www.ccr.ro/comunicat-de-presa-23-decembrie-2021/.

Once the leaders of the new Russian state fell out in 1992–93, the KSRF sided with the Russian legislature (then called the Supreme Soviet, an inherited name) in its death struggle with President Boris Yel'tsin. After his tanks fired on the legislature and burned down its building, Yel'tsin shut down the KSRF for more than a year and considered replacing it entirely. Ultimately he let it reopen, insisting only that Valery Zor'kin, the public face of its resistance to him, step aside as Chair but not leave the KSRF entirely.

Over the decades the KSRF reestablished its position as a sober and stabilizing force, building the rule of law incrementally rather than through flashy gestures. Early in Putin's first term as President it restored Zor'kin as Chair, a position he still holds. In 2008, it moved, at Putin's behest, to St. Petersburg. The government explained this gesture as part of a general project of correcting the balance between the country's two great cities, but the move gave off a whiff of fealty to the man from Leningrad (Putin's home town, and the name St. Petersburg had for most of the twentieth century).

The debt came due in the 2010s. Back in 2004, the Russian government had liquidated Yukos, the country's largest energy company, both to send a message to the oligarchs of the 1990s that they should remember their place and to implement a broad policy of renationalizing the country's great oil and gas resources. Enough of Yukos lived on outside of Russia and beyond the government's power to claw back its assets, however, to enable a prolonged legal counterattack. Litigation and arbitration in various courts and tribunals across Europe ensued and unfold still.

In 2014, the Strasbourg Court ruled that Russia's steps to destroy the company had violated the European Convention and ordered it to pay roughly $2 billion in compensation.[19] The same year an arbitral tribunal set up under the Energy Charter Treaty, a multilateral instrument to which Russia was a party, did even more. It handed down an award of roughly $60 billion to Yukos shareholders in compensation for what the tribunal regarded as the expropriation of the company.[20]

Russia responded to the Strasbourg judgment first. Under Russian constitutional law, compliance with international obligations has legal priority. A constitutional provision stipulates that any rule found in any of its treaties

[19] *OAO Neftyanaya Kompaniya Yukos* v. *Russia*, App. No. 14902/04 Eur. Ct. H.R. (2011), http://hudoc.echr.coe.int/sites/eng/pages/search.aspx?i=001-106308.

[20] *Hulley Enterprises Limited (Cyprus)* v. *Russian Federation*, PCA Case No. AA 226, Final Award, July 18, 2014; *Yukos Universal Limited (Isle of Man)* v. *Russian Federation*, PCA Case No. AA 227, Final Award, July 18, 2014; *Veteran Petroleum Limited (Cyprus)* v. *Russian Federation*, PCA Case No. AA 228, Final Award, July 18, 2014.

takes precedence over other legal rules. A post hoc determination that a treaty violates the Constitution would undermine this norm.

Accordingly, the law establishing the KSRF originally gave it jurisdiction to review all treaties for compliance with the Constitution before they entered into force, but not afterwards. This limitation avoided the potential embarrassment of having to invoke the Constitution to negate an existing treaty obligation. The framers of this legislation failed to anticipate, however, that a treaty body, such as the Strasbourg Court, might act in a manner that would violate the Constitution, even though the treaty submitting Russia to that court's jurisdiction by itself presented no constitutional issues. In 2015, the Russian legislature amended the law to allow the KSRF to review the judgments of the Strasbourg Court for compliance with Russian constitutional norms.[21]

The KSRF promptly wielded this new authority to assess the Strasbourg Court's *Yukos* judgment. To no one's surprise, it found the judgment wanting. Russia's Constitution requires all taxpayers to honor their obligations, the KSRF argued. It did not mention the companion part of that provision, which forbids the government from assessing taxes not based on law. As a result, the KSRF held, any compensation paid to the company for losses traceable directly to its failure to honor its tax obligations would function as a refund that would violate the constitutional duty to pay taxes. A judgment order for Russia to pay this compensation could have no force in Russia.[22]

Next up was the Energy Charter Treaty tribunal. Russia sued in the Netherlands, the designated home of the arbitral tribunal, to annul the $60 billion award. The Hague District Court in 2016 agreed with Russia's argument that the tribunal had a fatal flaw in its jurisdiction. Russia, the Dutch Court concluded, had not properly joined the Energy Charter Treaty as a matter of Russian law. As a result, the tribunal had no authority to issue its award. The shareholders appealed that ruling to the Court of Appeals of the Hague.

As part of the appeal, the shareholders' lawyers brought me in as an expert witness to address how Russian law applied to that treaty. Much of my testimony focused on a 2012 resolution of the KSRF that had established the constitutional validity of the kind of Russian treaty-making entailed in the Energy Charter Treaty. In February 2020, just as COVID-19 crept over the

21 Federal Constitutional Law No. 7-FKZ of December 11, 2015, On Introducing Amendments to the Federal Constitutional Law "On the Constitutional Court of the Russian Federation."

22 Resolution of the Constitutional Court of the Russian Federation No. 1-P of January 19, 2017, in the case concerning the resolution of the question of the possibility to execute in accordance with the Constitution of the Russian Federation the Judgment of the European Court of Human Rights of 31 July 2014 in the case of *OAO Neftyanaya Kompaniya Yukos* v. *Russia* in connection with the request of the Ministry of Justice of the Russian Federation.

horizon, the Hague Court of Appeals reversed the District Court and upheld the arbitral award. It largely agreed with me about the meaning of the KSRF's jurisprudence. Russia now faced a large debt that a well-regarded European court, not simply an ad hoc arbitral tribunal, had endorsed.

Perhaps because of COVID-19, the Russian government took a little longer to respond. Only in November of that year did the legislature again amend the law on the KSRF's jurisdiction to allow the Court to revise and reinterpret its earlier decisions.[23] The government promptly petitioned the KSRF to redo its 2012 opinion. It did so, producing one that followed closely the arguments that the Russian government had made before the Hague District Court. The decision argues, among other things, that allowing an international tribunal to consider whether a treaty imposed international liability for actions taken as part of a tax assessment would rob Russian courts of jurisdiction over that issue, in violation of the right of all Russians (including the government itself) of access to the domestic courts.[24] Nearly a year after the KSRF had its say, the Netherlands Supreme Court upheld the Court of Appeals on the award's jurisdictional issue, although it did ask the lower courts to consider a different challenge to the award.[25]

I may be too close to the matter to give a fair assessment of what the KSRF did. Still, it seems to me that these two opinions had no purpose other than to provide a veneer of legality for the government's defiance of a judgment of the Strasbourg Court, on the one hand, and of a treaty-based arbitral award confirmed by an important national court, on the other. Moreover, this defiance rests on considerations other than upholding the rule of law, international or otherwise. Indeed, the transparency of the process and the arguments marshalled by the KSRF convey not merely defiance, but contempt. I believe that the Russian leadership wants multiple audiences to understand clearly that it regards concepts such as the international rule of law as a risible ploy by the West to dominate Russia and its allies, a domination to which it refuses to submit.

* * *

[23] Federal Constitutional Law No. 5-FKZ of November 9, 2020, On Introducing Amendments to the Federal Constitutional Law "On the Constitutional Court of the Russian Federation."

[24] Decision of the Constitutional Court of the Russian Federation No. 2867-O-P of Dec. 24, 2020, on Clarification of Resolution No. 8-P dated 27 March 2012 by the Constitutional Court of the Russian Federation in the case of verifying the constitutionality of Article 23 Paragraph 1 of the Federal Law "On the international treaties of the Russian Federation."

[25] Supreme Court of the Netherlands, Civil Chamber, Case No. 20/01595, Judgment of Nov. 5, 2021, in the *Case of the Russian Federation* v. *Veteran Petroleum Limited, Yukos Universal Limited, and Hulley Enterprises Limited.*

The KSRF Court decisions seize the genie that escaped from the bottle in *Kadi* and *Medellín* – the argument that a domestic court may disregard the demand of an international adjudicatory organ if, in the domestic court's view, the international demand runs up against core domestic constitutional commitments. They demonstrate that, with a sufficiently tame domestic court, all orders of international courts fade into irrelevance because all domestic resistance can find a foundation in core constitutional commitments. This chapter's narrative begins with seemingly benign moves intended to protect international law from itself, and ends with a kind of legal *Götterdämmerung*.

During the 1990s, a prominent stream of legal scholarship foresaw a new age of judicial networking, of judges reaching out transnationally to support each other in promoting the rule of law, liberal democracy, and human rights.[26] Critics pushed back, myself included, but it remained open to argue that transnational judicial networks, if not yet up and running in the world, still might become a model that could shape future judicial behavior.[27] Those hopes, however, no longer work. Increasingly courts act like everyone else, fighting on behalf of local interests and culture and adamantly opposing liberal internationalist discipline. International tribunals find that the harder they press claims based on international law, the greater the local judicial resistance. Whether we ever had networks, now we unmistakably have battlegrounds.

[26] Anne-Marie Slaughter, *A Typology of Transjudicial Communication*, 29 U. Rich. L. Rev. 99 (1994); Harold Hongju Koh, *Transnational Legal Process*, 75 Neb. L. Rev. 181 (1996); Laurence R. Helfer & Anne-Marie Slaughter, *Toward a Theory of Effective Supranational Adjudication*, 107 Yale L.J. 273 (1997); William A. Aceves, *From Legal Transplants to Transformative Justice: Human Rights and the Promise of Transnational Civil Society*, 14 Am. U. Int'l L. Rev. 1335 (1999); Anne-Marie Slaughter, *Judicial Globalization*, 40 Va. J. Int'l L. 1103 (2000).

[27] Paul B. Stephan, *Courts on Courts: Contracting for Engagement and Indifference in International Judicial Encounters*, 100 Va. L. Rev. 17 (2014).

PART IV

International Law Futures

International cooperation based on international law seems a spent force, increasingly discredited rather than useful. Terrible threats – wars, nuclear proliferation, potent bioweapons produced by synthetic biology, new and worse pandemics, financial crises, catastrophic climate change, the rise of demagogues and authoritarians and the withering away of liberal democracy, ever greater surveillance and the death of privacy – await us. The knowledge economy that contributes so much wealth and amazing technology to the world also drives us apart and makes dealing with these threats even harder.

This part contemplates the consequences of these developments for international cooperation and law. Any one of these threats might set the world back decades if not centuries, with great suffering and misery. The world might come to embrace great power hegemony wielded by an authoritarian China as the only way out. Perhaps history will see liberal internationalism and the rule of international law as an inexplicable passing moment in its long march. Chapter 13 goes down this path.

Alternatively, the world might hold off the disasters long enough to discover means of rebuilding trust and cooperation among states, with some international institutions, likely very different from those made in the 1990s, helping along the way. Chapter 14 describes what that process might look like. It recalls earlier projects where international acceptance of a cooperative norm arose in spite of deep skepticism and widespread resistance. It explores how to duplicate these successes in the face of the new, terrible challenges that the world presents.

13

Dancing along the Precipice

This chapter considers a world where international cooperation and international law continue to unravel. The knowledge economy leads to widening class divides, social and political disruption in the rich world, and revisionist ambitions elsewhere, China in particular. Peace and prosperity face ever greater dangers that no single state can repel. Looked at in detail, the prospects seem dire.

DYSTOPIAN PROSPECTS

Consider all the bad things that can happen in the next five years. Iran can acquire nuclear weapons. China can invade and conquer Taiwan. Russia has already invaded Ukraine, with consequences to be seen but likely devastating. Increased risk of nuclear conflict as well as more wars of conquest seem both terrible and possible, if not yet likely.

If war isn't enough, what about plagues? Bioterrorists can launch a genetically engineered variant of, say, smallpox that pairs transmissibility with lethality. With restoration of international communication networks, a new respiratory virus with greater dangers than SARS-CoV-2 might pop up and flourish, without any help from malign engineers. We cannot rule out a new disease that will make the present pandemic seem inconsequential by comparison.

If you are tired of pandemics (and who isn't?), what about financial catastrophe? Bursting of the Chinese real estate bubble might take down the world financial system. The sanctions war between the West and Russia isn't helping. Ever more extreme weather events might cause flooding and storms that devastate large stretches of Europe or the United States. More countries might leave the European Union and Germany might not do anything to keep the enterprise alive. Ransomware attacks might shut down national power grids or financial systems. States might respond to destruction of the infrastructure of international finance and transportation with widespread embrace of protectionism and economic autarchy, much as they did in the 1930s.

And climate change will remain with us. It does not seem likely that the world will resolutely confront a potentially irreversible general catastrophe in the short term. Each year of delay in organizing an effective response, however, increases the cost of doing so, with the rate of increase probably more than linear. We may not recognize the point of no return until we're long past it.

If this parade of horribles is too depressing, consider threats to our dignity, self-worth, and self-rule. Cyberspace promises to become an even more malignant environment. With all this chaos unfolding, national populists might come to power in even more states, and Trump might get reelected in 2024. Performative politics will become an ever greater obstacle to organizing cooperative responses to international crises. Anyone within the grasp of an authoritarian state who seeks to challenge the status quo will suffer the consequences. And the roster of authoritarian states is likely to grow.

Perhaps international law and the international cooperation it underlies cannot do much about these grave risks. But to understand what we lose when the limits of international law no longer work, consider the possibilities. I start with the threat and use of armed force.

WAR

In deciding whether to radically revise the international status quo, either by acquiring nuclear weapons (Iran) or by seizing neighboring territory (China and Russia), the aggressor state would have to consider likely reactions. What kind of economic sanctions would follow, and at what price to those imposing the sanctions? What kinds of boycotts would ensue? In the case of Iran and Russia, would the offended states find a way of embargoing their oil and gas sales? Would states bar the international sale of Chinese-manufactured goods or knowledge products? What about rare earths, an essential ingredient in technology hardware for which China is the dominant exporter? Can the West, starting with the United States, get by without Chinese finance? Could it freeze all Chinese international banking operations? Would the West's retaliatory cyber operations inflict terrible pain on the aggressor's civilians? Would states with those capacities run the risk of even greater counter-retaliation?

This list of questions does not address possible military responses, not because armed force involving nuclear powers is inconceivable but because a state contemplating a provocative action will consider more likely responses first. The basic calculus of retaliation, non-military as well as armed, depends fundamentally on the answer to two questions: will retaliating states succeed in organizing a collective response, and will they persist in the face of mounting costs as their retaliation unfolds?

We already can see in Russia's war against Ukraine the difficulty of organizing a collective response to armed aggression. Current trends point to future breakdowns in cooperation and resilience. Organizing a boycott of Russian or Iranian energy products would require great trust among the participants, who would recognize the gains from shirking (buying at a discount). Shutting down banking channels would increase the value of work-arounds in discreet bank havens such as Vienna, Luxembourg, or Singapore, the benefits from which might be too tempting to resist. Scrambling to bolster its place in the world after Brexit, the City of London also might get in the game. Similar arguments apply to boycotts of Chinese-manufactured goods, knowledge products, and the rare earths. The Trump administration's inability to put together a worldwide boycott of Huawei's 5G systems shows how easy it is to fail at international coordination.

Moreover, leaders in the United States, the United Kingdom, and Europe would sense the limits of what their people would tolerate. Leaders in China, Iran, and Russia can take these limits into account. Already unhappy and discouraged voters would scream at the inflation, supply chain delays, and other costs flowing from the contemplated sanctions. Counting on a quick collapse of concerted retaliation, to the extent any concertation emerges at all, seems the better bet.

Were the potential retaliating states bound together in a dense network of security, political, and economic ties, each underlaid with trust and expressed through legal commitments, the chances of defection from a retaliatory coalition might be lower. Each member of the coalition might believe that defection from any single obligation might impair the entire cluster of commitments. Losing the cluster, as opposed to degrading an isolated obligation, might represent sufficient costs to deter defection. All this is to say that extensive ties undergirded by law reinforce each other, while the unraveling of these networks increases the frailty of remaining commitments. The hypothetical adversary – Russia, China, or Iran – should care about the density as well as the extent of connections among the states whose cooperation would make or break any retaliatory measures. The lower the density and extent, the less credible the threats of retaliation.

Any increase in violence and displacement, whether in the Middle East, Ukraine, or the Far East, likely will create new groups of emigrants fleeing to the West. They would add to the already large numbers that most, if not all, of the rich world's destination states find beyond their power to manage. The resulting turmoil is not likely to add to the resilience of these societies.

One last point needs making. I focus on retaliation as a potential means of deterrence because the existing international legal order by itself poses no hindrance to any of the revisionist states contemplating transgressions. None of the revisionist states has a clear stake in the international legal status quo, even if none wishes anarchy as the alternative. Any of the aggressive acts under consideration would qualify as flagrant violations of the international rule of law as understood in the West. Yet Iran, China, and Russia each has its own conceptions of international law that would let them do what they want here. Forcing the countries of the West to see how hollow their beliefs about the rule of law are would be, for these countries, a feature, not a bug.

PLAGUE

Enough of war. Consider instead the consequences of a new pandemic, whether an act of bioterrorism or another natural course correction imposed on humanity by the biosphere. We can take great loss of life as well as terrible sickness and misery as a given. Those awful costs aside, will it lead to economic and social rebounds, as did the influenza pandemic of 1918–19 and the Black Death in Europe in the mid-fourteenth century, or instead do such damage to social foundations as to upend our world for some time?

With COVID-19 we saw both the best and worst of modern capabilities in the face of a pandemic. Holding a highly transmissible disease at bay requires testing, safety equipment, effective quarantines, and, as quickly as possible, the development and deployment of effective vaccination and treatment. How we did this time might allow us to predict what future responses might look like, but there is so much we do not know.

We are years away from developing the data to determine, as to COVID-19, which societies did best in terms of morbidity and mortality. It will be even harder to link differences in these outcomes to how well each country executed the responses and how much each cost to implement. A preliminary assessment, however, suggests that geographically isolated, rich, and high-social-capital countries – Australia, Japan, New Zealand, and South Korea – did well. When the dust settles, Russia may end up leading the world in mortality and morbidity, but fights over the data to back up that assessment will persist for years to come. Russia has the world's longest international border, few natural barriers to keep out population movements, is not rich, and has low social capital. These seem to be the factors that determine the success of quarantines and, perhaps, vaccine rollouts.

Beyond these tentative hypotheses, there is the matter of the pandemic's enduring impact on social capital. As Chapter 5 describes, much of the rich world's pandemic responses became the site for inflamed political, economic, and social conflicts. Rather than pulling together in the face of a common enemy, as their national myths insist they did in World War II, nations fell apart. The loss of connection and trustworthiness might yet be the pandemic's greatest blow to these societies.

Another such challenge may make things even worse. Political and economic dysfunction could undermine each prong of the response, from testing to social distancing to the development of new therapies. Urban violence and rural opioid overdoses, both alarmingly high in the United States during the late pandemic, might skyrocket. Other societies might discover fault lines they did not even know about. Domestic turmoil might make international cooperation even harder than it was for COVID-19. Larger pockets of unprotected populations around the world could strengthen the disease's resilience and lethality. The economic and social settlements that allowed many people to move their lives online might break down. The world economy might never come back.

As with issues of peace and security, successful pandemic responses require international cooperation and trust. Fighting a disease depends first on opening up medical and epidemiological data, no matter the consequences. Public health authorities must quickly share insights and discoveries as to what works to fight the disease. Physical goods that support the fight – first protective equipment, then medical equipment, vaccines, and therapeutic drugs – must go where needed, not be stockpiled against future local threats. However, each of these measures can succeed only if trust and a desire to be seen as cooperative exists. Law is not essential for establishing trust and cooperation, but it is as good a tool as any to sustain these qualities.

As of this writing, the work of the international institutions and international law as to the current pandemic leaves much to be desired. The WHO dithered and created a perception that it acts at the behest of China, a serious problem given debates over the virus's origin. The WTO did little to promote sharing or to check protectionism in the face of pandemic panic. In the early days of vaccine rollout, the European Union embellished its reputation as a bureaucratic obstacle to timely and effective responses to real emergencies. The prestige of the US Center for Disease Control (CDC) and the Food and Drug Agency (FDA) suffered from mismanagement, misjudgment, and a failure to overcome bureaucratic inertia. Going into a new pandemic, we cannot call on the public to trust the health authorities as much as we would like.

FAMINE

If war and pandemic seem too painful to contemplate, consider instead financial collapse. The world still has not shaken off all the effects of the Great Recession. Many workers have not returned to the formal economy in the wake of the pandemic. A financial crash followed by a seizing up of the real economy, unfolding on a worldwide basis, could overwhelm an already vulnerable world.

The postwar institutions of international economic law – the IMF, the World Bank, and the GATT, now the WTO – were meant to serve as speed bumps to slow a downward spiral heading toward worldwide depression. By that standard – not repeating the 1930s – the system has worked, even though individual large countries – Russia in the 1990s, China from the Great Leap Forward to the end of the Cultural Revolution – suffered 1930s-equivalent hyperinflation, pain, and disruption. China cannot blame these institutions for its problems, although Russia to some extent can. Yet, however much the regime has accomplished, history teaches us that all systems fail eventually.

Chapter 11 shows why the international financial system and the world trading regime are not good candidates to withstand another severe shock. COVID-19 recovery has left the United States fiscally overstretched and unlikely to serve as a source of liquidity for the rest of the world. The trade dispute mechanism itself, not just the rules to prevent a slide toward depression, has come undone. China might have the economic resources to close the finance gap, but doing so itself would denote a revolution in the world financial system. The lack of trust between China and the West, based on a mix of mutual ignorance and genuinely sketchy behavior, probably would thwart cooperation even in the face of dire need.

Serious economic misery might not just shut down international economic ties, but also provoke mass expulsions of scapegoats. Chapter 10 describes the drift toward border controls to keep out new immigrants. In a real crisis, states may go further and expel those who had made it past those controls without regularizing their legal status. They might even strip people of valid naturalizations. Myanmar's treatment of the Rohingya shows how it might work. The liquidation of low-human-capital immigrants as a source of support to knowledge workers would play havoc with the knowledge economy, but a full economic meltdown would render that mode of production irrelevant anyway.

STORMS

Next, consider climate change. Chapter 9 discusses the fundamentals of the problem and the kinds of international cooperation and joint sacrifice that meeting the challenge demands. It should be clear that the foundations for such actions do not exist at the moment. I consider another obstacle to putting together a collective response to a collective problem, a profound divergence in priors (in the Bayesian sense) among people concerned about this issue.

Confronting climate change means guessing about future technological developments and economic consequences of particular policies. The stakes are great but the knowledge base for making the guesses is not. People necessarily must bridge the gap with conjectures. The hard problem, at least from a Bayesian perspective, is setting a prior as well as determining what kinds of evidence will justify resetting that prior and by how much. Public debate indicates a profound difference between those who assume that clever people will come up with solutions as the prospects for rewards grow (technological optimists) and those who believe only significant lowering of the level of carbon-based activity can save the planet (technological pessimists). At one end, the odds of not only clean energy but new extraction technologies and adaptations through geoforming seem good. At the opposite extreme, only radical reduction in human activity, and perhaps in the number of humans, will suffice.

Both perspectives necessarily begin with a leap of faith, neither irrational as such. The problem comes when new evidence arises that might prompt resets. Where the space between priors is as great as it is for climate change, and where the level of uncertainty is so high, resistance to resetting priors will abide. As the gap persists, so does the difficulty of building support for any one approach. If the debate is nested within a broader social environment of distrust, suspicion, and political dysfunction, getting people to take new evidence seriously becomes even more difficult. Our incapacity to grapple with the threat becomes even greater as the risks grow.[1]

Without an international settlement, law has only limited use as an instrument to manage climate change. The current approach, exemplified by the Paris and Glasgow agreements, focuses on transparency and confidence-building, rather than on outcome commitments. As I argue in Chapter 14, these kinds of low-cost, high-visibility legal obligations may serve as a workable path toward a more complete and deeper regime. At present, however, we have only this and no reason to expect more for some time.

[1] Jonathan Z. Cannon, Environment in the Balance: The Green Movement and the Supreme Court (2015); Jason Scott Johnson, Climate Rationality: From Bias to Balance (2021).

LIES AND THEFT

Degradation of the public space for presenting data and arguments will further complicate efforts to bridge deep disputes over evidence and policy with respect to climate change. Climate policy will engage normal politics, not simply workshops and seminars led by scientists. These politics will take place in an environment poisoned by emerging information technologies. Further inroads in data security and privacy, coupled with growing use of disinformation and deepfakes, will fuel paranoia and make reasoned assessment of the available evidence nearly impossible.

For all these reasons, making a new body of international law to limit carbon emissions and manage climate change seems unimaginable, absent profound changes in contemporary science, engineering, and politics. Liberal democratic politics seem blocked in too many significant states to permit international agreement to take costly and risky measures to reach the optimal level of carbon emissions. We can't even agree on the cost–benefit calculus for the right targets, no matter the targets themselves.

Perhaps, a reasonable person might conclude, the world can no longer afford liberal democratic politics. Great challenges – war, plague, economic collapse, environmental catastrophe – demand effective responses. If one approach to self-governance gets in the way of staving off terrible outcomes, should we consider others?

In academic circles, plenty of people who see themselves on either the left or the right respond with a cheerful affirmative to this question. If international law and politics throw up too many obstacles to effectual collective action, then perhaps we should do away with whatever obstructs the common good. In the world as we find it, the choices are more limited. There is only one candidate to serve as a global hegemon that faces no immediate problems from liberal domestic politics. That, of course, is China.

THE RISE OF A NEW HEGEMON?

Chapter 8 raises the possibility of China's relative prosperity in a world that combines the knowledge economy with rising autarky. Here I extend the thought experiment and consider the possibility that China can resolve the prevailing international turmoil on its own terms. China does not have to amass enough military and economic power to dictate to the rest of the world. It may suffice that, in some future global epidemiological, financial, or environmental disaster, it qualifies as the only plausible candidate to exercise the kind of leadership needed.

A growing body of scholarship and punditry explores China's paths to international power. It has, of course, the world's largest population and has invested heavily in education, both domestically and abroad. It brings to bear state control over fundamental economic choices coupled with superior surveillance tools to detect and neutralize domestic resistance to the leadership's choices. It has largely eradicated extreme poverty but tolerates great economic inequality. It values liberal equality to the extent that this principle promotes talent but also prefers traditional social norms, including sex and gender roles, where they conflict with the principle. Han racism remains a strong social force. It has transformed its economic basis from labor-intensive manufacturing to state-of-the-art technology, especially in communications and data processing. It aspires to lead the world in big data resources and the attendant AI capabilities that depend on big data.[2]

Perhaps these qualities, along with the fecklessness and disarray of states in the West, will permit China to become the world power that can shape an international response to pandemics, economic crises, and climate change. Perhaps it will exploit its authoritarian practices, rebranded as promotion of general welfare and social harmony, as a solution to the sticking points that liberalism, with its emphasis on deliberation, agency, and consent, throws up in the path of rapid and incisive social choice. It will insist, and others will agree, that some problems require commands, and not bottom-up distributed decision-making, as the best way of getting to solutions.

The case that the twenty-first century will be the Chinese one turns on two broad arguments. First, it reflects a belief that modern world history follows a pattern. Using Europe's discovery of the New World as a starting point, the pattern encompasses rises and falls of world powers. The Habsburg Empire of Charles V, the early beneficiary of New World conquest and exploitation, gave way by the end of the sixteenth century to the Netherlands, followed by Great Britain in the late seventeenth century and the United States in the twentieth. This narrative, of course, reflects the perspective of the dominant states of the twentieth century and leaves out

[2] Kai-Fu Lee, AI Superpowers: China, Silicon Valley, and the New World Order (2018); Peter Frankopan, The New Silk Roads: The New Asia and the Remaking of the World Order (2018); Jonathan E. Hillman, The Digital Silk Road: China's Quest to Wire the World and Win the Future (2021); Ryan Hass, Stronger: Adapting America's China Strategy in an Age of Competitive Interdependence (2021); Jacob Helberg, The Wires of War: Technology and the Global Struggle for Power (2021).

that part of the world economy that unfolded across the Eurasian continent.[3] As a general argument that no state can expect to remain on top for long, however, it has some force.

The second set of arguments focuses on the relative rise of China compared to the relative decline of the United States and Europe during the present century. People have a tendency to project trajectories based on short-term data, often to their regret. Still, looking at things such as growth in GDP per capita, indicators of technological innovation, and rise in international influence based on economic power, China's delta looks pretty good over the last two decades. Especially when compared to the West's disorder, China's prospects seem better than those of any other country.

Contemplating a future of Chinese leadership, free of the drags that liberal internationalism inflicts on international cooperation, is not crazy. If so, perhaps the looming crises won't be so bad after all, even if we end up missing liberal democracy. Perhaps China will do good as it does well. It could, for example, structure an effective worldwide climate change response that increases demands for its technologies and products, further building its economic power. It might actually build common prosperity, not simply promise it. A self-interested Chinese solution might be preferable to no response at all.

Still, even the incompletely reassuring outcome of Chinese hegemony rests on dubious assumptions. Because China has made great technological strides in the recent past, observers assume similar gains are likely and sustainable in the future. But it is not obvious that a system that privileges leadership discretion over accountability is the best fit for the knowledge economy, and unlikely that any state can exercise worldwide influence without the knowledge economy.

As Chapter 6 relates, reliable legal rules bolster the knowledge economy in many ways. The knowledge economy depends on ongoing investments – costly discovery in search of knowledge, whether in the laboratory or in the wild – that pays off only in the future. Credible legal commitments drive up the discount factor and thus increase the value of those future returns. A culture of corruption and arbitrariness that flouts the law does the opposite, discouraging the investments that bring future knowledge breakthroughs.

At the risk of repeating myself, it is not law itself that gives people confidence in the future. Legal forms – judges and their published opinions, statutes, elaborate procedures used to validate public or private measures – mean little if a society supposedly bound by that law regularly resorts to informal workarounds to avoid inconvenient outcomes. Symmetrically, legal rules that

3 Peter Frankopan, The Silk Roads: A New History of the World (2017).

predictably produce regrettable outcomes also are likely to mean little, because they will drive the affected actors to find alternatives. Legal commitments are valuable, in the sense that they help people go forward in the face of an uncertain future, only if they are credible. Credibility turns on a social practice of compliance in the face of what economists call regret contingencies.

Legal commitments need not be clear-cut to enable people to manage undertakings with a delayed payoff. Legal theorists recognize a form of legal commitment that allows people to adapt to an uncertain future through delegation to a trusted decision-maker. The legal rule conveys bounded discretion to the decision-maker. The form works best when people entering into an undertaking expect new information, hidden at the time that the undertaking begins, to clarify the meaning of the commitment and trust the decision-maker to take that information, and not extraneous factors, into account when enforcing the commitment.

Can a state that desires private investment in knowledge but also subjects outcomes to the unreviewable discretion of its political leadership strike the right balance in reconciling private returns to investors with public benefits? Is China that state? As a matter of theory, the answers to both questions could be yes. But there are good reasons to doubt that.

In China's favor, the fact that Mao and his lieutenants looked to Stalin's Soviet Union as a model for their system, and that the Soviet Union had structural features that thwarted the development of the knowledge economy, does not mean that the same features do the same kind of negative work in the contemporary Chinese economy. Deng Xiaoping's reforms represent a significant break from the Stalinist model that Mao had followed so disastrously. They leave far greater room for individual initiative, and their methods of administrative control emphasize flexibility, rather than the unworkable rigidity that characterized Soviet economic law.

At the same time, unaccountable discretion exercised by a self-perpetuating political leadership may not represent an effective long-term adaptation to the challenges of the knowledge economy. A lack of accountability does not guarantee stability. From the start of the Great Leap Forward until the beginning of Deng's reforms, China went through decades of chaos brought on by jockeying for position within the leadership. The human suffering as well as material losses devastated the country. The economic advances of the last forty years may represent not much more than the natural effect of relief from the ending of terribly harmful policies.

Moreover, much of China's economic progress since Mao's death occurred under a regime that relied on a leadership consensus. Both under Deng's tutelage and afterwards, it avoided the kind of retributive struggles that characterized the Mao period and the elevation of a single person above the rest. Over the last decade, however, the country has returned to personalized leadership. The steps taken to make that change, especially the suppression of the peers of President Xi who might have challenged his authority, seem from the outside to have gone smoothly. But even with the advanced surveillance technologies now at the regime's disposal, maintaining the ongoing authority of a single leader is hard. Anticipating challenges, the leader may pounce, producing disruption rather than stability. Knowing that the leader may pounce, others may take precautions that increase their prospects for survival but not for doing useful things.

The knowledge economy thrives on certain kinds of disruption – those that arise from evident shortcomings in the status quo that cry out for creative destruction. It does not do as well, however, when there is no status quo, when fundamental questions such as the boundary between public power and private life are in play. Some of the most recent technology policies emanating from Beijing, such as reining in the buildup of big data in private firms and denying those firms access to western capital markets, bolster the goal of building a state monopoly over big data and its AI potential. Others, such as shutting down online gaming and tutoring, rest on a paternalism that may not play well among the masses. Common prosperity sounds good, but its implementation may breed resentment and battles over rents. Leadership conflicts may follow.

As China accumulates economic power while adhering more closely to a supreme-leader model of governance, the stakes for becoming the supreme leader also go up. Becoming an international hegemon only amplifies that dynamic. Chinese history is not unfamiliar with warlord competition supplanting imperial centralization. If this becomes China's path, the reasons to fear the future grow, and the incentives to make knowledge decline.

* * *

The world crisis may come to a bad end. As threats grow ever worse and people become even more desperate, international life may revert to a nasty anarchy. The knowledge economy may fall apart in the face of the disruption, denying the world what fixes it might otherwise provide to stem the threats.

Even an unhappy second-best outcome – a Leviathan based on Chinese hegemony – might not save us. An authoritarian regime brings its own baggage and can turn on the knowledge economy the moment it sees that mode of production as threatening its status and power. All the knowledge economy has accomplished – the increases in life expectancy, the elimination of extreme poverty, the extraordinary tools that extend humanity's mastery of the world – may end up not mattering. In that world, where people live in fear and misery and power slips in and out of the hands of the ruthless and cruel, international law will have nothing to do. It will either disappear altogether or survive as an antiquated ritual, its meaning eluding everyone.

This bleak forecast is plausible, but not inevitable. It may take some effort to find grounds for optimism about the future of the world economy and international law, but they do exist. Chapter 14 does that work. It presents the case for the survival of a prosperous international society that sometimes draws on law.

14

What May Endure

Perhaps a look into the abyss may do the trick. The parade of horribles is so long and terrible that, faced with no alternative, states may grope their way toward accommodations that stave off the worst outcomes. People may make their peace with the knowledge economy, finding ways to dampen its bad effects while retaining the good things it does.

If we do pull out of the steep dive, international law also might enjoy something of a revival. I do not mean to suggest that international law can lead us to a better future. Rather, if enough states find ways to cooperate in the face of peril, they may use international law as part of the toolkit to shape and guide their cooperation. This does not mean that making more international law necessarily indicates progress. This book presents plenty of evidence that international law can represent an empty gesture that breeds distrust and dysfunction. But the promises made through international law need not be hollow.

This chapter considers how, in the face of the world crisis and growing unrest with the knowledge economy, states might adapt, rather than surrender, to the challenges. It focuses not on describing good outcomes, but rather good process. It shows how states have made enduring norms not by fiat, but by adopting measures unilaterally that end up becoming collective. The process entails learning by doing, as states discover that practices thought to be disruptive and dangerous provide substantial benefits and few, if any, harms. It emphasizes smallball over imaginative leap and the dramatic gesture.

This chapter first considers features of the present top-down international legal system that may fade into irrelevance if they do not disappear altogether. It then looks at how in the recent past bottom-up rules promoted by individual states have become international standards. It applies this experience to several areas where future action by norm-entrepreneur states might support confidence-building and ultimately greater international cooperation in the face of collective problems. It does not insist that such innovation will necessarily come from the West. The point is that the pathway exists, not whether the West or the South will lead the way.

OBSOLETE ORGANIZATIONS

International law is no more immune from the "March of Dimes" effect than any other social enterprise. The March of Dimes began during the Roosevelt administration as a private foundation dedicated to fighting polio, a malady that had robbed the President of much of the use of his legs and outbreaks of which terrified communities. After the Salk and Sabin vaccines effectively ended that scourge, at least in the rich world, the foundation might have declared victory and liquidated itself. Instead, it repurposed itself as a fighter against birth defects and for quality prenatal care.

The OEEC presents a close analog in the world of international organizations. After the Marshall Plan had achieved its goal of rebuilding Europe as a bastion of liberal democracy and economic health, the interested states might have shuttered the organization and returned its wonderful Parisian real estate to the French government. Instead, they remade it as the OECD, an international organization focused on maintaining and building prosperity in the West, adding members as it did so but keeping the great OEEC properties for its staff and state representatives. The World Bank has a similar backstory: it was meant to do the job that the Marshall Plan took over, but rather than shutting down it found a new mission as a sponsor of international development on the side of the West during the Cold War.

The list of international organizations that have lost ground to populist backlashes and the general press of events include the WTO, ISDS, the European Union (including its Court), the Strasbourg Court, and the ICC. The WTO lost its Appellate Body, the most direct means of giving its rulings the force of law. ISDS faces challenges from many national populist regimes across the South as well as several prominent states in the West. The European Union hangs by a thread as national populism marches on. A growing number of states flout the Strasbourg Court's rulings, although few talk about withdrawing from the European Convention. The ICC's focus on Africa provokes sharp criticism, yet its few forays outside of that continent have led to grief.

What these organizations have in common is a claimed authority to impose binding law on states and, in the case of the European Union and the ICC, individuals. Their authority is "claimed" in the sense that it rests on conventional rules about legal domains that enjoyed wide acceptance not too long ago, but face challenges today. They share a common risk of not surviving demystification in the face of attacks.

No one can predict whether these organizations will carry on as vestigial entities of no great consequence, have a March-of-Dimes moment, or disappear outright. Partly their fate will turn on how hard they push for their own authority; greater efforts to establish their mandates make rejection more likely. The WTO's Appellate Body is to date the only organ to disappear, and the others might survive with reduced scope and influence. This chapter imagines a world where none of these incumbent organizations has much of an impact on governance or politics. The precise form in which they manifest their irrelevance is less important.

NORM ENTREPRENEURS AND REMAKING INTERNATIONAL LAW

All these failing organizations came out of collective action taken by states and formalized through international treaties. The alternative path to development of an international legal order entails one or a few states leading by example. A state may insist on a norm that it knows others do not accept, and indeed will regard as transgressive and destabilizing, if it believes in the rightness of its cause. It will bear the opprobrium that results from imposing the norm if it thinks that, over time, evidence will accumulate that the norm does good work and others will embrace it. The outlaw will become a prophet.

Three examples of this process illustrate how it works. All involve international economic law rather than general international law. All also involve the United States, which may complicate the story. Perhaps the evolution of the norms in question reflects nothing more than a hegemon's ability to impose its will on the rest of the world. But a fair reading of these narratives is that the United States anticipated sooner than other states the need for new norms due to changes in the structure of the world economy. After decades of facing international resistance, the United States had the satisfaction of seeing other states recognizing that its norms fit a need.[1]

These three examples arose against a general background rule in international law that a state may not regulate the behavior of persons over whom it could not claim allegiance unless those persons act within that state's territory. The definitional elements of "allegiance," "act," and "territory" each have some flexibility, but the core idea is that a state cannot respond to overseas behavior by people not its subjects and not within its grasp, even if it that

[1] Paul B. Stephan, *Antibribery Law*, Is the International Order Unraveling? 338 (David Sloss ed., 2022).

behavior, due to the integrated nature of the world economy, causes it or its subjects harm. The examples all involve fashioning exceptions to that fundamental principle.

The first exception adjusts the principle of territorial sovereignty to allow effective responses to international cartels designed to manage or eliminate market competition. Membership in a cartel requires a firm to forgo sales it otherwise could make by adhering to the cartel's territorial allotments. The international cartels of the interwar period, for example, carved up the world into exclusive marketing regions for each of the industrial giants that belonged. Consumers suffered due to less competition, higher prices, and an inferior array of products. Because the cartel members that protect other members' monopoly did nothing on the territory of the country where the victimized consumers lived, their (in)action did not meet the traditional standard for exercise of regulatory (also called prescriptive) jurisdiction by the consumers' state. Yet the consumers indisputably suffered economic injury easily traceable to the cartel members.

The United States responded by asserting a new norm, that prescriptive jurisdiction extends to action or inaction occurring outside a state's territory if the extraterritorial behavior has a direct, substantial, and reasonably foreseeable effect on the well-being of people in the regulating state. On this basis, it imposed criminal anticompetition penalties on foreign firms that took part in cartels, beginning at the end of World War II.[2] Other states fiercely opposed these actions, even imposing their own penalties on persons who complied with US enforcement measures. By the end of the 1980s, however, most states had come around to the position that international cartels present an economic threat of common concern and that unilateral acts by injured states comply with customary international law even when the regulated person had not undertaken any positive activity on the territory of the regulating state.

The second story involves a norm against tolerating the payment of bribes to foreign government officials. The immediate victims of these bribes are foreign nationals who suffer because disloyal governmental officials betray them for their own private purposes. The United States shifted the narrative by arguing that corrupt officials affect the world economy as a whole, not just those people to whom they owe a special duty of loyalty. It developed a rule forbidding the payment of bribes, enforced by criminal and administrative penalties, that applies not only to its own nationals and to people who use US territory to pay bribes, but also to any firm that seeks access to US capital

[2] *United States* v. *Aluminum Co. of America*, 148 F.2d 416, 442–45 (2d Cir. 1945).

markets. When the United States adopted this legislation in 1977, no other country had such a rule, and many states treated such bribes as ordinary business expenses eligible for tax deductibility.

During the 1990s, the United States pushed the members of the OECD to take similar action against their own bribe-payers. An implicit threat to unilaterally increase the pressure on foreign firms if their home countries did not get on board helped. A treaty signed in 1997 obligates most of the world's rich countries to embrace this norm. In the twenty-first century the United States remains the foremost enforcer of the anti-bribery norm, but other countries have made great strides in its direction.[3]

The anti-bribery norm represents an incomplete response to the problem of corruption, but its incompleteness is part of its genius. It focuses on the supply side – actors that pay bribes, typically multinational companies doing business in states with weak legal systems and low social capital – rather than the demand side – corrupt officials who extort payments as a condition of doing business. In a perfect world, an international regime would do both. Once states start going after foreign officials, however, the temptation to confuse the anticorruption principle with the regular rough and tumble of international politics becomes too great. Because it does not provide a license for states to attack foreign governments directly, the anti-bribery norm is not necessarily a prisoner of geopolitics.[4]

A third story applies to regulation of international banks. The United States conditions access to its banking system on compliance with rules that have a worldwide scope. It forbids a financial institution doing business within its jurisdiction from practices that conceal financial crimes such as money laundering or sanctions evasion, even if the entity has foreign nationality and the concealment occurs outside the United States. These rules reflect a general anti-concealment norm – that banks cannot help clients hide criminal transactions because such fraud affects a bank's general trustworthiness. During this century, the United States has brought dozens of criminal proceedings and collected hundreds of millions of dollars in fines from foreign banks that violated this norm. National governments expressed reservations about these measures, but, research by Pierre Verdier demonstrates, have

[3] Rachel Brewster, *Enforcing the FCPA: International Resonance and Domestic Strategy*, 103 Va. L. Rev. *1611 (2017); Daniel K. Tarullo,* The Limits of Institutional Design: Implementing the OECD Anti-Bribery Convention, *44* Va. J. Int'l L. *665 (2004).*

[4] Paul B. Stephan, *supra* note 1.

come to accept them as a necessary means of protecting financial integrity, and ultimately the viability of international banking.[5]

Putting to the side a story about US hegemony in the second half of the twentieth century, the factors that explain these outlaw-to-prophet stories involve a reframing of the regulated conduct. Many states had seen international cartels, bribery of government officials, and bank-aided financial crimes as matters of parochial concern, rather than as systemic threats to an increasingly interconnected world economy. The United States was the first country to see these behaviors as undermining the integrity of advanced capitalism and thus creating general problems for the world. Not only did a growing number of states come to accept the US perspective as legitimate, but they also saw US practice in enforcing the norms as not skewed toward its own parochial interests (unless protecting advanced capitalism counts as an inherently American parochial concern).[6] US behavior convinced others that the norms provided systemic benefits and, in the hands of the state that propounded it, did not lead to substantial impairments of the legitimate interests of other states.

These examples suggest a more general model, a template for bottom-up reform of international law. Each begins with a significant national actor – a norm entrepreneur – announcing and complying with rules that constrain its behavior (regarding, as a kind of constraint, obliging oneself to take action against certain conduct). The norm entrepreneur has the capacity to engage in the behavior that the rule constrains, and thus has a plausible case that compliance with the rule means sacrificing some short-term interests. Accordingly, the norm entrepreneur can convince others of its willingness to pay a price to achieve the long-term benefits of the rule. The entrepreneur's behavior demonstrates that the rule does not provide one-sided advantages to itself, but plausibly generates systemic benefits that substantially exceed the costs of compliance.[7]

The remainder of this chapter looks at opportunities to take the norm-entrepreneur approach to the formation of international norms. In every case, the question arises whether the norm benefits primarily the entrepreneur, or instead represents a desirable response to a general problem. There is no guarantee that norm entrepreneurs will succeed, much less who the more

[5] Pierre-Hugues Verdier, Global Banks on Trial: U.S. Prosecutions and the Remaking of International Finance (2020).

[6] Katharina Pistor, The Code of Capital: How the Law Creates Wealth and Inequality (2019).

[7] Martha Finnemore & Kathryn Sikkink, *International Norm Dynamics and Political Change*, 52 Int'l Org. 887 (1998).

successful entrepreneur will be. The point is only that, if increased international cooperation with some reliance on law emerges out of the present crisis, it is more likely to result from this approach to norm formation.

RETHINKING TRADE AND INVESTMENT LAW

Unwinding the free trade commitments that the Uruguay Round agreements meant to establish remains high on the agenda of populist movements throughout the West. The Biden administration, while deploring the style of its predecessor's approach to diplomacy and international law, has done very little to undo Trump's most consequential attacks on the WTO regime and has given at least soft support to supply chain onshoring. As of this writing, it has neither indicated a pathway toward restoring the WTO's Appellate Body nor backed away from a view of the national security exception that provides a loophole for nearly every WTO obligation. Because of the disappearance of the Appellate Body, none of the ad hoc panel decisions seeking to rein in that exception has any legal force. If onshoring supply chains really takes off, as seems likely, even greater breaches in WTO rules will occur.

Eviscerating the WTO as a formal legal system, however, does not have to mean throwing out the organization and its values altogether. Imagine what might happen under present conditions, with no Appellate Body and broad discretion for states to invoke the national security exception to all WTO rules. In this world, the WTO functions not as a lawmaker, but as a proposer of compromises and a venue for negotiations. States remain free to reject its interventions, and a strong and consistent pattern of such rejections would indicate that it no longer serves much purpose. But irrelevance is not inevitable.

The GATT system that preceded the WTO had these features and yet seemed to do important work. It offered ad hoc arbitration to states with trade disputes, but the arbitral awards bound no one until adopted by consensus to become law. It also had a national security exception that seemed to rely on self-judging, or at least the United States so asserted.[8] That system had its shortcomings: it did little for the global South and excluded China and Russia. Nonetheless, it kept trade disputes from going off the rails and contributed to the West's economic ascendancy. Returning to that system, but with great involvement of the South, need not lead to deadlock and impotence.

[8] Report of the Panel, United States: Trade Measures Affecting Nicaragua, L/6053 (1986).

The Biden administration, while not reversing any of the significant steps undertaken by the Trump administration, has made one small gesture that might show how a scaled back WTO could work. In late 2021 it allowed a case – *Antidumping and Countervailing Duties on Ripe Olives from Spain* – to take effect even though it did not like the outcome. The dispute involves retaliatory duties imposed on imported olives to offset advantages that the producers enjoyed from unfair preferences in their home market. The panel ruled that the United States had failed to prove that a particular benefit provided to EU agricultural producers affected the exported product. The United States explained why it would not block the panel decision. The panel had rejected most of the European Union's arguments and thus had preserved US authority to retaliate against what it regarded as unfair support for exports. It objected to one of the panel's conclusions but interpreted that part of the decision as specific to the facts of the case and therefore not as an obstacle to attacking similar trade practices in the future. As it could live with the decision, it would do nothing to obstruct it.[9]

No one should make too much out of a single incident. The dispute involved an industry – large-scale agriculture – that largely falls outside the knowledge economy, and the protection of which has, in the view of many observers, held back the European Union, and the European Communities before it, from becoming a platform for economic dynamism. What the case does is map out a process by which important states can accommodate themselves to the technocratic and legalistic advice of the WTO without surrendering control over trade issues. It works as long as the participants find accommodation preferable to blowing up the system. That preference can survive as long as the pretensions of the system do not become intolerable.

As for international investment, many overlook an alternative means of dispute resolution that competes with ISDS and may yet emerge as the preferred alternative for protecting investors. Before the rapid growth of BITs in the 1980s and 1990s, many states as well as private firms provided political risk insurance. This mechanism breaks up investor protection into two components – a contract between the insurer (typically a state entity) and the investor, governed by the insurer's law of contract, and a right of subrogation in the insurer to seek compensation from the host state, typically under

9 Statement of the United States at the Meeting of the WTO Dispute Settlement Body, Geneva, Dec. 20, 2021, at 9–10, https://uploads.mwp.mprod.getusinfo.com/uploads/sites/25/2021/12/Dec20.DSB_.Stmt_.as_.deliv_.fin_.pdf.

customary international law or a treaty. In the case of public providers of political risk insurance, agreements between the underwriting state and states that host investments (called investment incentive agreements) create a framework for addressing these issues. Private claims against host states based on international law drop out of the process.

The United States incorporated a political risk insurance program into the Marshall Plan. In 1969, Congress created the Overseas Private Investment Company (OPIC), a state-owned entity, as a means of institutionalizing this service for US investors on a worldwide basis. OPIC also provided finance, in the form of debt and equity, to investors. Congress in 2018 restructured the US system by replacing the OPIC with the International Development Finance Corporation (DFC). OPIC and then DFC signed many investment incentive agreements with host-state governments that link settlement of insurance claims to provision of finance and other forms of support for investment.

A recent article by Rebecca Lamb, a lawyer in private practice whose research I supervised, shows how political risk insurance avoids some of the shortfalls of ISDS.[10] The state issuing the policy can impose its own terms on an investor's access to the system, lowering the risk of opportunistic behavior by powerful multinational firms. Private firms have no say in what adjustments, if any, the host country makes to its domestic policies or what compensation it pays. Instead, contractual bargaining with the issuer state shapes the investor's incentives, while state-to-state negotiations form the host state's stake.

Replacing ISDS with an insurance model does not require coordinated international activity. A single underwriting state can move the market. China and the United States might even compete for the position. Host states that wish can sign investment incentive agreements and denounce BITs. As BITs fall away, demand for insurance will increase. No one can guarantee that a virtuous cycle will unfold, but the path toward one seems clear enough.

The broad point is that international trade and investment can achieve its fundamental goals without depending on formal legalism manifested as mechanisms that subject states to third-party dispute resolution. Organizations like the WTO can provide technical expertise and trusted data collection without giving national populists a backlash target. Investors can spread their risks without feeding populist narratives. The world can find new ways to

[10] Rebecca Lamb, *The New Political Risk Insurance: An End to Corporate Nationality and a Substitute for Investment Arbitration*, 32 AM. REV. INT'L ARB. 245 (2021).

balance the benefits of an open international economy with the regulatory needs and policy goals of individual states without reenacting the disaster of the 1930s.

CLIMATE CHANGE AND ACCOUNTABILITY

As Chapter 9 makes clear, climate change may pose the single greatest threat to peace and prosperity across the planet in the medium, if not near, term. Yet many enormously consequential choices depend on future technologies, such as alternative means of energy production, carbon extraction, and emission monitoring, about which we currently know little. A battle over priors aggravated by distrust of evidence presented by those whose priors differ makes bargaining over amelioration even harder.

As awful as this predicament may be, recent international approaches to the problem may offer some modest hope. Rather than holding regulatory intervention hostage to deeply contested questions such as the appropriate distribution of cost, the two most recent international agreements – the 2016 Paris Agreement and the 2021 Glasgow Climate Pact – focus on bottom-up promises. This strategy does not require states to commit to any measures to reduce carbon emissions. Instead, it provides a forum for states to post their commitments with the understanding that other states have the right to monitor their progress and determine whether they honor their promises.

Critics dismiss these agreements as empty because they lack a mandate to do anything specific in the face of a looming disaster. The criticism, however, assumes away the obstacles to forging a collective response, not least the great divide over how to determine the sufficiency of the evidence and the nature of expertise. What the Paris–Glasgow agreements do is allow states to position themselves as norm entrepreneurs, holding themselves out as capable of meeting promised standards. They shift the focus from choosing the right target – something that is very hard under current conditions – to acceptance of accountability, something that individual states can do and that third parties can assess.

Again, the point is not that the commitments entailed in the Paris–Glasgow agreements constitute a sufficient response to the problem of climate change. Rather, they represent a modest but still necessary step in the direction of a sufficient response. Establishing the credibility of any promise to reduce atmospheric carbon dioxide levels is a prerequisite to choosing the promises that states must make. Proceeding in the manner we have blunts the force of populist objections to mandates emanating from supposedly corrupt technocratic élites. It also sets up the possibility of a virtuous competition among states seeking to demonstrate their technological capabilities.

RESTORING CYBERSPACE

Cyberspace as it has evolved over this century presents two kinds of threats to real-world life. First, it breeds misinformation and lies that exacerbate political and social divisions. The prospect of deepfakes promises to amplify this baleful effect. Second, as a greater portion of life – political and social as well as economic – moves online, it offers greater temptations to those seeking to exploit cyber insecurity. Predators can both shut down online activity, as with ransomware, or steal the information stored in cyberspace, with real-world repercussions including suppressing of dissent and the destruction of lives.

Cleaning up cyberspace, if even possible, will require concerted action by states and the cyber giants. Coming up with a widely accepted understanding of misinformation seems unlikely. Perhaps smart technologists will find ways of exposing deep fakes and market their services to victims. Ending the arms race between predators seeking information and defenders of cyber security seems unlikely. But individual states, acting without benefit of formal coordination with others, might attack one form of pollution: the exploitation of security breaches to extract real-world material benefits.

Ransomware involves extortion predicated on a security breach. The extortionist may threaten to disclose commercial secrets or embarrassing information or bar the owner from access to the data by imposing its own security barriers. The victim pays a ransom in the hope that the extortionist will honor its promise not to do any more harm. The skills and technology to undertake these attacks often have their origins in the public sector, even where the operations are private. Whether the bandits that run ransomware act on behalf of the state, use capabilities acquired from the state, or rely solely on their own resources and take no direction from the state, they operate in cyberspace, a place where several important states have growing capacities for surveillance and action.

A norm-entrepreneur state might use its cyber capacities to detect, thwart, and punish bandits seeking to become extortionists. Part of those efforts might include alerting states with real-world access to the bandits and pressuring them to respond. Conversations between the Biden and Putin administrations, while largely screened from public scrutiny, seem (if press reports are right), to point in this direction.

Limited cooperation along these lines may reflect a shared interest in limiting public power to public purposes. The analogy to anti-bribery measures seems close: both bribe-taking and extortionate uses of cyber capabilities constitute the privatization of public assets. States that develop offensive capabilities in the cyber world, the argument goes, should want to preserve those tools for operations such as espionage that directly benefit that state. Allowing those tools to fall into the hands of people acting for their own private purposes diminishes the value of those tools to the state (if only because it exposes that state to costly retaliation) and amounts to a kind of theft of public property. Thus states should at a minimum not obstruct the actions of other states to deter and punish people who derive private profits from cyber tools developed in the public sector.

In accordance with this logic, anti-extortionist states might articulate and follow attribution rules to determine appropriate targets for deterrence. Measures might range from taking down computers and networks to freezing or appropriating online assets (cryptocurrencies in particular) to arresting and punishing bad actors. Other states, recognizing the value of protecting their cyber capabilities from embezzlement, might undertake their own operations. Without any formal coordination or commitments, states might either compete to take down cyber bandits or, at a minimum, not get in the way of those states that do.[11]

Again, greater state activity to fight extortionate uses of compromised data will not restore cyberspace to the libertarian nirvana to which people aspired back in the 1990s. Ameliorating one of the pathologies of online life does not amount to cleansing the entire system. The point, rather, is that tractable approaches to containing one particular problem with cyberspace do exist, that states can take these measures without the need of treaties or other formal means of international coordination, and that a norm-entrepreneur state can lead others toward a virtuous cycle. Successful cooperation, however implicit, in one area need not spill over to similar behavior in others, but it can't hurt.

HUMAN RIGHTS

The withering away of the ICC need not end all efforts to deter the atrocities prescribed by international human rights law. Concentrating prosecutorial power in a single entity with self-determined jurisdiction proved a mistake. Faith that widespread moral clarity about core human rights commitments would overcome the world's geopolitical divisions was unfounded. But norm-entrepreneur states remain free to keep the project afloat.

A recent article by Pierre Verdier and me shows how states might adapt the modern anti-bribery regime to reach human rights violations by multinational corporations. The United States enforces its multinational rule – don't pay

[11] Paul B. Stephan, *The Crisis in International Law and the Path Forward for International Humanitarian Law*, 104 Int'l Rev. Red Cross 2077 (2022).

bribes to foreign government officials – by tying it to access to US capital markets. We demonstrate that only minor adjustments in current US law are needed to outlaw corporate complicity in serious human rights abuses such as genocide, torture, human trafficking, and grave war crimes.[12]

Any state that controls an important node in the world economy might link access to that node to submission to its rules on human rights compliance. As a principal financial center, the United States can use its capital markets for this purpose. The justification for this condition follows that for anti-bribery rules: investors need to know whether a business undertakes projects that rest on terror and turmoil. Those projects are not just repugnant, but risky. It is the business of capital markets regulation to segregate certain risks. Projects that depend on murder and mayhem present exactly the kind of risks to which investors should not be exposed without clear notice.

What our proposal would not do is provide a means to hold foreign government officials accountable for their human rights abuses. Just as the anti-bribery approach developed by the United States concentrates on bribe-payers, not bribe-takers, our proposal would go after facilitators and accessories, not necessarily the worst wrongdoers. Companies that, for example, hire security forces to terrorize one side in a civil conflict so as to protect its access to exploitable minerals would face criminal prosecution, but not the local military commanders that do the terrorizing or the national leaders that command the atrocities.

This gap reflects the limits of law in a world of states. Influential states can weaponize charges of human rights abuse, like accusations of corruption, as a means of geopolitical competition. Rather than risk conflicts over this confusion, states generally confine themselves to indirect measures. Prosecuting facilitators such as multinational corporations honors the purpose of deterring serious violations without the ramifications that measures taken directly against state officials entail.

Our article addresses US law because it already comes closest to our recommended result. Other states can do likewise, even if they have further to go. If it does not come undone, the European Union could insist that firms that sell goods and services within its confines comply with its conception of international human rights law. So can China. As long as they impose their standards on firms, rather than foreign officials, the possibility of convergence exists. We might yet see virtuous competition to find the best rules for governing businesses that operate in places where human rights are endangered.

[12] Pierre-Hugues Verdier & Paul B. Stephan, *International Human Rights and Multinational Corporations: An FCPA Approach*, 101 B.U. L. Rev. 1359 (2021).

* * *

International cooperation does not always, and perhaps not even usually, require formal organizations, international courts, and top-down governance by disinterested technocrats. This chapter shows how individual states, acting as norm entrepreneurs, have managed to shift international standards in ways that arguably enhance global welfare. It builds a template based on these examples and identifies opportunities in other areas to make progress toward effective responses to worldwide challenges.

None of the opportunities this chapter describes represents a complete response to admittedly grave risks threatening people around the globe. Rather, they provide examples of incremental measures that might restore some degree of trust among essential states. They show how the next system shocks, whatever they may be, need not completely upend the global community and push the world further toward desolation and despair. They show how small steps might lead us to others that, over time and with sufficiently modest expectations, might prevent the worst possible outcomes.

15

Conclusion

Writing off the WTO, ISDS, ICC, and European Union may seem extreme, even bizarre. These organizations consume thousands if not millions of lawyer-hours annually, not just private-sector billables but the work of many in government, civil society, and the legal academy. Their collapse would leave a gigantic hole in the lives of many people, not just lawyers. More importantly, it would indicate that the world had come to a dangerous place, a destination where no one should want to arrive.

This book does not envision that world because I wish it to come about. The people who made the 1990s got a lot right. They failed to foresee, however, three consequences of the changes they launched. Each became manifest, even pervasive, in this century.

First, the reformers and institution-builders of the 1990s assumed that low-social-capital societies could easily switch over to systems that depend on trust and cooperation to make their economies and politics work. Second, they took for granted that societies would address the needs of people displaced or disadvantaged by the rise of the knowledge economy. Third, they did not anticipate the dark side of the knowledge technologies that shape cyberspace. E. O. Wilson warned that humanity occupies "a social world of Paleolithic emotions, medieval institutions, and god-like technology."[1] Whatever the general truth of his claim, no one captured cyberspace better.

Fixing the effects of these oversights while holding on to the fruits of the knowledge economy will take time, resources, and political transformations. Not that history necessarily repeats itself, but it is worth recalling that it took two world wars as well as the Great Depression and the Russian and Chinese revolutions to push the winners of the industrial revolution, the predecessor to

[1] E. O. Wilson, The Origins of Creativity 90 (2018).

the knowledge economy, to a place of resilient entente, if not full solidarity, with that epoch's losers. Marx failed to anticipate what the reconciliation of the contradictions spawned by the nineteenth-century version of advanced capitalism would entail, but he understood as well as anyone that the contradictions existed and had to be resolved.

Law by itself can do very little to advance this process. If anything, the opposite is true: law depends on some kind of social settlement to do any work. The modern failed state, a feature of the post-Cold-War period, shows us what a no-law zone looks like. To the extent that the world ceases to be a community, international law similarly will slip away.

In today's world, where communal values are at risk but worldwide collapse has not yet happened, law can help, but only if expectations are kept in check. States can take steps to address problems in the international system while providing legal justifications that invoke continuity. The success of these initiatives can encourage others to get in the game. Slowly and incrementally, international law can become plausible again. Success can build on success, however, only if projects can be seen as accomplishing something good. Those that overpromise, that assume transformations in the interests and values of states and society rather than working with those that exist, will undermine international law's restoration.

This boring conclusion is not a satisfying one. The world faces terrible challenges. Alerted to these dangers, any reasonable reader would wish a commensurate response. Learning that international law can contribute to the solution, but that the heavy lifting must come from somewhere else, seems a letdown.

The first step in solving any problem, however, is not making it worse. International law too often overpromised. When it failed to deliver either peace or prosperity, people not only lost faith but, in some circles, portrayed it as a tool of corrupt actors. National populism and revisionism in the global South might have prospered in this century even without international law, but the West's ambitions for it did their part.

Modest international-law projects can help to rebuild the crumbling international order. The main task of humanity over the next twenty or so years is not to dismantle the knowledge economy but to adapt it so as to build dignity and solidarity across societies and to rein in the worst uses of the godlike technologies. International law can define and manage discrete steps in this task, whether attacking ransomware, inducing multinational enterprises to stay away from atrocities, or helping states experiment with technologies to reduce carbon emissions.

Expecting everything at once likely means getting nothing at all. That part of liberalism that emphasizes learning by doing and trial-and-error applies here. In the battle for the future, international law can help. That it cannot guarantee success should not keep us from doing what we can.

Index

CPSIA information can be obtained
at www.ICGtesting.com
Printed in the USA
LVHW031116010223
738322LV00007B/315